Library of
Davidson College

Defoe's Fiction

Ian A. Bell

BARNES & NOBLE BOOKS
Totowa, New Jersey

© 1985 Ian A. Bell
First published in the USA 1985 by
Barnes & Noble Books, 81 Adams Drive,
Totowa, New Jersey, 07512

Library of Congress Cataloging in Publication Data

Bell, Ian
   Defoe's fiction.

   1. Defoe, Daniel, 1661?-1731 – Criticism and interpretation. I. Title.
PR3407.B44   1985   823'.5   84-28296
ISBN 0-389-20559-1

Printed in Great Britain

CONTENTS

Acknowledgements	vi
List of Abbreviations	vii
Introduction: Defoe?	1
1. Reading Defoe	14
2. Reading Popular Fiction	42
3. *Robinson Crusoe* and Adventure	73
4. *Moll Flanders*, Crime and Comfort	115
5. *Roxana*, Scandal and Tragedy	153
Conclusion: Novels and Romances	189
Index	198

To my parents

ACKNOWLEDGEMENTS

A great many people have helped me to write this book, though most of them will be happily ignorant of the fact. My indebtedness to the great Defoe scholars and critics must be obvious. I am also especially indebted to the supervisor of my Ph.D. on Defoe, John V. Price of the University of Edinburgh, and to the examiners, Geoffrey Carnall and Paul-Gabriel Boucé. Their patience and kindness prevented me from making a fool of myself more times than I care to remember. My present colleague, Duncan Isles, has also helped my thinking greatly, and been supportive throughout the gestation period of these pages. Mrs Morfydd Radford gave invaluable secretarial assistance. I owe all these people my gratitude, as I do innumerable friends and students. Any mistakes and misconceptions that remain are my responsibility alone.

Ian A. Bell
University College of Wales, Aberystwyth

ABBREVIATIONS

Boulton *Selected Writings of Daniel Defoe*, James T. Boulton (ed.) (Cambridge, 1975).
CJ Daniel Defoe, *The History and Remarkable Life of the Truly Honourable Colonel Jacque, Commonly call'd Col. Jack* (1722), Samuel Holt Monk (ed.) (London, 1970).
CS Daniel Defoe, *The Life, Adventures and Piracies of the Famous Captain Singleton* (1720), Shiv K. Kumar (ed.) (London, 1973).
FA Daniel Defoe, *The Farther Adventures of Robinson Crusoe* (1720), in *The Shakespeare Head Edition of the Novels of Daniel Defoe* (Stratford-Upon-Avon, 1927; reprinted, 1974).
JPY Daniel Defoe, *A Journal of the Plague Year* (1722), Louis Landa (ed.) (London, 1969).
MF Daniel Defoe, *The Fortunes and Misfortunes of the Famous Moll Flanders, &c.* (1722), G.A. Starr (ed.) (London, 1971).
RC Daniel Defoe, *The Life and Strange Surprizing Adventures of Robinson Crusoe, of York, Mariner* (1719), J.D. Crowley (ed.) (London, 1972).
RC3 *Serious Reflections during the Life and Surprising Adventures of Robinson Crusoe: with his Vision of the Angelick World* (1720), in *The Works of Daniel Defoe*, G.H. Maynardier (ed.) (Boston, Mass., 1903–4), Vol. III.
Review Daniel Defoe, *The Review*, A.W. Secord (ed.), 22 vols (New York, 1938).
Rox Daniel Defoe, *Roxana, The Fortunate Mistress* (1724), Jane Jack (ed.) (London, 1964).
Tour Daniel Defoe, *A Tour thro' the Whole Island of Great Britain* (1724–6), G.D.H. Cole (ed.) (London, 1927; reprinted 1968).

INTRODUCTION: DEFOE?

Any new study of Daniel Defoe's fiction has to establish itself as worthwhile, novel and provocative. Twenty-five years ago, the very fact of a book-length study of this author would in itself have satisfied all three demands. Until the late 1950s, Defoe was on the margins of literary study, popping up briefly as a forerunner in the evolution of the novel, or resting impatiently in footnotes. Academic critics seemed to treat him as Dante would treat an especially virtuous pagan — worth special mention, but certainly not to be allowed into the circles of privilege. However, since 1957, Defoe has become increasingly prominent.[1] The often confusing facts of his biography have been clarified, his astonishing canon has been more or less defined, his Puritanism has been analysed and his psychology has been laid before us. His role in the development of the form we call the novel has now been discussed and re-discussed until it seems at least as unclear as it did in those earlier days. Why has there been this growth in interest?

The most obvious answer lies not in Defoe's intrinsic interest but in the 'publish or perish' academic world. Unlike virtually all the other eighteenth-century novelists, Defoe's position was open to publishable question, and seemingly endless exploratory questions were published throughout the 1960s and 1970s. Yet I want to argue that despite all this subtle and intelligent attention, Defoe remains undefined and often obscured. There has been an enormous development in what we know about Defoe, but much of it has been misused, or applied to special pleading, or simply ignored. One critic, trying to sum up the situation in 1973, unwittingly revealed the problem:

> After many years of scholarly and critical attention, Defoe remains an enigma . . . Was he a mere venal time-server? Was he a man whose convictions changed with the political weather? Was his religion mere bourgeois rationalization? Was he so subtle that it is a mistake to impute subtlety to him? Or was the author of *Robinson Crusoe* and *Moll Flanders* far more ironical, far more conscious of the double-edged sword he brandished over a corrupt society than his readers took him to be? Or — best

of all — was he unconscious of his penetrative powers, serving up helpings of middle-class apologetics, all unaware that he was delineating the grim economic imperatives of the world he represented so well that he could not see his own (or anyone else's) role in it?[2]

If these are really the questions to ask, then Defoe is very likely to remain an enigma. I take it that the questions are not rhetorical, and that the alternatives offered are exclusive. But are they? The structure of thesis/antithesis/synthesis in the list is a fair reflection of the debate, but it is surely generated more by the formal procedures of academic criticism than by any idiosyncracies in Defoe. The idea that the most subtle answer is 'best of all' is certainly questionable, and there is also room to query the whole location of the debate.

Are the questions listed above the most appropriate ones to pursue? I think not. The discussion of Defoe's irony and his conscious intentions has often been penetrative and stimulating, but it has become arid through the inappropriateness and redundancy of the critical categories which it draws on. The underlying supportive distinction between direct and indirect statement is, I hope to show, inappropriate to Defoe's period and cultural position. The audience he was addressing in his fiction did not have such firm distinctions between art and artlessness, fiction and fact, or distortion and verisimilitude. Defoe's cultural position, and his own perception of that position, are much more important in understanding his fiction than critics have so far shown. Furthermore, his relation as storyteller to his readers needs to be clarified, along with the storytelling conventions they were habituated to as readers. My approach in the rest of this book will be to try to re-insert Defoe into his literary and paraliterary culture, which I see as being corrective to all the critical efforts to place him in, or keep him out of, a literary tradition of a more exalted kind.

Of course, like all critical enterprises, this one starts from the recognition of similarities throughout the fictions. As I shall discuss in more detail later, each of Defoe's major narratives seems to exploit the ideas of jeopardy and security which can be seen in his biography. Any glance at Defoe's career shows an extraordinary combination of caution and recklessness, of prudent gradualism destroyed by ill-judged flamboyance. The most flagrant examples can be seen in 1685, when the recently married, prosperous Defoe rashly took part in Monmouth's rebellion, and luckily escaped severe punishment. Or in 1702 when, having become increasingly successful under the reign of William, Defoe infuriated the new Tory ministry under Anne with his *Shortest Way With Dissenters*. This miscalculated pamphlet forced Defoe into hiding, and led to his spells in the pillory and in Newgate. The odd conjunction of dour Puritanism with showy displays of boldness is hard to reconcile psychologically, and is interestingly repeated in the rhythms of all the narratives.

In each of the fictions, the central activity is the escape from jeopardy, or the attempts to avoid it. The pattern of deferred success recurs in each narrative, except the dark, late *Roxana*. Crusoe makes his initially disastrous error of running off to sea, then spends the rest of the narrative staving off the consequences and reconstructing a liveable existence. Singleton is rootless, and has to find some way of surviving in a series of hostile environments. At the end of the tale, he is a successful and prosperous ex-pirate, a rare phenomenon indeed. Moll is continually finding herself in positions of extreme difficulty, from all of which she extricates herself. Colonel Jack makes error after error in his life, but escapes the consequences through some vestigial sense of gentility. This theme of escape and survival, so persistently offered, is summed up by the narrator's final words in *A Journal of the Plague Year*:

A dreadful Plague in London *was,*
  In the Year Sixty Five,
Which swept an Hundred Thousand Souls
  Away; yet I alive! (*JPY*, p. 248)

The strongest temptation when faced with this insistent dramatisation of escape is to read it as an allegory of the author's own career. It is possible to see the aura of Defoe's own imprisonments, arrests and deliverances in the turbulent adventures of his characters, and indeed there is one clear occasion where Defoe invites just such a reading. In the Preface to Crusoe's final volume, *Serious Reflections During the Life and Surprising Adventures of Robinson Crusoe*, 'Rob. Crusoe' makes the following claim:

There is a man alive, and well known too, the actions of whose life are the just subject of these volumes, and to whom all or most part of the story most directly alludes; this may be depended upon for truth, and to this I set my name. (*RC3*, p. ix)

Some writers have taken this veiled history seriously, and have tried to find exact parallels between Crusoe's fortunes and Defoe's. The shipwreck, they claim, represents bankruptcy. Or Crusoe might actually represent Defoe's patron Robert Harley, and Defoe himself appear as Friday. The attempts at strict correlation seem overstrenuous, to say the least, but from 1719 onwards both sympathetic and unsympathetic critics have tried to find allegorical re-workings of the author's life in his works. The earliest commentary provoked by *Crusoe* was Charles Gildon's *The Life and Strange Surprizing Adventures of Mr D— De F—, of London*, a parodic re-writing of the original text, with a sceptical distaste for Defoe's character being the animating idea behind it.[3]

I will return to the reception of Defoe's work in the next chapter. For the moment, I want to suggest that however close the circumstances of the tales are to Defoe's own life, and however much they may be given energy by his personal involvement, there is no reason to see the books as being primarily expressions of the author's private experiences. In writing of danger, escape and turbulence, Defoe was offering the satisfactions of broadly shared experience, not of personal commitment. His fiction maintained patterns of freedom and entrapment as vicarious experience for readers, as escapist fiction for a broad public. Defoe's own life was odd and unrepresentative of his times, and that may have allowed him sufficient distance to create patterns of experience which were sufficiently close to, yet sufficiently far from, the experiences of his readers to provide satisfying narratives for them. Defoe's earliest readers found in the books fantasies of survival and resilience which responded to some wide cultural need. In order to avoid an arid repetition of the question of Defoe's intentions, I will try to approach his fiction through its results, not through its aims. It seems to me more appropriate to concentrate on what impression people actually receive from these tales, than on what Defoe may have tried to portray.

In the ensuing pages, I will be arguing that Defoe has to be seen as a popular, or populist, author, providing stylised, distanced versions of his audience's experience. Defoe himself may have been trying to do something entirely different, but his books were certainly used as sources of vicarious experience. It is difficult to reconstruct the earliest audience, but the notion of escapism is surely clear from the content of the fictions. First of all, it seems remarkable in a writer as politically conscious as Defoe, who had spent the

20 years before *Crusoe* engaged in virulent political pamphleteering, that the fictions make so few references to history. Crusoe is on his island for 28 years, but on being rescued, asks no questions about the events in the world during that time. Moll lives through the Civil War, the Plague and the Great Fire, but makes no references to them. The most engaged narrative may be *Colonel Jack*, where the Jacobite rebellions are present in the story, though are not prominent. And in *Roxana*, the implied comparison of the Georgian court with the licentious days of Charles II is managed very obliquely and may even slip by unnoticed. The only explicitly historical narrative is *Memoirs of a Cavalier*, a dramatised military history, largely in tribute to Defoe's great hero Gustavus Adolphus. The remarkable absence of direct political or historical allusion in the main body of the fiction indicates the degree of distance from the lives of the readers. The much more analytic writings of Swift and Pope can be seen as attempts to confront contemporary experience, and to account for it. Defoe's fiction is much more indirect than that, and seeks to show history from below, or from outside.

The experience of reading one of Defoe's pseudo-autobiographies is that of observation and semi-participation in an adventure. The fantasies are minutely detailed, and grounded in recognisable circumstance, but the tales remain romances, giving the audience some re-working of their own experience without the accompanying pressure. With the exception of *Roxana*, all the narratives offer the reassurance that the narrator will survive and reach a state of comfortable retrospection. The pleasure of the fantasy is that of seeing a life unconstrained by political pressures or public events, motivated by personal desire or accident. The adventurer's mobility gives the audience some reassuring illusion of social mobility, even if only during the activity of reading.

That last sentence may sound odd, since we have grown accustomed to seeing the early-eighteenth century as a period of increased mobility. The move to the cities, and the development of a boisterous urban culture, has been seen as very important in the development of the novel. However, for all the evidence of mobility that we can find, the experience of the period still looks very rigidly stratified and hierarchical to many observers. For those in the lower orders, or even the middle classes, the range of social possibilities was remarkably restricted, and basic literacy may have been for many the only access to a range of experiences. It is worth remembering Defoe's own very rigid social scheme, given in his analysis of the constituents of society. The seven classes in society seen by Defoe were:

1. The great, who live profusely
2. The rich, who live very plentifully
3. The middle sort, who live well
4. The working trades, who labour hard but feel no want
5. The country people, farmers etc., who fare indifferently
6. The poor, that fare hard
7. The miserable, that really pinch and suffer want (*Review*, vi, p. 142)

Defoe is rarely concerned with the first two categories, and his fiction shows a concentration on individuals moving into and out of the third and fourth groups. As can be seen from the groupings, the vast majority of Defoe's potential readers came from groups three and four. Those above would have been unlikely to take an interest in anything as undignified as a romance, and those below would be illiterate, and too poor to obtain books anyway. The narratives provide a reassurance that the 'middle station' is the most secure one possible for readers, while at the same time they offer some imaginative flight from that station. Natural disasters may disrupt the rigid calmness of experience, as shown in *A Journal of the Plague Year*, but even there, the central motif is that of resilience and survival. In *Roxana*, the narrator may end in misery, but her career has taken her significantly above her readers in experience, and her downfall is the result of her trying to maintain a position above that allotted to her.

Defoe's fiction, then, exploits the need of a stratified society for a more mobile image of itself. He offers his readers a combination of vicarious jeopardy and eventual reassurance, by taking the narrators sufficiently far beyond recognisable constraints, yet maintaining an otherwise clear verisimilitude. If Swift's satire is in some ways a compensation for his own self-perceived political impotence, Defoe's fiction is a compensation for its audience's self-perceived limitations in experience. The move from authorial expression to audience reception is, thus, essential to my reading of Defoe's fiction, and one which needs more discussion.

The evidence for Defoe's popularity is often anecdotal and unreliable. It is inevitable that his readers should not record minutely their responses to his narratives, or their reasons for reading them in the first place. For one thing, many of those readers would have been semi-literate, that is, able to read but not write. However, the association of Defoe's tales and the lower orders is traditional and plausible. There is an early record of this association in the couplet:

> Down in the kitchen, honest Dick and Doll
> Are studying Colonel Jack and Flanders Moll.[4]

Charles Gildon, in the hostile parody mentioned earlier, elaborated on this, claiming 'There is not an old woman that can go to the price of it, but buys thy *Life and Adventures*, and leaves it, as a legacy, with the *Pilgrim's Progress*, the *Practice of Piety*, and *God's Revenge against Murther* to her posterity.'[5] It is hard to be clear about the layers of Gildon's irony, but it is certain that this is more of an accusation than an enconium. Writing for old women and the lower orders was not highly regarded by Defoe's high-class contemporaries, and it was seen as a rather squalid extension of Defoe's trading instincts, which had earlier led him to deal in hosiery and civet-cats, amongst other items.

The books Gildon lists with *Crusoe* are interesting, in that they are all instructive or devotional works, and his 'old woman' is implied to be using *Crusoe* rather as Gabriel Betteredge does in *The Moonstone*. It seems unlikely, however, that the edition imagined is like any one we might now use. The first edition cost five shillings, which may have been slightly less than the usual price for a book of this length and format, but still represented a substantial outlay — the sum is approximately equivalent to two days' wages for someone in the relevant social class.[6] It is more likely that the book's extraordinary popularity arose from the numerous chapbook editions and serialisations, and that it established Defoe's name more gradually amongst readers. Since that name did not appear on the title page of any of his works of fiction, it is more likely that they achieved such popularity as they did through their content and effect than through any kind of brand loyalty, to use an anachronistic phrase.

Whatever the actual process of the spread of Defoe's popularity amongst the general reading public, it is enough to know that his sense of the public taste was for once accurate. There is a pleasing story in William Lee's biography of Defoe, which shows his position in the public mind at a much later date. Lee was so dogged in his researches that he went to the site of Defoe's pantile factory in

Tilbury in 1860, in the hope of unearthing a few genuine Defoe bricks. He was in luck:

> Large quantities of bricks and tiles had been excavated, and thrown into heaps, to clear the land for its intended purpose. The pantiles appeared to have attracted very little notice; but the narrowness of the bricks, and the peculiar forms of certain tobacco-pipes . . . had excited some little wonderment among the labourers. I asked several how they thought these things came there, and was answered by an ignorant shake of the head. But when I said, 'These bricks and tiles were made 160 years since by the same man that made "Robinson Crusoe"!' I touched a chord that connected these railway 'navvies' with the ship-wrecked mariner, and that bounded over the intervening period in a single moment. Every eye brightened, every tongue was ready to ask or give information, and every fragment became interesting. Porters, inspector, and station master soon gathered round me, wondering at what was deemed an important historical revelation.[7]

Lee's splendidly Victorian desire to legitimise Defoe's dealings does not allow him to go on and account for the failure of this business, but it has left us with a lovely vignette of the popular Defoe.

It would be wrong to draw any more from this anecdote than some broad recollection that Defoe's audience has been persistent and populist. But why did Defoe seek to address this section of society? I think the answer lies in the intersection of his notion of trade and his political ideas. It can too easily be forgotten by literary critics that Defoe spent the major part of his life engaged in trade, and that to his contemporaries he was seen as a theorist of trade much more than as the author of fiction. So much of Defoe's writing engages with the notions of fair trading, or with some aspect of commerce. Despite the repeated failure of his own business dealings, Defoe clearly saw himself as the poet laureate of the commercial interest. The most obvious example of this attachment comes throughout *A Tour thro' the Whole Island of Great Britain*, where the lands encountered on the journey are anatomised in terms of their commercial possibilities, industrial potential and prominent trades. But Defoe did not confine himself to theory. His biographer reminds us that in 1724, Defoe not only produced the *Tour* and *Roxana*, but also did some dealings in bacon, cheese and oysters.[8]

Defoe's interest in economics was so great that he felt it went beyond the limits of decent affection. In the last issue of his *Review*, he talked of trade as the whore he 'really doated upon', and that sense of lascivious lingering does come across. His frequent writings on trade can be seen as interventionist Whig tracts, defending the monied interest against the land interest. Defoe's economic sympathies were always on the side of activity and bustle. His notion of business was not the calm accumulation of capital, but the shrewd, at times opportunist attempt to increase the circulation of cash. His simple delight in currency can be seen in the recurrent hymns of praise to cash which permeate the *Review*:

> O money, money! What an influence hast thou on all the affairs of the quarrelling, huffing part of this world, as well as upon the most plodding part of it! Without thee Parliaments may meet, and councils sit, and kings contrive, but it will all be to no purpose; their councils and conclusions can never be put into execution! Thou raisest armies, fightest battles, fittest out fleets, takest towns, kingdoms, and carriest on the great affairs of the war. All power, all policy is supported by thee; even vice and virtue act by thy assistance. By thee all the great things in the world are done; thou makest heroes, and crowns't the actions of the mighty. By thee, in one sense, kings reign, armies conquer, princes grow great, and nations flourish. (*Review*, IV, p. 106)

That extract comes from a very long analysis, in which money's power to bribe and corrupt is balanced against its power to encourage honesty and provide liberty with its defenders. Defoe claims to know only two leaders whose purposes have been higher than money, Gustavus Adolphus and King William III, but sees the solid businessman as the centre of the community:

> Subjects honestly labouring, honestly possessing, ought to be left quietly, enjoying what they are masters of; and this is the foundation of what we call law, liberty, and property, and the like modern words very much in use. This is the end of parliaments, constitutions, government, and obedience; and this is the true foundation of order in the world, and long may it be our privilege to maintain it . . . (*Review*, IV, p. 106)

Defoe's notions of trade here become inherently political, and also become indicative both of the audience he sees himself as addressing, and the duties he has towards that audience.

In his economic writings, Defoe adopts a fairly conservative, moderate position, aligned to mercantilism. He tries to steer a course between the extremes of protectionism and free trade, with pragmatism being always the prime consideration. He was, for instance, one of the strongest advocates of England's renewed trade with France after 1713, arguing that the wealth of the nation was of greater consideration than the party policies involved. In *Some Thoughts upon the Subject of Commerce with France* (1713), he reiterated his earlier argument that trade should have continued even during the war, and that a regulated trade should now be revived. The importance of these and similar arguments for assessing Defoe's audience lies in his sense of plain-dealing, and in the notion that the business community is central to a nation's culture. Defoe was thus not addressing himself to the landed gentry or even the richest (classes one and two in his anatomy of Britain), but to the intermediaries, the middle sort and below. As a writer of fiction, late in life, he assessed the market for adventure stories, and engaged in yet another trading exercise.

In his more overtly political writings, Defoe set great faith in the people as the final arbiters of power. His clearest notion seems to have been that moderation must triumph over extreme passion, privately, publicly and politically. Indeed, it is possible to argue that Defoe's whole career was based on the desire to moderate between factions, and to show the horrors of absolutism of all kinds. In terms of early eighteenth-century politics, this prevented Defoe from putting absolute trust in either parliament or the monarchy, and he argued for the traditional Whig view of the necessary separation of the executive and the legislature. At moments of crisis, however, it was the freeholders of England who were the final guarantors of stability, and upholders of liberty. This theme runs through many of Defoe's oppositional pamphlets from 1701 onwards, but was most prominent in the affair of *Legion's Memorial* in 1701. The occasion of this issue was the illegal imprisonment by the Commons of five gentlemen from Kent, who had petitioned Parliament to attend to the nation's defences in the face of what looked like French preparations for war. The high-handed and illegal behaviour of the Commons was a matter for wide public concern, and on 14 May 1701, Defoe presented Robert Harley, Speaker of the House of Commons, with a very provocative series of demands in a pamphlet reminding the assembly that its power came only from the electors:

they that made you members, may reduce you to the same rank from whence they chose you; and may give you a taste of their abused kindness, in terms you may not be pleased with.⁹

This plain-speaking, forthright pamphlet is a very clear statement of the Whig position, and certainly singled Defoe out for unwanted attention later on. However, its argument has more importance for Defoe than simply its role in the Kentish petition episode. Defoe here put forward his view of the unimpeachability of the electors, a view which also appears in his later Whig pamphlets, such as *The Original Power of the Collective Body of the People of England* (1701). His populism, then, ran very deep. Political power was delegated from the people to Parliament and the monarch, and government was properly conducted when the responsibilities of each party were fairly carried out. Defoe was indisputably on the side of the electors here, and his hostility to an agitator such as Sachervell arose from that speaker's attempts to arouse the 'mob' to party strife.

Defoe's alignment with the people is, of course, an alignment with only a certain part of the people — the freeholders, business community and electors. However, as a writer of fiction, he was able to reach beyond that community because of the methods of proceeding within that community. In his most extended analysis of the duties and responsibilities of trade, *The Complete English Tradesman* (1725), Defoe discussed the appropriate written style, showing how the world of trade can be more generally accessible:

> easy, plain, and familiar language is the beauty of speech in general, and is the excellency of all writing, on whatever subject, or to whatever persons they are we write or speak. The end of speech is that we might understand one another's meaning; certainly that speech, or that way of speaking which is most easily understood, is the best way of speaking. If any man was to ask me, which would be supposed to be a perfect stile, or language, I would answer, that in which a man speaking to five hundred people, of all common and various capacities, idiots or lunatics excepted, should be understood by them all in the same manner with one another, and in the same sense which the speaker intended to be understood, this would certainly be a most perfect stile.¹⁰

The tradesman is thus required to avoid obscurity, ambiguity and bombast, and to write good plain English of the type Defoe learnt at Morton's dissenting academy at Newington Green. The impulse towards this clarity of expression may have been mercantile, but it reached beyond that in its effects. The clear English of the tradesman could be read by the semi-literate, and so Defoe's economic sense opened up a new audience amongst the lower orders.

So far, I have been arguing that Defoe's notions of trade, joined to his political leanings, determined the nature of his enterprises. When he took up the writing of extended fiction in 1719, it was as a new trade amongst many. There is no evidence to suggest that Defoe felt any special vocation towards the writing of fiction, or considered that it should be accorded greater privilege than his other activities. Although his pamphlets are all filled with illustrative anecdotes, the impulse to longer fiction seems to have been subdued until that late date. By then, there was an existing market for fiction, and Defoe entered that market as yet another trader, not as an innovator or as a radical modifier of the forms. Defoe offered his trading readers the vicarious pleasure of watching recognisable opposites of themselves, replacing caution with recklessness, plans with adventures. The complete English tradesman was advised to be cautious in his pursuit of pleasure, to avoid diversion unless it be in some ways rewarding to him. In all the extended narratives, Defoe offered this useful form of diversion by combining the stories of escape with digressions on morality and economics. The tales were then offered as both instructive and entertaining, and could be taken as cautionary and prurient at the same time.

For the lower orders, the tales offered a different fascination. The readability of the plain English placed the stories into existent generic categories of travel tales, criminal biographies and the like. The source of delight was then not the cautionary element, but the fantasies of social mobility, the fiction of escape. It is this last notion that I will be most concerned with in the remainder of my text. Having looked at the economic and political bases for Defoe's 'popularity', and for his appeal to his contemporary readers, I want to look more closely at his role within literary culture. As a Whig pamphleteer and tradesman, often commissioned by the Tory party, Defoe's position became conciliatory and mediatory. His literary enterprises in his own culture were simply an extension of his trading practice, and, therefore, it is not appropriate to read literary issues of sincerity and irony into his work. His divided and combative society exerted pressures on, and set limits to, Defoe's career as an author, and it is that sense of intimacy with his readership which I seek to investigate. Removing Defoe's works from the popular culture they were written in and for is seriously distorting. I will look at the history of that distortion in the next chapter, and try to offer a clearer methodology of reading in the following chapters. For the moment, it is perhaps appropriate to remember one of Defoe's pieces of advice to his readers:

> I see nothing remains to say of me, or of my Book; they that search for Faults may find them plenty, and they that will mend them for me, shall always have Acknowledgement for the Kindness: But he that wou'd make Faults where there is none, has little Charity and less Honesty.[11]

Notes

1 The choice of the year 1957 reflects the importance of Ian Watt's *The Rise of the Novel*, first published in that year. Preceded by A.D. McKillop's *Early Masters of English Fiction* (1956) and followed by John Robert Moore's standard biography, *Daniel Defoe: Citizen of the Modern World* (1958), it marks the moment when sophisticated modern study of Defoe became possible.

2 Unsigned review of John Sutherland, *Daniel Defoe: A Critical Study* (Cambridge, Mass., 1971), *TLS*, 28 April 1973.

3 The allegorical readings and Gildon's contribution are discussed in Pat Rogers, *Robinson Crusoe* (London, 1979), pp. 66–7.

4 Quoted in James Sutherland, *Defoe* (1937; 2nd edn, London, 1950), p. 236, from the *Flying Post*, 1 March 1729.

5 Quoted in Sutherland, *Daniel Defoe*, p. 228, from Charles Gildon, *The Life and Strange Surprizing Adventures of Mr D— De F—, of London* (1719).

6 See Peter Earle, *The World of Defoe* (London, 1976), p. 164. Also Rogers, *Robinson Crusoe*, p. 5.

7 Quoted in Sutherland, *Daniel Defoe*, p. 51, from William Lee, *Daniel Defoe: His Life, and Recently Discovered Writings*, 3 vols (1869).

8 See Sutherland, *Daniel Defoe*, p. 253. The fullest treatment of Defoe's commercial theories is in Maximillian E. Novak, *Economics and the Fiction of Daniel Defoe* (Berkeley and Los Angeles, Calif., 1962).

9 *Legion's Memorial* (1701), p. 2. See Earle, *The World of Defoe*, p. 12.

10 *The Complete English Tradesman* (1725), Letter III, 'Of the Trading Stile', in James T. Boulton (ed.), *Selected Writings of Daniel Defoe* (Cambridge, 1975), p. 227.

11 *A True Collection of the Writings of the Author of the True Born Englishman* (1703), sig. A3r.

1 READING DEFOE

In the introduction I gave a brief sketch of Defoe as a figure in the very various culture of the early-eighteenth century. With his interests in trade and politics, his life looks diverse and full. He is certainly an unusual figure, with his dissenting background, his failed businesses, his spying, his pamphleteering and eventually his fiction, but the period affords comparably busy and eccentric figures. We need only remember the extraordinary careers of John Dunton, Arthur Maynwaring, or John Tutchin, to see that there was a kind of unorthodoxy which became almost conventional. Later in the century, the mass of Grub Street authors share Defoe's hectic activities, without achieving his permanence. Indeed, had he not written *Robinson Crusoe*, Defoe would have been only another intriguingly glimpsed minor figure, and no Victorian biographer would have bothered to dig up his bricks.

Seen within his culture, Defoe makes sense, but seen within a constructed notion of literature, he looks a lot more puzzling. Within the broad category of English literature, his incredible fecundity looks very odd. With well over 500 authenticated titles to his name, ranging from the briefest of occasional pamphlets to the massive body of the *Review*, it is tempting to think, as George Orwell thought of Frank Richards, that there must have been several authors at work under the one name.[1] It may be reassuring to read one scholar's view that this massive canon shows 'an inner consistency of purpose', but it becomes very difficult indeed to identify that purpose, or to be confident of its consistency.[2] It is safest to arrive at a flexible uniform assessment, as the normally unsympathetic Dr Johnson did when announcing that Defoe 'had written so variously and so well'.[3] When faced with this great pile of writing, it is best to be tentative or selective, but any full critical analysis of Defoe has got to make clear the grounds for its selectiveness, and not pretend to be dismissively comprehensive.

The earliest responses to Defoe's writing came long before *Crusoe*, and were provoked by his poems and pamphlets. As a prolific and controversial author, Defoe was in the firing line from the very first. The responses to his work were, to say the least, direct, and arose more from personal and political hostility than from any disinterested delight in literary criticism. An early example of this unabashed literary correspondence can be seen in the commentator who described him simply as 'a loathsome Thing, shap'd like a Toad'.⁴ In fact, Defoe attracted as many vile caricatures and lampoons as Pope did, and was attacked in print as often as Swift. The Scriblerian writers, Pope, Swift and Gay, seem to have held him in special contempt, often expressed by a kind of mock-pitying condescension. Swift groaned that Defoe was 'so grave, sententious, dogmatic a Rogue, that there is no enduring him'. John Gay, less sweepingly but no less damningly claimed that Defoe 'had excellent Parts, but wanted a small Foundation of Learning', and saw him as 'a lively instance of those wits, who . . . will endure but one Skimming'. And Pope, in the most damaging and hostile deed of all, gave Defoe a passing mention in the *Dunciad*, amongst the fools and frauds associated with literature, making sport of Defoe's spells in the pillory.⁵

Some of this lofty hostility may be taken as Tory contempt for an author who was at best a Whig and at worst a turncoat, available for hire. In part, too, it can be seen as the contempt the learned gentleman feels for the trading classes. The class basis for the Scriblerians' hostility can be illustrated by a look at Defoe's class and religious background.⁶ Defoe's father, James Foe, was a respectable tallow chandler and butcher of Cripplegate in London, eventually a prominent member of the Butchers' Company. Defoe was born in 1660, the year of the Restoration, and seems to have been deeply influenced by the early events of his life. The importance of the urban commercial background is obvious, but the Foe family religion was also extremely formative. James Foe was a latter-day Puritan, a worshipper at the church of Dr Samuel Annesley. The Puritan movement, which had been so strong during and after the Civil War, had by this time been politically marginalised, and in 1662 Charles II passed an Act of Uniformity, requiring all clergy to accept the new prayer book, to approve of episcopal ordination and to swear unconditional non-resistance to the king. These conditions were totally unacceptable to dissenters, who were driven underground. Annesley was thus unable to preach from his pulpit any longer, and moved from meeting house to meeting house.

There are many implications of these events for readers of Defoe. The sense of belonging to a persecuted minority never left him. The almost clandestine nature of Puritan worship contributed to his life-long love of secrecy and disguise. The strong emphasis on doctrines of conscience and the innate sense of right and wrong surface throughout his fiction. More materially, there was the effect that belonging to the dissenting minority had on Defoe's education. Unable to attend the universities, Defoe was sent to the Rev. Charles Morton's academy at Newington Green, where the curriculum was conspicuously more 'Modern' than elsewhere. Defoe's concern with the shaping of individuals is obvious in *Moll Flanders*, *Colonel Jack* and *Roxana*, where he analyses the kinds of training which are necessary for personal survival. Also, he kept returning to the question of education in his discursive pamphlets, from his suggested academy for women in *An Essay Upon Projects* (1697) to the proposed university and musical academy in *Augusta Triumphans* (1728). His notion of the formative nature of education, and his sense that his own training was special, come from his days at Morton's academy, which provided him with his 'Modern' self-image, and the appropriate learning to establish it.

In the Scriblerian attacks on Defoe, the most frequent accusation was that he lacked learning. If learning was defined as a knowledge of the classics, then the accusation was justified, but Defoe strongly countered the taunt by seeking to prove the greater merit of his own skills. The curriculum at Morton's put great emphasis on reading and writing clear English, and on being conversant with modern history and the modern European languages. These were Defoe's most valued abilities, and the ones he most conspicuously flaunted in his writing. The most flagrant counter-attack on the Scriblerian accusation came through the *Review* in 1705, when he challenged any of his accusers to translate the modern European languages as quickly or as skilfully as he could. A purse of £20 was offered, and given Defoe's characteristic unwillingness to put his money where his mouth was, that can be taken as a very confident declaration of accomplishment.

Defoe's class background, then, gave him a sense of social mobility, confirmed in his own rise from furtive dissenter to the advisor to four monarchs. Yet his religious background and his education forced him into opposition to the dominant literary culture of his day, which was predominantly classicist. The division between the 'Ancients' and the 'Moderns' in the early-eighteenth century must be obvious to any reader of the literature. It is most graphically articulated in Swift's *Battle of the Books* and Pope's *Dunciad*, where the Ancients' views are given prominence, and most violently present in *A Tale of a Tub*, where the Moderns are seen as stupid, arrogant and evil. The distinction can be seen in terms of alignments: Ancients were aligned with the Classics, satire and retrospection; Moderns were aligned with contemporary writing, celebration and projection. Ideologically, the Ancient sensibility held that the world was in a state of irreversible decline, and that the individual's role was to alert others to that decline, and to become reconciled to it, however reluctantly or spiritedly. The Modern sensibility put much more emphasis on improvement, and on man's ability to impose order on the world by the exertion of his mind and will. Crusoe, building a small, coherent empire on his island, is the Modern mind at its most outgoing. Defoe himself, with his energy and adaptability, can be seen as the quintessentially Modern author.

In 1710, Defoe defended the Modern position in the *Review* by showing the inappropriateness of polite learning in the contemporary commercial world. The 'Mother Tongue' is seen as more enabling and alive than any amount of antique scholarship, especially in the political world:

> I know a Man at this Time a Minister, he is a Critick in the Greek and Hebrew, a Compleat Master of the Latin — Yet it would make a Man blush to read a Letter from him, sleep to hear him Preach, and sick to read his Books — He is a Master of Languages, and buried in Letters, but cannot spell his Mother Tongue, knows nothing of the World, and has never look'd abroad — Such learning, I confess, I despise; and covet to be illiterate rather than thus a Scholar.

This is defensive, even petulant, but it does lay out Defoe's pride in his achievements. He had travelled extensively as a merchant, and believed that a knowledge of the customs of Europe was essential to learning. This view is satirised by Swift, whose portrayal of Gulliver shows the Modern man becoming more deluded the farther he roams. Defoe shows his commitment to modernity here, and shows the fluency with which he himself can handle the 'Mother Tongue'. He shows, too, the combative literary world in which his writings existed. At this stage in his career, before 1719, all his writing was interventionist and aggressive, all of it defending the positions Defoe adopted. The political stance may vary, dependent on the occasion of the utterance, the patronage (i.e. Tory or Whig, Defoe wrote for both), and the temper of the debate, but there is a consistency in the broadly Modern alignment, arising in this case from the dissenter's background.

Defoe was regularly accused of unscrupulous behaviour, and even the most sympathetic biographer cannot fully cleanse his business dealings. The accusation of turncoat is easier to deflect, by remembering Defoe's professional status as a writer, and by seeing the ways in which he did seem to be maintaining a relatively moderating role throughout his political work. His modernity raises some problems, however, as seen in the following passage:

> I have often observed, both in Prose and in Verse, that some Persons of strong Genius, well acquainted with the World, and but of little Learning, have made a better Figure in some kinds of Writings, than Persons of the most consumate Literature, not blessed with Natural Genius, and a Knowledge of Mankind.
>
> The preference of Genius to Learning is sufficiently demonstrated in the Writings of the Author of *The True Born Englishman* . . . This Author is characteriz'd as a Person of little Learning, but of prodigious Natural Parts; and the immortal *Shakespear* had but a small share of Literature.[7]

The argument here is conventional enough. The distinction between 'Learning' (i.e. the classics) and 'Natural Parts' underlies all the Moderns' defences of writing, and the appropriation of Shakespeare to their party was a common strategy. What makes the passage interesting is that its exalted defence of the author of *The True Born Englishman*, with its air of scrupulous objectivity, is rather dispersed by discovering that it was written by that author himself; in other words, by Defoe. He makes no reference to his authorship at any point in the pamphlet, and hides behind his anonymity, a typically Modern device. This may come from his delight in subterfuge and secrecy, which is the other side of his plain-dealing business ethic, and it gives rise to many of the persistent problems of attribution which face Defoe's editors. However, it reveals the embattled position Defoe felt himself to be in, and offers a glimpse of the cut-and-thrust literary world in which he was prominent.

It is essential to keep in mind the radically divided nature of early-eighteenth-century literary culture. The divisions already mentioned — Whig/Tory, Ancient/Modern, conformist/dissenter — are only some of the splits, though they are the most pertinent ones for study of Defoe. The literary world was combative, aggressive and inherently politicised. All the texts available were in some way political, because of the overt politicisation of religion and learning, and of print itself.[8] In order to understand Defoe's autumnal move into extended fiction, we need to know what precipitated it, which will in turn depend upon Defoe's earlier role in the literary culture.

We in the present day, where the supremacy of Swift and Pope is acknowledged, have a different perception of the first 20 years of the eighteenth century from those who were alive then. We become so familiarised to *A Tale of a Tub* and *The Rape of the Lock* that we forget their radical unrepresentativeness. We overlook too the disparity between contemporary taste and those works which are alleged to have stood the test of time. Of course, this applies to later historical periods just as obviously — I suspect that Victorian poetry is associated in more people's minds with the then unknown work of Gerard Manley Hopkins than with the enormously popular work of Sir Lewis Morris. However, in the understanding of Defoe, some attempt at an archaeology of taste is essential. It is rarely mentioned now that Defoe's name would have been associated in eighteenth-century readers' minds with poetry rather than with prose. The first collection of his writings, published in 1703, was called *A True Collection of the Writings of the Author of the True Born Englishman*, and contained 22 poems and tracts, and the first authenticated portrait of Defoe. Before 1707, 17 other poems and pamphlets had been signed with this ascription. Certainly, *The True Born Englishman* is a boisterous, readable long poem, by far the liveliest of Defoe's verse pieces, and it has a kind of survival in its tokenist presence in the big anthologies such as *The Oxford Book of Eighteenth-Century Verse*. However, it was much more important and influential in the early-eighteenth century than this vestigial remnant of its potency might suggest.

In an anonymously published pamphlet called *A Vindication of the Press* (1718), Defoe claimed that his poem had 'Sold beyond the best Performance of any Ancient or Modern Poet of the greatest Excellency, and perhaps beyond any Poetry every printed in the *English* Language.'[9] In the preface to the second volume of his authorised *True Collection*, he was more specific, and claimed that over and above the legitimate editions, pirated broadsheets were sold 'in the Streets', making the total sales up to somewhere around 80,000 copies.[10] Of course, these statements may be exaggerated, to make some point against the Ancients, but they serve to remind us that Defoe was a popular author in the most obvious sense of selling a lot of copies of his work, and that his historical placement is at that fascinating moment when literature and literacy intersect. After the original publication in 1701, *The True Born Englishman* remained in print until at least 1749, when a twenty-fifth edition was published in Dublin.

The genesis of the poem is revealing. With the apparent mobilisation of French troops having continued after the Treaty of Ryswick in 1697, there was much English discussion of the desirability of maintaining a standing army. Parliament was against the expense of such a commitment in peacetime, but King William was strongly in favour of being in a state of readiness to meet any French threat. Defoe's position, as we would expect, was on William's side, and he joined in the controversy with a number of activist pamphlets, most notably *An Argument Shewing, that a Standing Army, with Consent of Parliament, is not Inconsistent with a Free Government* (1698). In that early pamphlet, there is a very characteristic Defoe argument, in which the requirements of liberty are balanced against the equally essential need to safeguard property. The fairly even temper of the debate was not persistent, and by 1700, a strain of xenophobia had crept into the anti-William arguments. The king's attempt to retain his Dutch troops was rejected by Parliament, who insisted that the very small force permitted should consist entirely of native Englishmen. The anti-Dutch element in this censure was obvious, and was reiterated in some of the popular literature accompanying the measure. Defoe was moved to intervene, as he recalled in his quasi-autobiographical pamphlet, *An Appeal to Honour and Justice* (1715):

> During this time, there came out a vile abhor'd Pamphlet, in very ill Verse, written by one Mr. *Tutchin*, and call'd, THE FOREIGNERS: In which the Author . . . fell personally upon the King himself, and then upon the *Dutch* Nation; and after having reproach'd his Majesty with Crimes, that this worst Enemy could not think of without Horror, he sums up all in the odious Name of FOREIGNER.[11]

Moved by 'a kind of Rage', Defoe composed *The True Born Englishman*, in similar verse, as a scathing reply.

The argument of the poem is simple. There can be no such thing as 'Englishmen ab Origine', for the English nation was composed from the blend of Romans, Gauls, Greeks, Lombards, Saxons, Danes, Scots, Picts, Irish, Normans and Welsh:

> From this Amphibious Ill-born Mob began
> *That vain ill-natur'd thing, an* Englishman.[12]

The undoubted popular success of Defoe's poem was his first, and least disastrous, important political intervention. It gave him access to the king's confidence, and brought him to prominence as a vigorous campaigner in popular political rhetoric. Of course, replies were written scorning and vilifying Defoe's position, as in the anonymous poem *The True Born Hugonot* (1703), where Defoe is caricatured as:

> A true Malignant, Arrogant and Sour,
> And ever snarling at Establish'd Power . . .[13]

As well as these counter-arguments, Defoe's popularity brought out imitations of a less scrupulous kind. Since his poem had appeared anonymously (as was the norm of such pieces), it offered the possibility of sly cashing in by imitators, trading on Defoe's name. Defoe denounced such practices in a characteristically mercantile way:

> The Mob of wretched Writers stand
>   With Storms of Wit in every Hand,
> They bait my Mem'ry in the Street,
> And charge *me* with the Credit of their Wit.[14]

From the point of view of popular success, prestige, and incisiveness, this episode marks Defoe's greatest political involvement, and the least damaging.

If Defoe's intervention in the standing army controversy arose from his Williamite sympathies, his next, disastrous pamphleteering adventure came out of his dissenting background. The great popular success of *The True Born Englishman* gave Defoe a kind of unfortunate celebrity, and made him something of a marked man after William's death in March 1702. The first Parliament of Queen Anne's reign was Tory dominated, and sought to bring pressure to bear on the Whig-supporting dissenters. With little opposition, a Bill to prevent Occasional Conformity made its way through the

Commons and on to the Lords. For dissenters, this was a major threat, and was seen as coercive. A political crisis broke out when the Bill was blocked in the House of Lords, setting the two houses against each other, and raising suddenly the temperature of an already over-heated debate. It was at this point that Defoe made his ill-judged intervention. Instead of pursuing his normal path of lively but judicious argument, or racy polemic, Defoe chose a fundamentally ironic strategy, and sought to ridicule the high Tory position by exaggerating it slightly. *The Shortest Way With Dissenters* took the ironic form, now familiar to us through Swift's *A Modest Proposal*, of the *reductio ad absurdum*. For Defoe, the most extreme statement of the threatening case had been made by Sachervell, in a sermon in Oxford, where he 'told his hearers that whoever was a true son of the Church, or wished well to it, was obliged to hang out the bloody flag of defiance against the Dissenters'.[15] Such rabble-rousing was inimical to Defoe's understanding of the relationship between orators and crowds, and his own pamphlet is an attempt to rely on the good sense of the audience. All effective irony depends on subtle, tacit understanding between speaker and listener. In this case, no such understanding was reached.

The Shortest Way starts from the premise that the dissenters must be suppressed, and that the apparently harsh penalties of the Bill are nowhere near strict enough:

> 'TIS vain to trifle in this matter, the light foolish handling of them by Mulcts, Fines, &c. 'tis their Glory and their Advantage; if the Gallows instead of the Counter, and the Gallies instead of the Fines, were the Reward of going to a Conventicle, to preach or hear, there wou'd not be so many Sufferers, the Spirit of Martyrdom is over: they that will go to Church to be chosen Sheriffs and Mayors, would go to forty Churches rather than be Hang'd.
>
> If one severe Law were made, and punctually executed, that who ever was found at a Conventicle, shou'd be Banished the Nation, and the Preacher be Hang'd, we shou'd see an end of the Tale, they wou'd all come to Church; and one Age wou'd make us all One again.[16]

This inflation of Sachervell's case was meant as a devastating satire, revealing the intellectual paucity of its speaker, and the inhumane severity of his arguments. Unfortunately, Defoe had wholly misjudged the temper of the debate, and the pamphlet was taken by some high Tories as a succinct and clear statement of their case. Naturally, when they discovered they had been taken in by a hoax, they were furious. Defoe also enraged fellow dissenters, who were terrified by the arguments offered, and equally taken in. Though the pamphlet sold very well, its popularity was of the wrong kind for Defoe's liking, and it had terrible consequences for his career.

In 1703, the Bill again passed through the Commons and was again blocked by the Lords. Defoe's pamphlet had been so divisive and injurious to the government's case in one way or another, that a warrant was issued for his arrest, the charges being serious ones and the possible punishments grave. It has been suggested that *The Shortest Way* was only a pretext for Defoe's arrest, a trumped up charge to get him into custody, where he might be pressed to betray his Whig masters as traitors.[17] Whatever the case, the charges were sufficient to send Defoe into hiding, and to lead him to try throwing himself on the mercy of his arresting officers. He tried various means to try to escape imprisonment, such as promising to raise a troop of horse for the queen, and serving at the head of it in the Netherlands. However, these were all rejected, and Defoe was eventually found and imprisoned. Stranded in Newgate, his businesses unattended, his family unprovided for, Defoe had time to consider the wisdom of his apparently spontaneous deed. The recklessness which had involved him in Monmouth's rebellion had burst out again, but with more disastrous consequences, and the sentence he received was surprisingly severe. Despite his apparent offer to betray his accomplices, he was sentenced to a sizeable fine, and to three spells in the pillory. The offending pamphlet was to be burnt by the common hangman, and Defoe totally discredited in public. Having sought to pacify and bring about moderation, Defoe now found himself labelled as seditious, as an agitator. His mistake confirmed him in his self-image of moderation, and created his later literary *persona* of the calm moderate. Only rarely after 1703 did he attempt extended irony, and then much less grandly.

As he stood in the pillory, Defoe made available the most explicit statement of his populist politics. While on bail, he wrote his poem *A Hymn to the Pillory*, a verse re-working of the accusatory position expressed in *Legion's Memorial*. It reads as a direct appeal to public feeling, based on the notion that 'Justice' is higher than party strife, and that Defoe was a victim of jealousy and malice. The poem is daringly direct and racy, particularly in its conclusion, where Defoe asked the pillory to proclaim his integrity:

> Tell them it was because he was too bold,
> And told those Truths, which shou'd not ha' been told.
>   Extoll the Justice of the Land,
> Who Punish what they will not understand.
>   Tell them he stands Exalted there,
>   For speaking what we wou'd not hear;
> And yet he might ha' been secure,
> Had he said less, or woud' he ha' said more.
>   Tell them that this is his Reward,
>   And worse is yet for him prepar'd,
> Because his Foolish Vertue was so nice
> As not to sell his Friends, according to his Friends Avice;
>
> And thus he's an Example made,
> To make Men of their Honesty afraid,
>   That for the time to come they may,
>   More willingly their Friends betray;
> Tell 'em the Men that plac'd him here,
> Are Friends unto the Times,
>   But at a loss to find his Guile,
>   They can't commit his Crimes.[18]

It is obvious that the irony here is a lot less hidden than in the originally offending pamphlet, and that Defoe was seeking to avoid indirectness. But it was a bold move to have the poem on sale at the foot of the pillory in which he stood, and transformed a humiliation into a partial triumph. Instead of being bombarded by fruit and vegetables, and even seriously hurt, he turned the crowd on his side by an act of literary intervention.

   The audacity, skill and perhaps above all the speed of composition of the *Hymn*, reinforce the view that Defoe used literature as a vehicle for immediate political expression. The vigour of *The True Born Englishman*, *The Shortest Way* and the *Hymn* all testify to an informed, populist author, following his own principles as they got him into and out of scrapes. Up until this point, Defoe had persistently written along Whig, Williamite, dissenting lines, and his work was thoroughly consistent. It defended commerce, religious toleration and William's policies against France. It also tried to move political debate beyond the strict confines of party faction, by appealing to the middle ground of moderate Whigs and Tories alike. After the pillory, however, Defoe's political support had collapsed. Despite the personal triumph of the *Hymn*, Defoe was still in the political wasteland. With the king dead, and Parliament increasingly Tory, it must have seemed to Defoe as though the moderating voice had been wholly silenced.

It was at this point that Defoe was taken up by Robert Harley, the Speaker of the House of Commons, and the idea of his writing a newspaper on the government's side was put forward. Harley is the most important single figure in shaping Defoe's later career. As the instigator of Defoe's periodical work, he deserves some attention. In 1703, he was a moderate Tory, having earlier been a Whig. He was a Church of England man, but had dissenting connections. A shrewd and secretive politician, he saw himself as a statesman, pursuing the general good rather than a party's advancement, and was himself at this time becoming much more prominent in the nation's affairs. His aims look sufficiently similar to Defoe's for the two to be politically compatible, and so Defoe's move over to his party is perhaps not the sell-out it might appear from the outside. In *An Appeal to Honour and Justice* (1715), Defoe offered a version of Harley's intervention which makes it seem like a kind of religious deliverance, and he justifies his own later behaviour by grounding it in 'Gratitude and Fidelity'.[19] Whatever the reasons for Defoe's acceptance of Harley's support, its effects were great.

Under Harley's tutelage, and with the support of the Lord Treasurer, Godolphin, Defoe started a twice-weekly (later thrice-weekly) newspaper of the moderate line. Its full title is indicative of its mood, and its political position, *A Weekly Review of the Affairs of France, Purged from the Errors and Partiality of News-Writers and Petty Statesmen of all Sides*. The title is misleading in its reference to France, for in fact the subjects covered throughout its nine-year run were extremely varied, but the notion of impartiality is nearer the mark. It is impartial in the sense of following Harley's middle-of-the-road line, and couching its arguments in balanced and judicious language. Very rarely did the *Review* rise to heights of passion, or deal out invective. Unlike other periodicals of the time, it sought to offer itself as reasoned, forward looking and beyond petty squabbles. It was certainly not a newspaper in the modern sense of providing up-to-the-minute details of contemporary events — the official publication, the *London Gazette*, came nearest to fulfilling that role. Rather, it offered commentary on issues of note, broadly ruminative, and articulated Defoe's public concerns recurrently. Most of the other contemporary papers carried their party alignment very clearly, and sought to demarcate Tory and Whig concerns much more exclusively than before. The *Review*, on the other hand, sought to avoid direct association with the Tories, and to appeal to that section of the political community which thought itself beyond sectarian interest. The attacks on Defoe continued, and there are a number of issues of the *Review* where the unnamed editor defends the conduct of Daniel Defoe. However, Defoe's association with Harley, and the long labour of this paper, gave him status and renown as a commentator, and disengaged him from the more dangerous areas of controversy.

During the Tory ministry of 1704 until 1714, Defoe worked for Harley or Godolphin in a number of capacities, including a prolonged, clandestine period in Scotland, reporting public feeling on the Act of Union. Despite this hectic life, he still managed to write a great deal, and just as it is important to remember that Defoe's writing was always professional, it is necessary to recall that writing was only *one* of his trades. In this period, he relied much more on anonymity than before, and developed the ability to write on controversial, but relatively safe subjects. In his more successful later pieces, direct political involvement was replaced by civil or domestic concerns, obliquely referring to wider issues. His later non fiction dealt with the supernatural, with the treatment of servants or criminals, or with civil projects. He wrote some hefty historical volumes, and developed a new facetious side in the 'Scandalous Club' section of the *Review*. By the time the *Review* was brought to conclusion by the combination of the 1713 Stamp Tax and the increasing influence of the extreme Hanoverian Whigs, Defoe was equipped to produce pamphlets and tracts of a less dangerous kind. His last mistakes were to write more ironic pamphlets in favour of the Hanoverian succession in 1713, *Reasons Against the Succession of the House of Hanover* and *And What if the Pretender Should Come?*, which landed him in prison briefly again. He was granted pardon by the queen in November 1713, and kept out of bitter political controversy from then on.

By 1715, then, Defoe was out of political favour, no longer in touch with the seats of power, and lacking in steady employment. He was tried for libel in 1714, but no action was taken. He managed to come to terms with the Whig administration to some extent, and was employed by them as an editor. His role in periodicals such as

Mercurius Politicus was a curious one — to put the Tory view forward in a moderate way in a paper set up by the Whig Ministry. This moderating and controlling role continued in his work for *Mist's Weekly-Journal* and *Applebee's Weekly Journal*, where Defoe's furtiveness and secrecy were at their most extreme.

The aim of this history of Defoe's political status as a writer has been to show the shaping forces at work in his literary career up to 1719 when he wrote *Robinson Crusoe*. His career shows the twin features of personal intervention and professional accommodation, and I see the fiction as belonging to the second of these tendencies. Apart from his covert Whig work, Defoe's later writings are much more distanced from the political world than his earlier ones. They seek to confront more domestic issues of the day, and only treat the recurrent issues of sovereignty, foreign policy and religious toleration obliquely. His fiction is informed by these areas of debate, but they are not prominent. Defoe's later career is much more cautious and discursive, much less aggressive and adventurist. When dealing with the lives of adventurers, Defoe was himself drawing away from adventure, returning to the persona of the sound man of trade and business sketched in the *Review*. His fiction was a means of professional engagement with, and personal or political disengagement from, the issues of the day. The use of the first-person narrators allows Defoe the space to be unattached to the ideas offered, and that space can be seen to have grown in his use of the *Review* and the later journalism. When dealing extensively with jeopardy in the fiction, Defoe found ways to keep out of personal jeopardy.

The more austere, authoritative tone of the later work can be seen in the various conduct books, starting with *The Family Instructor* (1715). Defoe was here drawing on his dissenting background, and articulating the issues of conscience and duty in the various relationships within the family. This first conduct book was certainly the most successful, in terms of sales and influence. It was described later in the century as having become 'as much a Standard Book in this Country as Robinson Crusoe & the Pilgrim's Progress.'[20] The sales seem to have been steady, if unspectacular, and prolonged. There was a fifteenth edition in 1761, and a nineteenth in 1809. It was, we are told, 'a great favourite for school prizes' in the early-nineteenth century, and was translated into Welsh in 1818.[21] In 1825, the Religious Tract Society of London must have been confident of its lasting potency, for they issued an extract called *The Two Apprentices* as part of their admonitory campaign. So it looks retrospectively as though this distanced, authoritative voice was more popular for Defoe than his ironic or interventionist one. *The Family Instructor* now seems rather dreary and lacking in urgency, but it is enlivened by anecdote, illustration and the formation of characters, and can be seen as opening up the possibility of extended fiction for Defoe.

Popular conduct books are made possible by societies which are aware of rapid social change. Defoe's books show some consciousness of the conflict between the received ideology of Puritanism and the more volatile society in which the books appeared. It is as though the conduct books made explicit and vocalised the silences in the Bible, and offered clear instruction on issues where the Bible was unhelpful or enigmatic. Issues such as the treatment of servants, the education of children in the Modern world, and the Modern view of marriage were all treated in detail in these books. Essentially, they were populist and Modern, in their attempt to make moral guidance public and comprehensible. They were non-controversial, in tone as much as in substance, illustrating their message by the simplest of parables.

All this makes Defoe sound grave, authoritative and lofty. Yet the publishing policy to some extent contradicted the stance of the books. His attempt to deflect personal attention, and to retreat from controversy, can be seen in the way the books developed a persona as author. We know that Defoe always relished false names — even 'Defoe' is a variant on his given name, and he adopted several aliases in his spying days in Scotland. The conduct books disassociated themselves from the notorious, bantering Defoe by being attributed to one 'Andrew Moreton, Esq.', a social elevation as well as a deflection of curiosity. Though Moreton's personality is not the centre of attention of his books, it is still markedly different from Defoe's, and constitutes the most extensively used alternative personality in Defoe after 'Mr. Review'. Moreton was said to be responsible for the popular tract on servants, *Every-Body's Business is No-Body's Business* (1725), *The Protestant Monastery* (1726), *Parochial Tyranny* (1727), *Second Thoughts are Best* (1728) and *Augusta Triumphans* (1728). Moreton's success as a way of attracting readers can be confirmed by noticing the way originally anonymous works were reissued under his signature — *A System of Magick* (1726) was reissued thus in 1730. Moreton's views may be Modern in their address to the public, but they are couched in a tetchiness and consciousness of old age which is inherently backward looking. He was not convinced that the Modern world was the best of all possible, and shows a consciousness of its cruelties and injustices. Defoe created this persona as the most appropriate vehicle for moral instruction, and ignored the moral complexities of his subterfuge.[22]

At this advanced stage of his life, Defoe was drawing on his varied experiences to provide him with material. The Puritan background, and the richness of his own life, gave him the material for the conduct books and the Moreton pamphlets. His travelling and his interests in trade gave him the materials for his other great later work, *A Tour thro' the Whole Island of Great Britain* (1724-6), where again he presented the book as authoritative and helpful, rather than as interventionist and aggressive. In the Preface to volume I, he announced his subdued, conciliatory position, and made explicit the reversal from previous efforts:

> The author says, that indeed he might have given his pen a loose here, to have complain'd how much the conduct of the people diminishes the reputation of the island, on many modern occasions, and so we could have made his historical account a satyr upon the country, as well as upon the people; but they are ill friends to England, who strive to write a history of her nudities, and expose, much less recommend her wicked part to posterity; he has rather endeavour'd to do her justice in those things which recommend her, and humbly to move a reformation of those, which he thinks do not. (*Tour*, p. 2)

The possibility of the satiric anatomy of the kingdom is fleetingly offered, only to be grasped away again instantly. By this point in his career, Defoe wanted to tone down his hectoring style, and offered his book more 'humbly' than ever before. From this tone, he gained aloofness and the air of disengagement, which kept him out of damaging contention. It also allowed him to present his *Tour* as fair, incontestible and reliable. In all senses, it was a middle of the road report.

His approach to early-eighteenth-century Britain was prosaic and wholly businesslike. Defoe travelled with an eye to use and purpose in the landscape, not prominently concerned with beauty or inventiveness in writing. He set out to write a suitably weighty and solid description of the country, not to write either a panegyric or a denunciation:

> I intended once to have gone due west this journey; but then I should have been obliged to croud my observations so close . . . as to have made my letter too long, or my observations too light and superficial, as others have done before me.
>
> I shall sing you no songs here of the river in the first person of a water nymph, a goddess, (and I know not what) according to the humour of the ancient poets. I shall talk nothing of the marriage of old Isis, the male river, with the beautiful Thame, the female river, a whimsy as simple as the subject was empty, but I shall speak of the river as occasion presents, as it really is made glorious by the splendor of its shores, gilded with noble palaces, strong fortifications, large hospitals, and publick buildings . . .
> (*Tour*. pp. 172-4)

This is only one of many instances where Defoe denounces pastoral whimsy in favour of ringing tribute to economic expansion. In obvious contrast to the grumpy and retrospective Moreton persona, the Defoe of the *Tour* was progressivist and projecting. Whereas in the conduct books, Defoe was drawing on his Puritan past, to make the historically sanctioned moral issues clear, in the *Tour*, he was offering a tribute to the forward-looking Whig view of history. Though there were elements of pessimism and archaic conservatism in his economic thinking, Defoe was more advanced there than in his moral pamphlets. His sense of bustle and energy is more directly communicated when discussing trade than when discussing religion, and his more ruminative discussions of the issues late in life, in the *Tour* and in the massive *Atlas Maritimus & Commercialis* (1728), show his belief that only an active commercial life could animate the country.

Defoe's literary career, then, went through the stages of vigorous, bantering political intervention, more reflective and consistent periodical contributions and eventually ruminative essays on trade and religion. Where does his fiction fit into this scheme? And what features of the other writing does it display? At first sight, it looks as though at least some of the fiction draws on Defoe's interest in history, and was presented as fiction as part of a general safeguarding process of displacement. In *Memoirs of a Cavalier* (1720), for instance, the persona of the soldier hero is used to allow privileged access to historical events, and to introduce initimacy both with the great man Gustavus Adolphus and with the common soldiery. In the Preface, Defoe (or at least his editorial presence) claims that the book is authentic, but that it allows particular delights which more general histories cannot supply:

> almost all the Facts, especially those of Moment, are confirmed for their general Part by all the Writers of those Times, if they are here embellished with Particulars, which are nowhere else to be found, that is the Beauty we boast of . . .[23]

The notion of 'embellishment' is important here, for it reveals the way the fiction is redeemed. Instead of being some distracting kind of fancy, it is a form of shaping and moulding, which lets the historical events open out to show their true meaning. From a general abstract of the Civil War and Adolphus' campaigns, the Cavalier brings out some vision of the meaning of bravery, and provides a way of inspecting the soldierly virtues. Similarly to Defoe's other long soldierly narrative, *The Military Memoirs of Captain George Carleton* (1728), the narrative deals both with the broad historical sweep, and with the narrator's reaction to events. The theme of both books, if there be one, is the individual's role in history, and the proper behaviour of the soldier in wartime. Defoe's interest in this kind of biography grew out of his interest in historical narrative, not out of an interest in fiction itself.

The same could be said of the much better known narrative *A Journal of the Plague Year* (1722). Defoe wrote few dull things, but some of his historical narratives certainly lack zest. Even the very sympathetic John Robert Moore called Defoe's *The History of the Union* 'the nearest to a dull book that he ever wrote'.[24] The problem with that narrative is that it remains so plodding, and is so devoid of reactions. *Memoirs of a Cavalier* sought to invigorate history by plotting an individual's reaction to great events. So too *A Journal of the Plague Year* becomes a very animated version of history from below. Its tale of the saddler who stayed in London while most others fled, and of his graphically recorded recollections of the visitation, is compulsive and very easy to follow. The rather indigestible lumps of fact have been made palatable by the human centre to the tale, and 'H.F.' gives readers a way of comprehending the most ghastly of events. Both this narrative and Defoe's earlier work depicting extreme conditions, *The Storm: or a Collection of the Most Remarkable Casualties and Disasters which Happened in the Late Dreadful Tempest, Both by Sea and Land* (1704), convey the sense of first-hand experience which makes the events comprehensible, through the perception of scale. For *The Storm*, Defoe ran an advertisement in the *London Gazette*, soliciting any memorable anecdotes from witnesses (specifically from clergymen, who combined unimpeachability with literacy).[25] The result of this news gathering is certainly powerful, but it lacks the plausibility of H.F., in his fears and anxieties.

So it is possible to see those two long narratives as being Defoe's way of making historical storytelling palatable. Was this Defoe's aim in all his fiction? The *personae* I have mentioned so far — Moreton, H.F., the Cavalier, and the Tourist — have all been secondary to the events they reveal, and their role has been the provision of an individualised point of view on public events. It is possible to see some element of this in the major narratives. Crusoe and Singleton provide ways of seeing piracy, Moll and the Colonel provide individualised access to the discussion of crime. Roxana and Moll give scale to discussions of marriage and parenthood. Roxana also provides a human way of talking about prostitution. Jack shows us something about the rights and wrongs of slave-owning. It would be wrong to ignore this public side of Defoe's fiction, or to dismiss the way it repeats themes he worried over elsewhere. But for all that, these issues are never made central in the fiction, and I do not think it fair to argue that the narrators are merely subsidiary. Of course, first-person narrative makes the distinction between plot and character difficult to draw, and it is true that plot is probably more important than personality in these tales.

Before going on to a wider discussion of the popular direction of Defoe's narratives, it is worth trying to assess his attitude to fiction. He was certainly aware of the complexities and contradictions of inventing a narrative to tell the truth. In the Preface to *The Storm*, writing as 'the Age's Humble Servant', he said:

> I cannot be so ignorant of my own intentions, as not to know, that in many cases I shall act the Divine, and draw necessary practical inferences from the extraordinary Remarkables of this Book . . . And while I pretend to a thing so solemn, I cannot but premise I should stand convicted of a double Imposture, to forge a Story, and then preach Repentance to the Reader from a crime greater than I would have him repent of: endeavouring by a Lie to correct the Reader's Vices, and Sin against Truth to bring the Reader off from sinning against Sense.[26]

The moralistic anxiety expressed here is put more forcefully by the Moreton-like narrator of *The Family Instructor*, who approved of the mother who burnt all her daughters' trivial reading matter, such as novels and romances. Of course, the pose of moralist is paradoxical and self-defeating here, for the 'editor' has to lie and lie again to get nearer to the truth. An example of how combative and problematic this disdain becomes for the professional writer is seen in Defoe's introduction to *The Highland Rogue* (1723):

> It is not a romantic Tale that the Reader is here presented with, but a real History; not the adventures of a *Robinson Crusoe*, a *Colonel Jack*, or a *Moll Flanders*, but the actions of the *Highland Rogue*, a Man that has been too notorious to pass for a mere imaginary Person . . .[27]

The unerring way in which Defoe disparages his own creations here is delightful. It shows the victory of the committed professional writer over the anxious Puritan. The aim of each text is to acquire an audience, and any trading practice which will secure that is acceptable. Puritan scruples about the status of fiction have little place in Defoe's later narratives, as that fiction proved a lot less problematic and dangerous to him than his other writings had.

As a writer, Defoe was always much more concerned with the status of his trade, and with professional ethics, than with Puritan morality. Though the last component was a prominent feature in the content of his writing, it was suppressed in his practice and procedure. The most sustained discussion of the writer's role came in the *Review*, where Defoe returned regularly to the question of the regulation of the press. Talking of piracy and legislation, he came down strongly on the side of some form of legally enforceable restraint. Defoe, in his guise as altruistic projector, saw the piracy of printed texts as a threat to his professional status (and to his income), and denounced it soundly:

> The Practice is the Shame and Scandal of the Present Time — and gives a Liberty to daily Invasions of Property equal in villainy to robbing a House, or plundering an Hospital. Nor is this all; it is a Discouragement to Industry, a Dishonour to Learning, and a Cheat upon the Whole Nation. By this Practice, a Man, who had study'd several Years to perform the most elaborate Work; and perhaps been at 500*l*. Charge to print it, besides

all other Pains, and to whom such a Work might otherwise be an Inheritance, and to his Family, has his Labour destroy'd, his Expenses lost, and his copy re-printed by pyratical Booksellers and Printers, who eat the Gain of the poor Man's Labour, destroy and spoil the Work itself, cheat the Buyer by performing it imperfect, and ruin the laborious Author. (*Review*, VI, p. 363)

The argument here is similar to some of Defoe's other economic pronouncements. It rejects *laissez-faire* attitudes to the market economy, and seeks some kind of regulation to protect both producer and consumer. Yet it also rejects the most obvious solution, a return to the old pre-1695 system when all the presses had to be officially licensed. Defoe's somewhat sceptical view of human nature led him to reject the idea of a licenser immediately:

NO LICENSER, whatever you do — Partiality, Bribery, Siding with Parties, permitting Error, and crushing valuable Learning, were always the Consequences of a *Licenser* of the Press. (*Review*, VI, p. 416)

The author must be free from overt political pressure, and the press should strive to subdue partiality. These might seem odd notions from a writer as embroiled in political controversy as Defoe, but we must remember his persistently mediating role, and his recurrent desire to subdue party strife. Despite his rejection of the old system, Defoe still argued in favour of some profitable restraint — '. . . I cannot but agree that a Regulation, or due Restraint of the Press is a good Work.'[28]

Defoe's involvement in the proposals to regulate the press is informative both of his notion of what a writer ought to do, and of his rather different behaviour in the less than ideal world. The mixture of confident, firm argument, and furtive, opportunistic behaviour is typical. In the *Review*, he stipulated that it should be a punishable offence for any printer or publisher to issue a book or pamphlet without the definite consent of its author. Playfully, Defoe suggested that a suitable punishment for offenders might be to require them to read his *Elegy on the Author of The True Born Englishman* at least once a week (*Review*, VI. p. 416). More seriously, he suggested some financial punishment — '*5l. per* Sheet for the said Copy, to be paid Half to the Queen, Half to the Person injur'd' (*Review*, VI. p. 419). Such an extravagant sum would have served to remunerate an abused author, but any scheme of fines would only have worked if the printer or publisher could be apprehended and sued. The major drawback of the proposal, as far as Defoe was concerned, was that it only curtailed some of the practices of shady publishers, and did nothing about seditious publications, issued under their author's name — what he called the 'swarm' of 'Socinian, Heretical, Deistic, and Erroneous Books' (*Review*, VI. p. 403). To secure the restraint of these publications, Defoe suggested that 'every Author, who causes any Thing he writes to be printed or publish'd shall be oblig'd to cause his Name to be printed in the Frontispiece of the Book' (*Review*, VI.p. 420). In that formulation, the responsibility lay entirely with the author. Elsewhere, Defoe's position was more flexible, asking for some law which would 'oblige the Printer or Bookseller to place the Author's Name in the Title, or himself'.[29]

In these formulations of his proposal, no sanctions were named, but the author was being offered greater protection in return for a more responsible attitude to his production. Defoe's proposals about the regulation of the press were part of a widespread debate on the best way to replace the lapsed Licensing Act. His ideas were largely in line with Tory proposals, though he never went so far as to suggest that all printing presses should be registered — presumably that would have gone too far in the direction of restraining trade. During this debate, at least six bills were presented in Parliament, between 1695 and 1702, but none had reached the statute. The only law limiting book publication to come into effect was an act in 1707, which made it a treasonable offence to publish the Pretender's right to the throne. There were still laws of libel, of course, and Defoe was arraigned under one of them in 1714, for his editorial revision of a letter in the *Flying Post*, which seemed to suggest that the Earl of Anglesey was a Jacobite sympathiser. However, no action was taken against him after his trial. On wider issues, there was no law fully to regulate the behaviour of authors until Fox's Libel Act of 1792.[30] Defoe's role in the debate was to try fo emphasise the non-party interest, to offer himself as an honest broker, concerned with the broader issues involved, and to make suggestions which safeguarded both readers and writers from overt political pressure.

Despite Defoe's arguments against anonymity, and his demand for a kind of authorial accountability, his own works were most often unsigned, or pseudonymous. Of the 500 and more works now acknowledged as Defoe's, only 19 displayed the full name or initials of their author.[31] Certainly, Defoe's authorship might often have been recognisable in other ways. The *True Born Englishman*, though issued anonymously, was instantly ascribed to him, and this was confirmed when the *True Collection* included a named engraving of Defoe as frontispiece. Both *A Hymn to the Pillory* and *The Shortest Way* were quickly ascribed, and Defoe occasionally admitted his responsibility for anonymous pieces through his *Review*, for example, *The History of the Union* (III, p. 658), *Giving Alms No Charity* (IV, p. 27), and *The Consolidator* (V, p. 71). Even with all these means of acknowledgement, the canon's reliance on anonymity is very striking. Even the *Essay on the Regulation of the Press*, containing the proposals for compulsory signature, was unsigned. And most important of all, the major narrative fiction was issued anonymously, thus dissociating it from Defoe's known pamphleteering career.

My assessment of Defoe's literary career so far has emphasised his gradual withdrawal from the front line of hostilities, into a more conciliatory and ruminative position, sometimes put forward obliquely by a persona. His persistent engagement with the professional ethics of writing did not prevent him from taking advantage of such loopholes as existed, if they allowed him the distance from jeopardy which he sought. His literary career shows increasing furtiveness, and a dwindling of the direct connection between writing and society which was so obvious in the first three years of the century. The sense of openness and integrity which is expressed in the *Review* is a pose, for Defoe was always aware of the need for guile and secrecy in putting forward schemes. In one of his letters to Harley, he praised Cardinal Richelieu for his knowledge of the world:

How Many Miscarriages have happen'd in England for want of Silence and Secresy!

Cardinall Richlieu, was the Greatest Master of This Vertue That Ever I Read of, in the World, and if hystory has Not wrong'd him, has Sacrifyz'd Many a faithfull Agent, after he had Done his Duty, that he might be sure he should Not be betraid.

He kept Three Offices for the Dispatch of his Affaires, and One was so Private, That None was admitted but in the Darke, and Up a pair of back Remote Stairs . . . Tis Plain the French Out do us at These Two Things, Secrecy and Intelligence . . .[32]

He felt that improvement was more important than acceptance, and the Modern sensibility allowed for any subterfuge to be employed if it brought about the required end. Defoe's social policies were always forward looking in the respect that he felt that stability and comfort could be achieved, in the right circumstances, by effort and self-assertion. The backward-looking element in his writing comes from his reverence for the days of William, and his distaste for the Hanoverians. This balancing of human assertiveness and the yearning for comfort became much more prominent as his career progressed, and, as we shall see, it informed his fiction with its main themes and moods.

The role of secrecy in the fiction will be discussed later. It appears frequently in the earlier writing, as anonymity, and as covert self-advertisement. I referred earlier to the sly self-justification in *A Vindication of the Press*. Other examples of this engaging furtiveness can be found in the *Review*. In a discussion of a pamphlet called *A Letter from a Gentleman at the Court of St. Germains* (1710), Mr Review said, 'Whether that Letter be a Genuine Produce of a Popish Author, or no, I do not determine . . . The book is worth any man's perusal, and I refer to it' (*Review*, VII, p. 371). The pamphlet was, of course, 'one of Defoe's best and most characteristic writings'.[33] A more extended example can be found the following year, when a whole issue of the *Review* was given over to a laudatory discussion of the remarkable prophecies contained in *The British Visions* (1710). The writer described it as 'a little Book which I found at *Newcastle*, as I last came up from *Scotland*, and is Sold but for two-pence' (*Review*, VIII, p. 45). The implied exhortation to part with twopence is not informed by any suggestion that Defoe might have written the work himself. These are examples of Defoe seizing upon the possibilities of anonymous publication, while overall disapproving of it. In a better world, he would not have to do these things, but since things are as they are, he should not overlook the possibilities. We shall see this pattern again in *Crusoe* and *Moll*, and observe how it affects the characters.

The shaping of Defoe's fiction is, then, produced by Defoe's social position, his retreat from controversy and his professionalisation as a writer. Two other contributory factors need to be mentioned, his Modern tastes in reading, and his conception of his audience. It will never be possible to find out everything Defoe read, but the source studies of his fiction reveal a very eclectic taste, and voracity in reading.[34] Defoe's apparent appetite for reading all sorts of things, and vast numbers of books is made even more remarkable when we remember his other activities and business pursuits. In *A Vindication of the Press* (1718), he showed, or at least claimed, a knowledge of Cicero, Horace, Chaucer, Dryden, Spencer [sic], Shakespeare, Milton, Cowley, Otway, Jonson, Pope, Prior, Rowe, Congreve, Phillips, Farquhar, Addison, Steele, Oldsworth, Rochester and Butler. The fascinating thing about this list is its enormous bias towards the contemporary world. After all, only the first two authors on the list are classics, and only four others were not alive during at least some part of Defoe's lifetime. The Moderns were clearly Defoe's main reading, especially if we remember his great familiarity with travel literature, writing about economics and trade and dissenting literature. In the course of the *Review*, he referred to Aesop, Homer, Ovid, Tacitus, Virgil, Plutarch, Lucretius, Juvenal and Demosthenes amongst the Ancients, and, with markedly more conviction, Marvell, Suckling, Bunyan, Locke and Boileau amongst the Moderns. His attitude to reading and the literature that should be propagated is summed up in the following passage:

> the King of *France* outdoes all the Princes of *Europe*, where such Encouragement is given to Learning, that all useful Books in the World now speak *French*, and a Man may be an Universall Schollar, read *Virgil*, *Horace*, *Ovid*, and all the Antient Poets; *Cicero*, *Plato*, *Epictetus*, *Aristotle*, and all the Antient Philosophers; *St. Athanasius*, *St. Augustine*, and all the Primitive Fathers; *Plutarch*, *Livy*, and all the Antient Historians; and yet neither understand a word of *Greek* or *Latin*.[35]

As well as secrecy and intelligence, it seems as though the French excelled at making useful literature publicly available. Defoe's emphasis on the utility of reading is important here, as is his very Modern desire to reach beyond the obstacles of Greek and Latin.

The idea of the usefulness of reading and writing is inevitably associated with the reading public, and the writer's attitude towards it. I have been arguing that Defoe's persistent desire to get beyond party and religious differences leads him to try for the widest audience possible, and that the populist impulse is very strong in his work. Clearly, the very idea of writing fiction involves a populist approach, since that form is the most consonant to, and least directly challenging of, its audience's attitudes. Unfortunately, it is extremely difficult to reconstruct Defoe's audience, or to make anything other than guesses about its expectations of reading. It seems obvious that Defoe's fiction has to be seen as Modern, popular fiction, in its desire to please, enthral and enlighten. But it remains very hard to go beyond that to say just what it was that people received from reading Defoe. I have argued that for the author, Defoe's fiction was a way of re-addressing the public, without confronting that public, and without putting himself under pressure. The fiction addresses itself to notions of escape, freedom and mobility, which were comforting images for a constrained, immobile readership. Yet, the relationship between the readership, the society of the time and the shapes of the fiction is indirect and at times difficult to isolate. The enterprise of writing fiction was in itself Modern, and addressed to readers who were uninformed by the classics, or at least who were not required to be informed by the classics. The fictions are escapist in the sense that they offer very stylised versions of the audience's experience, in the form of adventure and peril.

All these complex questions of the role of popular fiction at the time, its generic divisions, and the satisfactions it offered, will be looked at in the next chapter. So far, I have sought to present a version of Defoe's career which stresses his business activities, his political adventurism and subsequent quietism and his dissenting background, and which has tried to show how these affected his writing in general. The fiction was a much more collaborative exercise, in that a covert Defoe was colluding with his readers' expectations to provide satisfying yarns. The possibility of reading his fiction simply as a kind of lying journalism, so prevalent in nineteenth-century estimates of Defoe, and retained by F.R. Leavis in *The Great Tradition*, is simply unsupportable. Apart from the more obviously historical *Memoirs of a Cavalier* and *A Journal of the Plague Year*, Defoe's fiction does not simply record or report. It always offers shaped, distorted versions of experience, sufficiently distant from the experience of readers to be enthralling, yet sufficiently similar to be recognisable. The combination of the bizarre and the familiar, of the adventurist and the domestic, makes Defoe's fiction resplendent with the author's interventions. However, the meticulousness of detail and sense of haphazardness distracts attention from his mediations.

In order to be able to discuss the uniqueness of these tales, it is necessary to assess their context. As popular fictions, they intervene

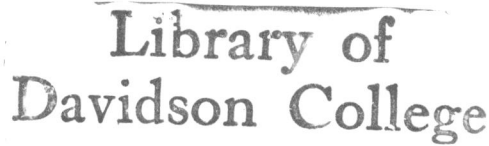

in a literary world, full of conventions, forms and received styles. Any attempt to remove them from that literary world is as futile as the attempt to remove Defoe from the culture in which he was active. It is only possible to read Defoe, and his fiction, as part of a full, divided culture, and it becomes essential to understand the role of popular writing within that culture before Defoe's texts can be fairly articulated.

My prior analysis of Defoe's political career, and of his attitude to writing, has shown a significant change taking place after the earlier adventures. Defoe's increasingly pacifying role after 1704, albeit in the service of his political masters, shows his alignment to moderation and order. These themes become clarified in his fiction, along with other recognisable issues from his life — education, loyalty and the rhythms of recovery from disaster. The discussion so far has not been background, but an attempt to reconstruct the experiences from which the narratives were formed.

Notes

1 The standard bibliographical tool for reading Defoe is John Robert Moore, *A Checklist of the Writings of Daniel Defoe* (2nd edn, Hamden, Conn., 1971), which will later be referred to in the notes as *Checklist*. There have been some emendations by scholars since 1971, but they do not yet seem to affect the texts I have chosen. Orwell's remarks on Richards will be found in 'Boy's Weeklies', in *The Collected Essays, Journalism and Letters of George Orwell*, 4 vols (London, 1968), I, p. 517.

2 John Robert Moore, *Daniel Defoe: Citizen of the Modern World* (Chicago and London, 1958), p. vii.

3 *Boswell's Life of Johnson*, G.B. Hill (ed.), revised and enlarged by L.F. Powell, 6 vols (Oxford, 1934, 1950; 2nd edn., V and VI, 1964), III, p. 268.

4 *The Fable of the Cuckoo* (1701), quoted in Pat Rogers (ed.), *Defoe: The Critical Heritage* (London and Boston, 1972), p. 10. Further references to this book in the notes will abbreviate the title to *Heritage*.

5 Swift, *A Letter Concerning the Sacramental Test* (1709); Gay, *The Present State of Wit* (1711), from *Heritage*, pp. 38, 39.

6 My discussion of Defoe's early life relies on James Sutherland, *Defoe* (1937, 2nd edn., London, 1950) and J.R. Moore, *Daniel Defoe*. I have also taken into account the work of F. Bastian, *Defoe's Early Life* (London, 1981), and the relevant parts of Peter Earle, *The World of Defoe* (London, 1976).

7 Defoe, *A Vindication of the Press* (1718), O.C. Williams (ed.), Augustan Reprint Society, no. 29 (Los Angeles, 1951), pp. 29-30.

8 See the controversial discussion of the political status of printing in Lennard J. Davis, *Factual Fictions: The Origins of the English Novel* (New York, 1983), pp. 85-102 and 138-54.

9 *A Vindication of the Press*, p. 29.

10 Defoe, *A True Collection of the Writings of the Author of the True Born Englishman*, 2 vols (London, 1703, 1704), II, sig. A3r.
Information about the sales of Defoe's poems, and about the circumstances of their

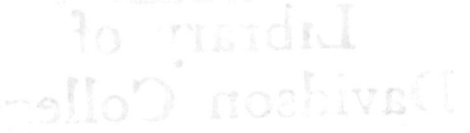

publication, will be found in D.F. Foxon, *English Verse 1700-1750*, 2 vols (Cambridge, 1975).

11. Defoe, *An Appeal to Honour and Justice* (1715), in Boulton, p. 168.
12. Defoe, *The True Born Englishman* (1701), in Boulton, p. 59.
13. *The True Born Hugonot* (1701), in *Heritage*, p. 34.
14. From Defoe, 'Elegy on the Author of the True Born Englishman', *True Collection*, II, p. 70. See also Foxon, *English Verse 1700-1750*, S442.6, L238, L162, N132, T513. Defoe wrote about one such spurious poem at some length in an early *Review* (4 April 1704).
15. 'An Unpublished Manuscript of Defoe', in Sutherland, *Defoe*, p. 279.
16. Defoe, *The Shortest Way With Dissenters* (1702), in Boulton, p. 96.
17. See Moore, *Daniel Defoe*, p. 348.
18. Defoe, *A Hymn to the Pillory* (1703), in Boulton, p. 109.
19. Defoe, *An Appeal to Honour and Justice* (1715), in Boulton, p. 172.
20. Quoted in E.P. Thompson, *The Making of the English Working Class* (revised edn., Harmondsworth, 1968), p. 118.
21. Walter Wilson, *Memoirs of the Life and Times of Daniel defoe*, 3 vols (London, 1830), III, p. 480.
22. For a discussion of Defoe's problems with the lying status of fiction, see Davis, *Factual Fictions*, pp. 154-73.
23. Defoe, *Memoirs of a Cavalier* (1720), James T. Boulton (ed.) (London, 1972), p. 4.
24. Moore, *Daniel Defoe*, p. 255.
25. See Laura Ann Curtis, *The Versatile Defoe* (London, 1979), pp. 279-80.
26. Defoe, *The Storm* (1704), sig. A3r.
27. Defoe (?), *The Highland Rogue* (1723), sig. A2v.
28. Defoe, *An Essay on the Regulation of the Press* (1704), Luttrel Reprints no. 7, J.R. Moore (ed.) (Oxford, 1948), p. 4.
29. Ibid., p. 24.
30. See Laurence Hanson, *Government and the Press 1695-1753* (1936, reprinted, Oxford, 1967), pp. 7-10.
31. Moore, *Checklist*, numbers 16, 31, 38, 41, 63, 85, 106, 117, 119, 143, 153, 161, 162, 167, 171, 173, 177, 307, 430.
32. *The Letters of Daniel Defoe*, G.H. Healey (ed.) (Oxford, 1955), p. 39.
33. Moore, *Checklist*, p. 77.
34. The best of the many source studies is A.W. Secord, *Studies in the Narrative Method of Defoe* (Urbana, Ill., 1924), which explores Defoe's use of travel literature.
35. Defoe, *An Essay on the Regulation of the Press*, pp. 12-13.

2 READING POPULAR FICTION

Defoe's fiction may look like a mere appendage to his pamphleteering and poetic career, in its evasion of direct political statement. Yet, as I have argued in the previous chapter, it shares with this later political work the desire to address as many readers as possible, and to address them above party divisions. When the 59-year-old Defoe came to write *Robinson Crusoe*, he had a lifetime of the most varied religious, mercantile, political and literary activity to draw upon, and a sense of a popular audience to address. Just as the populist aims of works like *A Hymn to the Pillory* or the *Tour* involved some knowledge of what the audience would accept, so the professional enterprise of the fiction demanded that he accommodate himself to his readers' desires for distraction. Above all, Defoe's fiction is popular fiction. It is escapist, diverting and enthralling, seeking to satisfy its audience more than to disturb them. Though the texts articulate large systems of thought, such as Natural Law or casuistry or Puritan thinking of all kinds, their aim is to provide the audience with recognisable, dramatised versions of heightened experience. Each narrative crams in more than any reader could expect to experience, and offers an image of life which was in some way comforting. Even *Roxana*, with its dark ending, comforts its readership by keeping them distant from the narrator throughout. Yet this notion of Defoe's fiction being fundamentally popular may sound disparaging. If 'popular' as a category is set against 'polite' or 'high' literature, then it might seem crude and unsubtle. In this chapter, I want to look more closely at what is meant by shifting Defoe's fiction from its place in a diachronically understood literary tradition to a synchronic, divided culture. This will involve some discussion of the nature of popular literature, and a look at what eighteenth-century readers would have understood by the term. Putting Defoe back into his culture, and seeing his role in that culture as the producer of tales, may require some defending, but only because he has previously been displaced.

In the relatively short history of English as an academic discipline, the central activity of its agents has been to demarcate a definite, isolated area of enquiry, and so to establish the subject by its uniqueness. Since reading itself has been such a widespread, undisciplined activity, the specialised study called 'English' has defended itself by generating and privileging a special kind of reading, or a reading of certain specialised, non-popular texts. It has sought to construct traditions and forms, and has broadly accommodated Defoe either as a forerunner of the form called the novel, or as a surprisingly vigorous purveyor of a technique called realism. But even within this diverse, pluralistic study, questions of selection and evaluation have become so centralised that they seem primary, and Defoe has not fared especially well. At times he has been cast into that group of writers who have merely some kind of historical interest, not true value. At other times, he has been allowed membership of the literary elite, but only when on his best behaviour, and only when he has left his political interests behind him.

Defoe's fluctuating fortunes would be worth a study in themselves, as an illustration of the way English puts forward its values. Whilst the main enterprise of establishing a canon is still continuing, and whilst Defoe is sometimes in and sometimes out, it is useful to examine the aims sought by the canon. At least some of the reluctance to accept Defoe arises from his obvious robustness, which can be seen as insensitivity. As early as 1785, long before the professionalisation of English, Defoe was regarded as suspiciously vulgar:

> Yet I am not convinced, that the world has been made much wiser, or better, by the perusal of these lives: they may have diverted the lower orders, but I doubt if they have much improved them; if however they have not made them better, they have not left them worse. But they do not exhibit many scenes which are welcome to cultivated minds.[1]

The association of Defoe with the lower orders is traditional, but not always even as indifferent as this. Hazlitt, for example, thought *Moll Flanders* 'calculated to do an infinite deal of mischief among the lower classes'.[2] Purveying fiction for the lower orders is bad enough, but purveying mischievous fiction is clearly not on at all. Defoe is ruled out of serious consideration here, because of the way the books blandly accept the demands readers might make of them. Defoe is seen, at best, as a good read, and at worst as a bad read.

The most obvious tactic that English has used to reinstate Defoe has been to turn him into a good writer *despite* his aims, his audience and his attachment to eighteenth-century society. The tone of regret permeates discussion of Defoe, even in the most helpful and sensitive books:

> Defoe was in a sense without successors, and because of his dubious reputation as a journalist and political agent, and because he wrote much of low life, and professed to pay little attention to literary canons, his great popularity was in large part sub-literary.

Defoe's energy or innovativeness may compensate for his dubious behaviour, but he seems to start off with a severe handicap. Yet, surely what has just been said is in itself very insensitive to Defoe's cultural position. He may have professed indifference to some 'literary canons', but his writing was informed by an extraordinary range of reading. His audience may in turn have been unlearned and unacquainted with what we now think of as the literary tradition, but surely the mere fact of their participation in a newly literate culture, seen in their reading of Defoe, makes the term 'sub-literary' weighted and prejorative. The implied hierarchy from the literary downwards is made more overt slightly later:

> It is hard to analyse a bygone reading public: we can only speculate about various levels and attitudes and their interaction, about the relation between the persistence of popular traditions of a semi-literary or sub-literary kind, and the emergence and acceptance of great innovators who change the course of things. Bunyan and Defoe, writers of high quality and superb ability, tended for generations to be re-absorbed into the popular current.[3]

With the metaphor of the 'popular current' and 're-absorbed', it is tempting to see this critic offering Defoe the kiss of life. He is obviously trying to wrest Defoe out of his popular readership, and looking for what he takes to be the really valuable, innovative features of his work. Certainly, Defoe might have welcomed this rescue mission, but it seems a weak way to describe the purpose of the books, and how they are actually read. The notion that some books 'change the course of things' would have delighted Defoe the projector, but it seems to make literature very central and powerful. In the early-eighteenth century, 'things' were changed by royal decree, by acts of parliament, by war, and by all manner of public events.

Writers may have assisted, provoked, or hindered those changes, but there is no evidence that their books were instrumental in historical change, whatever they might have said to the contrary.

The move to find some timeless value in Defoe, and to praise him in spite of his lamentable attachment to his public, derives its ideological support from Matthew Arnold, who saw the preservation of the higher, aesthetic values as a defence against barbarism. In *Culture and Anarchy*, he defined culture as 'the study of perfection', and critics of his persuasion are thus drawn to the identification of timeless perfection, and the advocacy of seriousness and solemnity in criticism. A canon of valuable works is thereby constructed, leaving out nearly everything that people have actually read. Arnold talked of that selectivity producing 'the best that has been thought or known in the world'.[4] In such a canon of productive perfection, a writer like Defoe, inconsistent, demotic and shifty, will have no place. Popular literature must also have no intrinsic value, since it seeks to satisfy the lowest common denominator, appetite, rather than the highest, most exclusive property, sensitivity.

The predominance of this kind of criticism in English has made writers on popular literature adopt frantically defensive positions. As C.W.E. Bigsby puts it:

> As an area of study, popular culture has a reasonably long, if fragmented history, but uncertainty over method, the absence of any generally agreed theory and the persistence of an academic tradition suspicious of material so generally available, has created an air of defensiveness which has still not entirely dissipated.[5]

In the face of such uncertainty and institutional hostility, many writers on popular literature have become humble and apologetic. With a deal of compassionate concern, they remind readers that life is after all short, and that any concern with low literature might seem like a waste of the few moments allowed to us. J.M.S. Tompkins opened a book on later-eighteenth-century popular fiction by saying 'a book devoted to the display of tenth-rate fiction stands in need of justification'.[6] She went on to apologise for wasting her reader's time with 'over-scrupulous gentleness' towards 'this inferior fiction', while reassuring us that she has kept her hands clean by treating the novel as 'a popular amusement rather than a literary form'. In fact, the book is lively and full of enthusiasm, but a reading of the exculpatory preface would make it seem dull and dour.

What worries me in such discussions is the casual conjunction of 'tenth-rate' and 'popular'. What justification can there be for dismissing the objects of most people's attention as trivial? Why are great books assumed to be central, and to have more importance by definition than widely-read ones? And must popular writing serve only as a dull background for the more subtle analysis of inherently subtle works? Unexamined evaluation of that sort can only be central to a discipline which sees itself in a moral position. That is, English has taken upon itself the role of scrutinising the books people ought to read (or ought to have read), rather than the ones they have actually given their time and attention to. In literary study, the moral emphasis can be seen in the shift in meaning of the word 'literature', from referring to something written, to its later reference to a privileged body of imaginative or creative writing. Alongside this selective use of 'literature' there is the connotation in 'popular' of vulgar, cheap, or trivial. The term popular literature, then, becomes an oxymoron for some critics, for whom literature must in no circumstances be popularised.

However, the various consequences of adopting the oxymoronic usage of 'popular literature' are highly undesirable, and especially distorting for Defoe's enterprise. The generating of a separate canon of approved works may satisfactorily demarcate a separate discipline, but it becomes a grossly elitist, enfeebling discipline. Any critical statements made from that stance, however subtle, are affirmative of the ideology which has constructed the canon, and become collaborative with the omissions from that canon. For the Arnoldian critic, the whole fabric of society, in which literature operates, becomes hostile, and an object little worthy of attention. It is obstructive to literature, and questions about it are reductive, of inferior interest. Taken to extremes, this can lead to ludicrous statements like 'political passions . . . distort the literary scene from, say 5 November 1709'.[7] The extraordinary idea implicit in such a statement that the literary scene is normally pure, and that political passions somehow cloud and sully it, shows the enfeeblement which results from excessively privileging the literary.

The attempt to relocate Defoe within the popular, and within the context of these 'political passions' is not in any sense an attempt to debase him, or to confirm his position outside the real literary canon. Rather, it is an attempt to understand him within his historical location, and to try to understand the way his fiction mediates between him, his society, and his readers. To call him popular, in this sense, need not imply crudity or vulgarity, but simply isolates his breadth of address, and his attempts to dramatise recognisable features of people's lives. Treating Defoe's fiction as popular lays emphasis on the way it was written for a specific readership, in forms with which those readers were at least partly familiar, and on the way it was shaped by social forces, just as Defoe himself was. The social nature of his productions is obvious from their persistent availability to other writers as well as to the reading public, as seen in the many hundreds of *robinsonaden*, or continuations of the original *Crusoe*. But it is surely a mistake to strive after the timeless qualities of a writer so intimately concerned in the affairs of his day as Defoe. It would be wrong to label so unusual a figure merely representative or typical of his times, but it remains difficult to find a terminology to describe his role within the culture, while maintaining a sense of his individuality. It has become commonplace to talk of Defoe as representing a new type of writer, appealing to a recently new type of reader. However, the critical writing which has sought to deal with this coincidence of novelties (most notably in Ian Watt's *The Rise of the Novel*) has relied too much upon broad generalities and a rather limp notion of *Zeitgeist*. Defoe may represent some spirit of his times, embodied in the development of the form we recognise as the novel, but he did write the startlingly popular *Crusoe*, and so stands out in retrospect from the culture of which he was a part. If we are to make sense of him fully, we have to see him as a popular author characteristic of the period, distinguishable from the others by his singular popular success, and his earlier political and religious views.

The distinction between popular literature and serious literature is too strongly emphasised by the critical tradition, and made too absolute, but it is not a wholly recent invention. In the eighteenth century, the distinction between popular and serious authors overlapped largely with the distinction between the Moderns and the Ancients I discussed earlier. The Moderns sought to address the widest possible audience of their contemporaries, whereas the Ancients wrote for a small group of intimates, always conscious of their embattled position. The literature of the Ancients, most familiarly Swift and Pope, is typically cryptic and allusive, often couched in the form of the intimate epistle, or the collusive private irony. Modernist literature, in this rather special sense of the term, seeks to popularise or capture as large an audience as possible, and so draws on narrative and fable, rather than on satire or epic. However, the internal evidence for popularity is often ambiguous, and it can be hard to assess whether a text is best treated as having been popular or not. Beset by the relative absence of information about sales, readership, or availability, the critic may have to rely on anecdote or surmise.[8] The notion that a popular text was one that many people had access to will not fit, for the more 'serious' works of Swift and Fielding were distributed as widely as Defoe's, though they were initially more expensive. Nor can popular here simply mean something like well-liked, for Defoe was singularly unpopular in that sense. Any man described as 'a loathsome Thing, shap'd like a Toad' is unlikely to win any popularity contests. The society of the period is too divided for such a general term to be pointed enough. 'Popular', in this context, must refer to the audience implied by the book, and the easy relationship that is invited between the book and its readers. Hazlitt, and Sir Walter Scott, saw Defoe's readers as the lower orders, and that may well have been the audience for popular literature in the period. In 1725, a writer in the *Dublin Journal* became agitated by fears that popular literature was spreading its tentacles upwards, into the middle classes:

> your Robinson Crusoes, Moll Flanders, Sally Salisburys and John Shepards have afforded notable instances how easy it is to gratify our curiosity, and how indulgent we are to the biographers of Newgate, who have been as greedily read by people of the better sort as the compilers of last speeches and dying words by the rabble.[9]

Defoe, it seems, was not only read by 'honest Dick and Doll', but also by the better sorts, and here the implied easiness of reading seems to have given the books access to the widest group of readers possible.

Not all Defoe's readers were artisans. Even Pope, who scorned Defoe in the *Dunciad*, found something to enjoy in *Crusoe*.[10] The voracious reading of these novels and romances seems to have permeated the society, and popular literature seems to have been a rather furtive pleasure for the upper classes. Lady Mary Wortley Montagu, for instance, took casual delight in light reading, even if she expressed her taste apologetically:

> I desir'd you to send me all the Books of which you gave a catalogue, except H. Fielding's and his Sister's, which I have allready. I thank God my Taste still continues for the Gay part of reading; wiser people my think it triffling, but it serves to sweeten Life to me, and is, at worst, better than the Generallity of Conversation.[11]

Wiser, or at least graver people did indeed think her taste trifling. Lady Walpole remarked caustically to Spence, 'I wonder how anybody can find any pleasure in reading the books which are Lady Mary's favourites!'[12] And in a chiding reply to Lady Mary's request for more of these trifles, Lord Hervey sternly (or mock-sternly) announced:

> I will get the Books you desire and send them to You by the first Opportunity, but they are really fitter for the Kitten you mention than for you, for tho the tearing the Leaves may give that happy playfull animal some Entertainment, it is . . . morally impossible that the reading them should give you any.[13]

Despite these pompous disclaimers, the taste for novels and romances was consistently growing in the period after 1715, and various justifications for reading them were developed.

Dr Johnson, who was enthusiastic about *Crusoe* and some of Defoe's other works, if not about Defoe himself, was never against the reading of romances and popular narratives:

> We must read what the world reads at the moment. It has been maintained that this superfoetation, this teeming of the press in modern times, is prejudicial to good literature, because it obliges us to read so much of what is of inferiour value, in order to be in the fashion; so that better works are neglected for want of time . . . But it must be considered, that we have now more knowledge generally diffused; all our ladies read now, which is a great extension. . .[14]

The contribution of popular narrative to this general diffusion would have been close to Defoe's heart. The role played by the growth of female literacy in the development is well known, and the educational side of popular writing must be obvious. Elsewhere, Johnson found a subtle justification for popular writing, based more on its capacity to enthral and delight than on its pedagogic role:

> I am always for getting a boy forward in his learning; for that is a sure good. I would let him at first read *any* English book which happens to engage his attention; because you have brought him to have entertainment from a book. He'll get better books afterwards.[15]

So for Johnson, popular literature is justified by its ability to diffuse knowledge generally, and its capacity to bring the unsophisticated towards the enjoyment of reading. Learning made simple, and reading made painless. In Dr Johnson's view, the Moderns were insufficiently grave, but still they could prove useful.

Moving on with the definition of popular literature, the attempt to isolate its audience has not succeeded, for it was read promiscuously. However, it seems clear that its function for that very broad audience was to divert or painlessly instruct. Popular literature seems to have been that branch of letters which people took up without serious intent, although surreptitious seriousness might still creep over them. This capacity to divert was clearly the kind of danger that the moralistic Defoe/Moreton figure was anxious about in *The Family Instructor*, where romances could distract impressionable young women more than was good for them. Of course, people could read all manner of things for diversion, not only the things designed for that purpose. And different classes of readers could take diversion from different kinds of book. To clarify the definition of 'popular' for Defoe's works, I want to suggest that his narratives are designed to divert and quietly inform those classes with seriously restricted leisure time. These classes may combine artisans, women, or children, and the restrictions may be various, but in each case, reading is seen to be a leisure activity, partly disguised as instruction. Such a very broad orientation is in line with that offered by Victor E. Neuberg: 'At its simplest, popular literature can be defined as what the unsophisticated reader has chosen for pleasure.'[16]

Defoe's narratives never patronise their readers, and cram in all sorts of information with their digressive plots. He was clearly aiming at a readership with time to dwell on a book, expectations of form and a desire for easy assimilation of information.

Of course, great questions are still being begged. Why do the fictions take *that* form? And why were *those* tales pleasurable? More immediately, it is worth asking if popular fiction existed as a clearly separate category from other popular narratives. The range of popular literature in the early-eighteenth century is vast. It included jest books, collections of riddles, horoscopes, speeches from the scaffold, almanacs, ballads and advertisements, not to mention the surviving oral tradition.[17] The popular narratives very rarely acknowledged themselves to be fictional, and drew more attention to their verifiability than to their imaginative uniqueness. Defoe's tales all start by denying their mendacity, most bluntly in *Crusoe*: 'The Editor believes the thing to be a just History of Fact; neither is there any Appearance of Fiction in it. . .' (*RC*, p. 1)

This exculpation might be seen as a purely Puritan exercise to allay the taint of lying, but it is more broadly conventional than that. The central convention in storytelling at the time was the attestation of truth, and it was adopted by most tellers, not only Puritans. Popular fiction seems most closely related to oral storytelling, where invented corroboration is so prominent, but the two forms of narration do not wholly overlap. Confessional tales and pseudo-autobiographies are the nearest that printed tales come to oral storytelling, but some distinctions have to be drawn.

In a provocative essay called 'The Storyteller', Walter Benjamin distinguishes between the role of the storyteller and the role of the early novelist:

> The earliest symptom of a process whose end is the decline of storytelling is the rise of the novel at the beginning of modern times. What distinguishes the novel from the story . . . is its essential dependence on the book. The dissemination of the novel became possible only with the invention of printing. What can be handed on orally, the wealth of the epic, is of a different kind from what constitutes the stock in trade of the novel . . . The storyteller takes what he tells from experience — his own or that reported by others. And he in turn makes it the experience of those listening to his tale. The novelist has isolated himself. The birthplace of the novel is the solitary individual.[18]

Benjamin is suggesting that the novel is the literary form appropriate to a specialised, alienated culture, whereas storytelling is a feature of integrated, whole cultures. The development of technology throughout the seventeenth century in England, which made the production of cheapish books possible, coincided with the specialisation of labour and the increasing professionalisation of crafts. The community of listeners was transformed into a market of readers, and the vicarious experience gained through reading a popular narrative was more consoling than the shared experience of listening to a recognised storyteller.

Of course, we do not know enough about the circumstances of reading to confirm Benjamin's insight. It may be possible that many people's experience of a text like *Crusoe* came through hearing it being read out loud to them. In any case, the point remains that the novel establishes the space between its readers and its participants, and grounds a foreign experience in recognisable circumstances. Benjamin encapsulates the vicarious experience of reading in a colourful phrase when he talks of the attraction of novels for a reader being 'the hope of warming his shivering life with a death he reads about' ('The Storyteller', p. 101). The reader as consumer is attracted to the texts by their estranged versions of his own life, heightened, stylised and made safe. The sense of participation which the economic circumstances have removed from lower-class readers is restored temporarily by the vicarious participation in a narrative. The most striking feature of the popular narratives of the early-eighteenth century is the way they situate themselves in a recognisable historical environment, and deal with unremarkable figures. The adventures may be remarkable, but the adventurers are not. These recognisable figures such as Crusoe and Moll and Singleton are subject to extravagant fates and take part in remarkable adventures, while remaining relatively unchanged throughout. As I shall discuss later, Crusoe learns nothing from his adventures, and is as prone to his 'wandering Disposition' at the end of his story as at the beginning. For readers, this juxtaposition of the familiar and the strange, of predictability and hazard, and of stability and mobility, offers some reassurance that life is both comprehensible and potentially exciting.

The mundane elements in popular narrative incorporate elements of its readers' experiences, and by offering them the solidity of print, ennobles them. By simultaneously showing the extraordinary, popular narrative confirms the boundaries of the likely and the unlikely, and so gives a transient social form the appearance of fixity. Popular narrative, thus, has a role to play in defining its readers' expectations, and satisfies by its offer of an understandable, comforting social hierarchy. It is clear from reading Defoe's fiction that the two elements in *Crusoe*, his 'Life' and his 'Strange Surprizing Adventures', would have been more readily discerned by a contemporary audience than they seem now. The object of grounding the marvellous in the familiar was to provide reassuring pictures of social mobility, which would also have been more identifiable by an audience that was more similar in some respects to Crusoe himself than is now the case.[19]

The process of identification with the participants, then, overrode the distinction between fiction and non fiction. The protestations of veracity were a way of incorporating something new (novels) into something already established (narratives). The fantasy element in providing these artificial pictures of reassurance had to be denied if it was to be acceptable. The tales did not have to be taken as true in every tiny detail, but unless they were presented as acceptably genuine, their power to satisfy would be seriously diminished. Our later absolute distinction between true and false was not so clear to readers of these yarns, who wanted aptness and plausibility above mean, precise accuracy of detail.

One distinction which is necessary for popular writing like Defoe's to flourish is the distinction between work and play. Such a distinction is only available in certain historical periods, and the later-seventeenth century in England is one. With the exception of the strictest Puritanism, which could not recognise the notion of play as important, all the social movements of the time were directed towards the segmentation of a person's life into wage-earning activities, or activities supportive of wage earning, and a more limited free time. The popular narratives of the period did not just happen fortuitously, but were professionally supplied to occupy such free time as readers had available, and to occupy that time usefully. Reading was only one such recreation, and may have been fully available to only a few.[20] However, the location of popular narrative was in the work life of its authors and in the recreational life of its readers, a distinction which helps clarify its various social roles.

Some literature, addressing itself to a leisured readership offers to beguile the time away. A life of almost constant leisure may be wearisome, and a book may transport readers out of themselves, and so help time pass. As Lennard J. Davis has argued, *Don Quixote* opens by offering the promise of learned diversion, exploiting the possibilities of fiction.[21] Defoe's texts, on the other hand, address themselves to readers whose leisure time is restricted, and who may be seeking illumination or instruction as much as diversion. Defoe's fictions offer the charade of an integration of work and play, transforming *homo ludens* into *homo faber* and back again. Just as *The*

Family Instructor and the other directional tracts spent some time analysing the proper uses of leisure, so the narratives show what happens when the categories of work and play become confused. Crusoe puts inclination above duty, and so places play over work. As a result, he is condemned to a life of making and fabricating a tiny kingdom, a truly childlike play version of the working world. Moll is also initially horrified by the notion of work, and seems to spend her life in games of theft and love, another kind of play. Roxana is trained only for a life of leisure, and when forced to work has little to draw on other than the attributes of a whore. In all these cases, the categories of work and play lie behind the narrative, and for a readership just beginning to understand them, the categories of public and private responsibilities are explored dramatically. The transition from popular storytelling to popular novels draws on the transition from *Gemeinschaft* to *Gesellschaft*, and Defoe's fiction explores such a transition, with all its gaps and duplications.

This issue of the relationship between the texts and the lives of the audience raises the more fundamental one of what popular literature was *for*. I have been arguing that it gave a distanced rendering of its readers' problems, in a suitably remote and comforting form. But its uses were various. Lady Mary Wortley Montagu saw it as a foolish but pleasing diversion; Johnson saw it as a way of inculcating the pleasures of reading in children. The notion of childlike absorption in stories underlies many descriptions of popular narrative from above. James Boswell saw it as a diversion, but as a more innocent, childish diversion than some of his other pursuits:

> here I must mention that some days ago I went to the old printing-office in Bow Church-Yard kept by Dicey, whose family have kept it fourscore years. There are ushered into the world of literature *Jack and the Giants*, *The Seven Wise Men of Gotham*, and other story-books which in my dawning years amused me as much as *Rasselas* does now . . . I bought two dozen of them and had them bound up with this title, *Curious Productions*. I thought myself like old Lord Somerville or some other man of whim, and wished my whims might be all as quiet.[22]

Boswell was certainly a man whose other whims could be boisterous and roaring, and his tone of reminiscent indulgence towards these narratives is telling. Popular tales were associated with an innocent state of docile receptivity. For the polite reader, these crude tales gave a naively rendered sense of basic human nature, which training might disguise as much as reveal. Joseph Addison found in the ballad of 'Chevy Chase', 'some peculiar Aptness to please and gratifie the Mind of Man', despite its being a production of 'the Rabble of a Nation'.[23] Less laudatory remarks can be found elsewhere, of course. Fielding gave an ironic catalogue of penny romances at the beginning of *Joseph Andrews*, wryly asserting that in such yarns 'Delight is mixed with Instruction, and the Reader is almost as much improved as entertained.'[24] He meant that no such instruction was offered, and that penny romances were cheap sources of pleasure only.

Polite readers, then, found in popular tales some reassuring evidence about the universality of human nature, and the correctness of the social hierarchy. The lower orders were just like themselves, really, but like themselves as children, untrained and credulous. The tone of lofty condescension lasted throughout the century, and was only altered by the Wordsworthian responses to ballads, where the common man was seen to be more dignified than the sophisticate. In the early part of the century, the readers of popular narrative were seen as gullible, simple and tractable, but basically decent. The tales were seen as sources of uninformed pleasure, which even the sophisticated might enjoy on occasions. The proper objects of scorn, in *A Tale of a Tub* and the *Dunciad*, were not the consumers of popular narratives, who knew no better, but the purveyors of them, who did. Authors and especially publishers were cheapening the whole world of literature by pouring out these easy tales, contributing to what Johnson called the 'superfoetation' of the press. The satisfaction deriving from seeing the lower orders as a naive version of the polite was tempered by the cheapening of literature which resulted, and by the growth of the mercantile purveyors of such stuff, including Defoe.

Popular literature, then, invited that mode of reading which academics find so hard, called 'naive involvement'. In the limited leisure time available, readers took to popular literature for its access to adventure, delighting in its covert reorganisations of notions of work and play. These tales could be prominently fantastic, such as *Jack and the Giants*, or more firmly rooted in experience, like *Crusoe* and *Moll*. It is difficult to state exactly what these members of the lower orders found so appealing in romances like Defoe's. It can be seen that tradesmen reading Thomas Deloney, for example, would have delighted to see their activities so ennobled. But the attraction of Defoe's tales is different. The question here is the broad one of the uses of reading, of which there has been little sustained examination.

For a later period, E.P. Thompson has shown the political uses of popular reading, and its social dissemination.[25] Elsewhere, J.R. MacDonald has discussed the creative role of the readership of Rousseau in the eighteenth century, and G.H. Ford has analysed the various readings of Dickens in the nineteenth century.[26] But for the period in which Defoe was most widely read, we know little about the circumstances of reading, or the various uses to which the narratives were put. The idea that a text may be read in different ways has been important in literary study, but the different ways have been seen to arise from inherent ambiguity or complexity of language. The notion that a text has a different existence for readers of different classes or times, depending upon what they seek from it, or the mode of enquiry they might be engaged upon, does not rest happily with the Arnoldian notion of the transcendence and integrity of the text.

The assumption that readings are historically relative is central to any study of popular narrative, and is allied to what sociologists call the 'uses and gratifications' approach. As John Hall puts it: '. . . there is more to be said for asking what the readers of popular literature want from their books than in simply asking what these books are doing to their readers.'[27]

Such an approach means that any text may be a popular text, if it has been read in a certain way. There is no inherent quality which may be identified as the popular element of a text, though some texts might make their suitability for a popular reading more obvious than others. This suitability will be seen in an avoidance of self-consciousness in language, an absence of literary allusiveness and a lack of distance from the audience. On the positive side, a community of readers may be invited to involve themselves naively with a text if it makes storytelling prominent, if it seems to be intimate with its readers and if it is readable — to use that familiar colloquialism. The meaning of a text read as popular is, thus, not something inscribed in it by the author, but the collective enjoyment of a community of readers. Neither reading nor writing is an isolated or wholly private activity, but depends on the social possibilities of reading and writing, and on the constraints imposed upon these activities.

But how does this approach avoid complete pluralism? How does it sanction some readings as appropriate and rule out others as inappropriate? The openness promised by the 'uses and gratifications' approach looks as though it could become wholly anarchic, leading to a kind of deconstructionist position, where 'the absence of an ultimate meaning opens an unbounded space for the play of significations'.[28] I want to argue that the 'space' was bounded at particular historical periods by the audience's horizon of expectation, and by the social status of their reading experience. The most immediate way of imposing a boundary on reading might be to establish the common themes, attitudes and ideas which emerge from the corpus of Defoe's texts, and to call them Defoe's themes, attitudes and ideas. The books then become the vehicle of personal expression. Tempting though this is, and helpful though it might be regarding Defoe's work, it is practically very difficult. If this writing were personal and consistent in its expression, then there would not be the recurrent problems of attribution which have dogged Defoe scholars for centuries. A typical example might he *The Military Memoirs of Captain George Carleton* (1728), which for many years was sometimes seen as genuine, sometimes seen as Defoe's. Only by the most scrupulous textual analysis, as late as 1974, was the attribution to Defoe accepted as reliable.[29] If Defoe was using his texts as vehicles for personal expression, with his recurrent themes being prominent, no such problems would really arise.

As well as these practical reservations, it is also possible to doubt the authorial approach on theoretical grounds. I have suggested that popular literature might be a collaborative exercise in reading, bounded by its audience's expectations. This would make the author a figure of less importance for readers. Such a diminishing in the role of the author may draw theoretical support from Roland Barthes, who put the case most flamboyantly in 'The Death of the Author' (1960). Barthes claims that the figure of the author has had excessive reverence paid to him by literary critics and the more informed general readers:

> The image of literature to be found in ordinary culture is tyrannically centred on the author, his person, his life, his tastes, his passions . . . The *explanation* of a work is always sought in the man or woman who produced it, as if it were always in the end, through the more or less transparent allegory of the fiction, the voice of a single person, the *author* 'confiding' in us.[30]

Barthes argues against the intimately confessional account of literature by offering a counter-tradition of disguised or absent authors, like Mallarmé, Valery, or Proust. He goes on to use some recent linguistic theory to usher the author out of consideration finally, by seeking to change the status of literature. Writing, he says, can 'no longer be designated an operation of recording, notation, representation . . . rather, it designates . . . a performative, a rare verbal form (exclusively given in the first person and in the present tense) in which the enunciation has no other content (contains no other proposition) than the act by which it is uttered' ('The Death of the Author', pp. 145-6). Literature is then categorised as a sequence of performative assertions, best understood as a self-sustaining body of texts, forming a kind of language, and best analysed structurally, independent of surmises about authorial expression. Barthes's very racy, and rather obscurely argued case would presumably cover all texts, not just popular ones, but his analysis has more force when applied empirically to a body of popular writing. I will argue later that while it is possible to see the author of a 'high' text exerting some control over its readings, the readings of popular texts are controlled by their place inside known literary systems. It might seem paradoxical to be so slighting of the author in a study devoted to one, but Defoe's position is in itself paradoxical. He has been plucked from his culture by later writers, and forced into representative isolation. In order to understand him properly, it is necessary to place his work back in its context, and to some extent that diminishes the importance of his personality.

The exact role of the author in the production of a popular text is obviously hard to define. The authorial approach to literature seems to depend on the presupposition that writing is a private activity, conducted almost in secret, which allows for greater personal expression than other activities. Such a notion may be aligned to some belief that literature is the work of great minds, transcending their circumstances and going beyond their personal conflicts. Critics may choose to emphasise the secret personal conflicts, as Edmund Wilson does in his study of Dickens, or to stress the grandeur of conceptions of a great author, as Leavis does in his study of Lawrence.[31] However, such single attention to a lonely generating figure has only limited use in other arts. In the study of film and television, it is very difficult to isolate the dominant creative figure behind any work, *auteur* theory notwithstanding. The nature of the enterprise seems collaborative, with writers, director, performers and technicians all contributing to the overall effect. So too with popular narrative, which seems inherently collaborative rather than personally expressive. It can certainly become tiresome, if not downright impossible, to detect the single creative mind behind a popular text. Many popular texts are quite obviously collaborative — from Head and Kirkman's compilation *The English Rogue* (1650) to the many works produced by two writers under the pseudonym 'Ellery Queen'. But collaboration is important in a wider sense than simply this obvious one of multiple authorship. In popular narrative, the writer needs to take less initiative than in high literature, since the work is hedged round by a number of known demands from publishers and readers. Popular narratives are repetitive not only in terms of form and content, but also in matters such as length, binding format and presentation. The author or presenter of a popular narrative collaborates with these demands, and the text arises out of the collaboration. The author of a popular text is, thus, only one contributor to its significance. The writing of popular texts is, after all, a business proposition, and such authors are more likely to make efforts to satisfy a known demand than to try to instigate a new one. The audience's demands are revealed by the system of *genres* existent at any time, from which their horizons of expectation may be measured.

It is obvious that popular literature is always much more easily grouped into genres than high literature. In the twentieth century, the dominant form of popular narrative has been the cinema, and it has always been strenous in its attempts to make clear its broad genres, so that prospective consumers may be lured in. The number of genres of popular film is large, but finite, and known to consumers as well as to producers, forming a way of communicating some advance knowledge of a particular film without divulging all its secrets. Any given film may strive after purity in its generic presentation, or it may mix its genres, and by this method, the popular film seeks to satisfy by simultaneously offering reassuring predictability and thrilling novelty. In the more recent period, the combination of recognisability and surprise has been clearly related to market forces and aggressive advertising. In times of booming cinema attendance, such as the 1930s and 1940s, the marketing emphasis was on predictability, and the films were more generically stringent. In times of dwindling attendance, such as 1960s, the emphasis was put on shock and novelty, the generic conventions were broken down.[32]

I would like to think of eighteenth-century popular fiction along the lines of a model of generic patterns, designed for easy consumption by readers. Prospective readers were lured to the texts by the promise that the narrative form was one they were familiar with, but the particular example was somehow special. The individual text thus gained its meaning by its expected conformity with, and partial disruption of, these recognised generic conventions. Reading such a text now may, however, be radically different, if we are reading it within a different set of expectations. Reading Defoe as a forerunner of the novel is, therefore, very different from reading him as a popular writer of his period, for the patterns of conformity and disruption we might detect are very different.

In any given historical period, literature can be thought of as offering two main ways of communicating its form to readers — by its participation in recognised genres, and by its presentation in known modes. Literature, as a signifying practice, presents itself at any time as a system, though as a system itself composed of many smaller, overlapping systems.[33] The reading of any one text within the system is not an isolated act, but an act of assimilation, informed by an anterior awareness of the components of the system. Any accomplished reader internalises the rules of the system, so that the recognition of familiarity and novelty is largely subliminal, though still pleasureable. Within the system of literature as a whole, the two most important conventions of signification or communication are genres and modes. It might be argued that this approach makes literature and reading too enclosed or self-reflexive as activities, severed from any connection with the external world, either empirically perceived or intuitively revealed. However, this is an objection that holds little force. Many recent studies have shown the greater problems in trying to define this extra-textual 'reality', and trying to keep it free of ideological commitments. For the present study, talking of literature as a self-enclosed system, albeit one generated by the externally determining features of reality, is the less problematic path.[34]

In this context, what is meant by genres and modes? Aristotle, followed much later by Northrop Frye, defined the available literature in universally recurring groups or categories, labelled, amongst others, epic, tragedy and comedy. These have often been taken as the basic, universal categories of literature, but have then become unworkably broad. When Frye took the whole body of literature non-historically, and attempted to find its recurring patterns, he came up with the broadest and vaguest of categories, with little discriminatory power.[35] Rather than follow this universalist scheme, I want to see genres as the various kinds of literature recognised at any given historical moment. In the period between 1700 and 1739, these genres are much more clearly definable, including the pirate tale, the criminal biography, the *roman à clef*, the traveller's tale and the pious polemic. Any given narrative may advertise itself as one or more of these, by its title and its self-presentation, and the reading of any one narrative is supervised by the expectations thus generated. The danger of doing a Polonius, and defining the tales out of existence, is certainly possible, but the categories I refer to would have been recognised by a reasonably self-aware reader of the period, even if they were not fully articulated.

Though it is best to define genres locally and historically, modes are best seen trans-historically, as recurrent possibilities of presentation. Historically, one may be more regularly employed at any given time than others, but all are still possible. The most obvious modes of presentation are tragedy, comedy and irony, but it might also be possible to see allegory as such a convention.[36] A mode such as tragedy, in which harmful elements overcome benevolent ones, can cut across generic boundaries, for in any genre, a narrative may show its protagonist defeated by some form of misadventure. So too, the events in a traveller's narrative might be presented comically or ironically. It is only necessary to think of the picaresque comedy of *Lazarillo de Tormes*, where the adventurer is eventually integrated into his society, and *Gulliver's Travels*, where the traveller is finally excluded, to see the variety of modal possibilities in the simple story of the wanderer. I suppose the traveller's tale rarely employs tragic presentation because of its regular use of first person narration, but the possibilities are still present. The fascinating question of the association of modes and genres is, then, partly a historical one. All modes are theoretically possible, but some are more likely than others, and the way to assess likelihood is to look for prevalence in a body of texts. In specific cases, such as asking whether *Moll* is ironic or comic, the evidence from the body of similar generic texts is inconclusive. In others, like asking if *Crusoe* is ironic, the evidence of prevalence in the genre indicates that it is not.

It will be clear that genre has a very specific and detailed referent here, and one which is more applicable to the grouped productions of popular literature than to the singular high texts. Indeed, one way of drawing a distinction between popular and high literature would be to stress the predominantly generic nature of the former and the modal nature of the latter. The most important way that a popular text has of signalling its form is by its generic references, its assimilation into a corpus. A high text, on the other hand, tries to signal its integrity and uniqueness, by stressing the singular way it supports its chosen mode. It is easy when talking about these modes to take trans-historical statements for universalist ones. For example, when Aristotle talks of tragedy dealing with people better than ourselves, and comedy dealing with people worse than ourselves, he seems to be offering some general statement about the components of these forms. However, what he is really doing is describing the type of action treated in comedy and tragedy in his own social formation, measured in terms of the social position of the audience. There is no reason to suppose that tragedy can only present the affairs of the more socially elevated, or that comedy can only show us the lowly. Rather, what has happened here is that the conjunction of genre and mode has been taken to be fixed, not variable. In a seemingly fixed social formation, that conjunction can seem more inevitable than it actually is, and the course of literary history shows the changing content of modal works. For instance, Shakespearean comedy often shows the foibles of characters more socially elevated than almost all the audience, and Hardy's novels show the tragic fates of weak, flawed characters in humble social positions. These fluctuations of mode and genre occur at dynamic moments in literary history. In calmer moments, when movement seems to atrophy, the available forms seem more rigid.

The early-eighteenth century is such a dynamic period. With the growth in extended narrative, the range of available forms was greatly extended, especially when in the hands of a partly literary character like Defoe. The modes available for narrative broadly speaking were comedy, tragedy, irony, allegory and *mimesis*. Examples of each can easily be identified, if we widen the historical period slightly to take in more obviously literary fiction — *Joseph Andrews* is comedy; *Clarissa* is tragedy; *Gulliver's Travels* is irony; *The History of John Bull* is allegory; and most of Defoe's fiction is that most apparently neutral of all modes, *mimesis* — where the act of shaping is not made prominent. In many high texts, more than one mode is hinted at in the course of one narrative, and more sophisticated terminology would be required to describe *Rasselas*, *Jonathan Wild*, or *Tristram Shady*. In each of these predominantly ironic texts, the disruptions effected by comedy, tragedy, or the sentimental require subtle combination of distance and involvement which is beyond the aims of popular fiction. Such high literature assumes a degree of self-consciousness and literacy on the part of the reader, which rules out the possibility of naive involvement. So much eighteenth-century literature is carried on at the level of allusion and implication that the required reader must be detached, at least sporadically, and alert to nuance. One need only think of the narrator of *Tom Jones* continuously disrupting the linear flow of the text to chasten and cajole readers to see that the prevailingly ironic mode creeps into texts which may broadly be comic.

Popular fiction, on the other hand, is much less purposefully miscellaneous in its attempts to delight. The linear narrative of popular tales may be thoroughly wide ranging and broad in scope, but it remains episodic rather than unified by any clear modal shape. One of Swift's targets in *A Tale of a Tub* was the Modern mind's inability to maintain any coherent narrative line, and its complete inability to integrate various items into an understood, shaped tale. Whereas high literature always had the playful element of surprising combinations of genre and mode at this time, popular literature did not draw on any modal inheritance, only on a generic stockpile. Any reader of any tale wants to know the answer to the basic question of how things are going to turn out at the end. A reader of *Tom Jones*, say, plays an elaborate cat and mouse game with the narrator, watching the transitions through various modal possibilities, before arriving at the comic ending. But a reader of *Captain Singleton*, for example, is sufficiently held by the linear movement of the narrative to defer questions of ending. Reading popular narrative seems a less teleological pursuit, and the occasionally perfunctory endings of Defoe's fictions are best understood in this anticlimactic sense. It might be possible to see some connections here between the life experiences of the respective required readers — the readers of high literature seeking some sense of purpose, being in control, taking delight in games; the readers of popular fiction experiencing life more as a flux, without eventual purpose, and without the possibility of climax. However, I will refrain from such grand links at the moment.

A more modest and appropriate question to ask is the question of the stockpile of genres. What was available to Defoe? And how innovative did his fiction seem to eighteenth-century readers? What were the extant varieties of popular fiction? And what were their recurrent patterns? The most reliable catalogue of narratives at the time is W.H. McBurney, *A Checklist of English Prose Fiction, 1700–1739* (Harvard, 1960), which lists the 391 appropriate discoverable works. McBurney makes the point that works of fiction are not fully separable from works of non fiction at this point, but he has tried to disentangle them as far as possible. His heroic endeavour in reading 86 per cent of these books transforms him instantly into an acceptable authority. His main criterion for inclusion is that the works should 'deal with characters and events which are largely or wholly imaginary, consciously invented by the authors' (p. ix), and he excludes narratives too brief to be seen as extended. So, despite ruling out many narratives because they are factual, or because they are too short, McBurney still dug up 391 extended fictional tales. The first interesting thing about his catalogue is the way it shows the novel trying continually to pass itself off as something else, as something not at all new, but rather commonplace and recognisable. The modern critical enterprise of unearthing the novelty of the novel to a great extent contradicts the activities of the early novelists, who went out of their way to disguise that novelty. McBurney points out the way the narratives were offered consistently as factual, calling themselves *history*, *memoirs*, *life*, *voyage* (*trip*, *travels*, *discovery*), *adventure*, *letters* and *account* (*journal*, *relation*). Such a concerted appropriation of the language of non fiction shows that there was more than just a Puritan uncertainty about lying behind the disguise. It shows a widespread desire for quasi-factual relations, which raises again the vicarious side of popular narrative, supplying experiences which its readers would not otherwise have access to. The diversity of the fiction is balanced by its consistency of deception, and its recurrent role in generating imaginary experiences.

Any attempt to be faithful to this diversity rules out two tempting critical procedures. The writer on early-eighteenth-century fiction is not in the enviable position of a taxonomist like Vladimir Propp, with a neat sequence of assimilable tales at hand, which can be analysed as a unified group with recurrent identifiable components.[37] Such strict morphological approaches simply cannot cope with the variety of styles and genres employed. Nor can the critic just isolate one topic, and either anthologise the literature pertinent to it, or paraphrase it.[38] That also falsifies the diversity. But some attempt has to be made to scan the material, and to identify its patterns. The most ambitious and successful attempt at this daunting task so far is that of John J. Richetti, *Popular Fiction Before Richardson:*

Narrative Patterns 1700–1739 (Oxford, 1969), to which I am greatly indebted. Richetti looks at a great many texts, also relying on McBurney's list, and tries to find in them the recurrent patterns of narrative which would supervise the reading of individual texts by individual readers. He has very little to say on the implied audience, and restricts himself to searching for what he calls the 'structure of feeling' (p. 13). This Raymond Williams echo is seen as the ideological basis for all the texts, and it is defined as 'a dramatic confrontation between two opposing attitudes to existence . . . "secular" and "religious" (p. 13). These very broad terms, kept snuggly within their inverted commas underlie all his discussion, Richetti goes on to argue that popular narrative portrays action as impious aggression against the natural order, or against virtuous, innocent characters. He sees popular fiction as being the graphic presentation of the fantasies of social order and disruption, and his insight into the social function of the narratives is confirmed by studies of the popular literature of more recently literate West African cultures.[39]

Richetti talks of the opposition between secular and religious as being the 'novelistic ideology' of popular fiction, and though the meaning of 'novelistic' is never fully clear to me, this definition leads to the enumeration of the generated genres of the period. It is slightly unfortunate that the book starts rather arbitrarily in 1700, for it thereby suggests an unlikely point of conception for these forms, and disrupts the continuity of the popular cultures into which the texts intervene. However, in the period he analyses most fully, Richetti uncovers five basic systems of patterning, which become apparent in genres — the literature of roguery, travel literature, the scandalous chronicle, the erotic novella and the pious polemic. In each pattern, the basic split between the secular and religious is rehearsed, and each pattern offers a received shape for the struggle.

Though it is never certain whether Richetti's patterns are to be seen as empirically identifiable features of the texts, or as *a priori* critical categories, or as both, their function is to act as supervisors of the reading of individual texts. It is obvious that they are immediately relevant to reading Defoe. Even from the mention of the categories, it is tempting to consign *Moll Flanders* and *Colonel Jack* to the literature of roguery; *Robinson Crusoe* and *Captain Singleton* to travel literature; and *Roxana* to some or all of the rest. Indeed, I will be arguing in the next three chapters that it is essential to read

Defoe's books in this supervised way, and that his contemporary readers would have been alerted to the generic categories by conventional signs. Perhaps it will be thought that this transforms 'honest Dick and Doll' into highly sophisticated, informed readers, protostructuralists even, when in fact they were naive, semi-literate and ill-informed. Maybe they were, but the process of reading any book, in however 'naive' a way, is extremely complex, and must involve the recognition of kinds of book at an early stage. The recognition of similarities and differences between stories, and the allocation of tales to groups, are not the activities of professional literary critics only; they are an intrinsic part of literary and narrative comprehension. No utterance, however long or short, can have its meaning in isolation. The supposition behind stringent New Criticism, that an innocent reader confronts an open text, can only lead to incoherent atomism. The comprehension of any hitherto unknown tale requires the act of provisional categorisation. Such categorisation is not definitive, and it could be revised at any point in reading — as it must do at some points in *Captain Singleton*, which combines a number of categories, such as the exploration story and the pirate confessional. It might even be misguided, and unhelpful, as would be the case if a reader failed to pick up the ironic mode of *Gulliver's Travels*, and read it as a straight travel tale. The preliminary categorisation is not arbitrary, of course, for it is based on internal evidence and external signs. The tone of narration, and the early events are clear signs, as are the title page and any illustrations. The early title page of *Roxana*, giving the book its most elaborate title, and including a woodcut of an elaborately dressed woman, invites immediate categorisation as a scandalous tale. Some of the conventional ways of indicating the appropriate category of narrative may now have been lost, and I will try to unearth them as I go through the books.

A reader of early-eighteenth-century popular tales would have had an extensive catalogue of categories to apply, and with which to govern the reading of individual tales. Since this system must have been both more definite and less extensive than the system of a widely-read and learned reader, the system of allusion looks cruder and less elegant than that in operation in high literature. The allusions in *The Rape of the Lock*, say, draw on moral systems present in Virgil, Homer and Milton, and offer a critique of the events inside the poem, subtly and obliquely. The allusions in *Robinson Crusoe*, on the other hand, draw on travel writing, confessionals and conduct books. But these allusions do not alter the weight of the events portrayed, or invite distance from them. Rather, they provide points of reference and similarity which make the story easier to understand, not more complex. Since these allusions are to near-contemporary books, now forgotten, popular literature seems much less resonant than 'high' books, and it becomes much harder to disinter. Polite literature draws its allusiveness from a frame of reference which is still available, at least amongst literary critics. This frame of reference is simply the literary curriculum up to the time of writing, the inherited canon, with the modal possibilities as we know them. Popular literature does not draw on this linear tradition, but on the other possibilities at any given time — it refers synchronically, not diachronically. In eighteenth-century terms, this contemporary allusiveness is strengthened by the Ancients/Moderns debate, but it is true at most periods that popular literature does not have an extensive sense of tradition, and is more concerned with novelty than with heritage.

Polite literature most emphatically signifies by its mode, by interpreting the experience it offers tragically, comically, or whatever, and by making that interpretation prominent. In contrast, popular literature most frequently restricts itself to the mimetic mode. Mimetic in this context does not mean making reference to some persistent and universally recognised reality. Rather, it describes works which do not draw attention to their act of shaping, to their distortions or interpretations of experience. All tales are constructions, selecting items for emphasis, and distorting chronology for some purpose. But the mimetic work does not draw readers into seeing this. It pretends instead that the conventions are transparent, and that they are not conventions at all, but windows to the world. The distortions in Defoe, principally to do with his handling of time, are well concealed and subtle, and conform to the mimetic conventions of the period, which are very different from ours. Whatever may be made of these distortions, it remains the case that popular tales are rarely wholly comic or tragic, and that they seek to present themselves more as documentary than as artifice.[40]

Accepting for the moment Richetti's five narrative patterns as the most prominent broad genres of the period, it is worth asking *why* they appeared as they did, and why they appeared *then*. The conventional answer in sophisticated genre criticism of high literature is to refer the narrative patterns to some system of archetypes, which may underlie the literature of all ages and cultures, and which may embody the fundamental patterns of human experience. Such an approach is conducted most forcefully and persuasively by Northrop Frye. Frye's insights into the broadest categories of literature, published in the 1950s, helped to re-establish poetics as a proper branch of literary study, and helped to displace evaluative questions from the centre of the literary debate for a spell. However, they re-occurred, and they were always implicit in Frye's work anyway. His exaltation of the category of romance revealed the ideological underpinning of his position. Since he saw literature as part of the process of civilisation, in its attempts to organise and systematise experience, Frye relied on a static conception of human nature, which consistently re-appeared in the archetypes he discovered. These archetypes were the ritual patterns which betrayed the persistence of human dreams and aspirations, commonly held by all cultures. Frye tried to restrict himself to the study of western literature, but the implications of a transcendent entity called human nature were always present in his work. His archetypes not only transcend individual books, they also supervise human history at large, and, as commentators have often pointed out, Frye ends up assuming that a specifically local bourgeois ideology is the basic pattern of human experience.[41]

Frye's experience brings out the problem that the genre critic is faced with. The critical procedure seems to offer two possibilities, each of which is somewhat undesirable. On the one hand, the critic can draw up an allegedly pure, empirical taxonomy, which compiles the recurrent patterns within the prose fiction of a specific period. The result is of little use to most readers, however, for it remarks only on local features, and may be subject to infinite regression. As is often pointed out, such a procedure can lead to the recording of innumerable genres, which may be trivial, such as the genre of tales in which the participants wear hats. On the other hand, such a critic can motivate the enquiry by some set of values, and seek to find the most important recurrences in fiction. As Jonathan Culler puts it:

> an account of genres should be an attempt to define the classes which have been functional in the processes of reading and writing, the sets of expectations which enabled readers to naturalize texts and give them a relation to the world. . .[42]

This is clearly a more productive procedure, but it is obviously much harder, and less open to empirical presentation. The impressionable just have to take it on trust that *these* conventions and expectations enabled . . . etc., whereas *those* ones were trivial. However, it is this second option that will reappear in the ensuing pages, and readers are asked to be as impressionable as they think fit. For popular fiction, the second approach is privileged, since the books are so self-classifying. The genres of popular fiction between 1700 and 1739, say, exist as empirically definable signs, and as recoverable mental codes which supervised reading.[43]

So much depends on how a book offered itself to its potential audience. The conventions of address in eighteenth-century popular fiction are much more prominent than those in polite fiction, since the former was much more eager to sell itself. So too, the characterisation within that popular fiction is much more obviously based on a popular typology than that in high fiction. Polite literature, of course, did draw on popular typologies, as Richardson did extensively in *Clarissa*, but it was used more obliquely, and might only be deciphered by an astute, sensitive and widely-read audience. The popular presentation of roamers, pirates, thieves, lovers and whores was stylised and familiar to all readers, even if the enterprise of an individual book might be to tamper with that received notion somewhat. Despite what Ian Watt claimed extensively in *The Rise of the Novel*, the early-eighteenth-century novel did not seek to individuate its characters, but to fit them into understandable categories, often generated outside fiction. These categories, of course, were never static, and were modified by every new book. However, the point remains that the tales offer themselves within known groups, and one of the later reader's jobs is to try to reconstruct those groups, and their bearing on individual books.

Defoe's fiction occupies a very interesting position with regard to the genres. Though the books all draw upon known groupings, and though their reading was supervised in the way I have been outlining, there is also an attempt to break out of this referential framework, and to produce more independent books. *Crusoe* might have been read by its earliest readers as just another traveller's tale, but its extraordinary popularity through the century, its translations and its adaptations, all suggest that Defoe had written something which *could* be read unsupervised. That was less true of the other narratives, which have never been as popular, but even there, the attempt at moving beyond the generic requirements is obvious. Defoe's fiction is as miscellaneous as earlier and contemporary fiction was, but it looks more purposefully miscellaneous. And there is, as I shall argue, an increasing concentration on the character and possibilities of the narrator from 1719 to 1724. The fact that Defoe has been removed from his culture and transplanted in the literary tradition is not accidental, for he very nearly seems to have requested it himself.

Defoe's literary enterprise in the extended narratives reflects neatly one aspect of his social position. Having risen steadily from a childhood of middle-class dissent to a role in the affairs of state, Defoe had become *déclassé*. He no longer fitted fully into the community he had left, or the one he had arrived in. This unsettled position is brought to life in the narratives, and reflected in their social role. The tales neither fully fit into the schematised system of popular literature, though they are based there, nor do they stand fully independent on their own terms. This oscillation between the received body of generic forms and the individualised work can be seen in each tale. *Crusoe* looks like a more lively example of the travel tale, until we see the vestigial ironies and complexities in it. *Moll* looks like a conventional criminal autobiography, until we see the development in the role of its narrator, and its comedy. *Roxana* looks like a scandalous chronicle, until we realise its unique presentation of its heroine's guilt and eventual fate. The persistence of popular forms must be articulated by any critic of Defoe, but so must the emergence of individuality. Reading Defoe's fiction with these *genres* in mind may help to restore Defoe to his culture, but we must remember his peculiar position within that culture.

To understand Defoe's fiction within the social formation of the early-eighteenth century, we must remember a great many things. We must remember Defoe's social and religious background, and its effect on his education. We must remember the combination of caution and recklessness in his behaviour. We must remember his career as a political writer, along with his insistent claims to write above party squabbles. We must remember his professional role as author, and his need to write in forms with which his audience was familiar. Yet we should not assume that he merely sought to duplicate these forms. He drew on them, and expanded them, just as he drew on everything else that was available to him. In some ways, Defoe's fiction effects a compromise between his adventurism and his desire for security — by letting his imagination take the risks in a fairly safe market. In the fiction, much more obviously than in his political writings, Defoe was taking the safest way out, but the safest way here involved innovation as well as conformity. In proceeding to articulate these issues in the books, I seek to come to terms not just with Defoe's abilities as a writer, but with the social origins of his expression, and with the dialogue in the fiction between familiarity and novelty.

Notes

1. George Chalmers, *The Life of Daniel Defoe* (1785), quoted in Rogers, *Heritage*, p. 62.
2. See *The Complete Works of William Hazlitt*, P.P. Howe (ed.), 21 vols (London, 1934), xvi, p. 390.
3. A.D. McKillop, *The Early Masters of English Fiction* (Lawrence, Kansas, 1956), pp. 1, 43.
4. The reference to Arnold is to *Culture and Anarchy* (1785), J.D. Wilson (ed.) (Cambridge, 1960), pp. 45, 70.
5. C.W.E. Bigsby, 'The Politics of Popular Culture', in *Approaches to Popular Culture*, Bigsby (ed.) (London, 1976), p. 3.
6. J.M.S. Tompkins, *The Popular Novel in England, 1770-1800* (London, 1932), p. vii.
7. Bonamy Dobree, *English Literature in the Early Eighteenth Century*, OHEL VII (Oxford, 1959), p. 73.
8. The best known discussion of the contemporary reading public is in Ian Watt, *The Rise of the Novel* (London, 1957), chapter 2. However, his conclusions have been seriously questioned by later writers. See Diana Spearman, *The Novel and Society* (London, 1966), *passim*; and Robert D. Mayo, *The English Novel in the Magazines 1740-1815* (Evanston, Ill., and London, 1962), pp. 1-11. There is still discouragingly little firm evidence, but what there is can be found summed up in Pat Rogers, *The Augustan Vision* (London, 1974), pp. 76-85. Two more specialised books, now rather old, are still helpful: A.S. Collins, *Authorship in the Days of Johnson* (London, 1927) and Leslie Stephen, *English Literature and Society in the Eighteenth Century* (London, 1904).
9. James Arbuckle, *Dublin Journal* (1725), quoted in Lennard J. Davis, *Factual Fictions: The Origins of the English Novel* (New York, 1983), p. 123.
10. See Joseph Spence, *Observations, Anecdotes, and Characters of Books and Men*, J.M. Osborne (ed.), 2 vols (Oxford, 1966), i, p. 213.
11. *The Complete Letters of Lady Mary Wortley Montagu*, Robert Halsband (ed.), 3 vols (London, 1967), ii, p. 473.
12. See Spence, *Observations*, ii, p. 583.
13. Montagu, *Letters*, ii, p. 241.
14. Boswell, *Life of Johnson*, Hill and Powell (eds.), iii, p. 332.
15. Ibid., iii, p. 385.
16. Victor E. Neuburg, *Popular Literature: A History and a Guide* (Harmondsworth, 1977), p. 12.
17. For a discussion of the relevance of the oral tradition, see Ruth Finnegan, *Oral Poetry: Its Nature, Significance and Social Context* (Cambridge, 1977), pp. 1-52, 244-72.
18. Walter Benjamin, 'The Storyteller: Reflections on the works of Nikolai Leskov', in *Illuminations*, translated by Harry Zohn (1970; paperback edn, London, 1973), p. 87.
19. For a discussion of the 'real' and the 'invented' in Defoe, see Pat Rogers, *Grub Street: Studies in a Subculture* (London, 1972), pp. 322-4.
20. The fullest discussion of the varieties of recreation in the period is Robert W.

Malcolmson, *Popular Recreations in English Society 1700-1850* (London, 1973).

21. See Davis, *Factual Fictions*, pp. 11-25.

22. James Boswell, *London Journal 1762-1763*, F.A. Pottle (ed.) (London, 1950), p. 299.

23. Joseph Addison, *The Spectator*, D.F. Bond (ed.), 5 vols (London, 1965), i, p. 297.

24. Henry Fielding, *Joseph Andrews* (1742), M.C. Battestin (ed.) (Oxford, 1967), p. 18.

25. See E.P. Thompson, *The Making of the English Working Class* (1963, revised edn, Harmondsworth, 1968), pp. 19-207.

26. The books referred to are J.R. MacDonald, *Rousseau and the French Revolution 1762-1791* (London, 1965) and G.H. Ford, *Dickens and his Readers* (New York, 1965).

27. John Hall, *The Sociology of Literature* (London, 1979), p. 82.

28. Jacques Derrida, *L'Ecriture et la Différence* (Paris, 1967), p. 411. Quoted in Jonathan Culler, *Structuralist Poetics* (London, 1975), p. 247, in his own translation.

29. See Stieg Hargevick, *The Disputed Assignment of Memoirs of an English Officer to Daniel Defoe*, 2 vols (Stockholm, 1974).

30. The essay will be found in Roland Barthes, *Image-Music-Text*, ed. and trans. by Stephen Heath (London, 1977), pp. 142-9. Page references will be to that edition.

31. See Edmund Wilson, 'Dickens: The Two Scrooges', in *The Wound and the Bow* (New York, 1941) and F.R. Leavis, *D.H. Lawrence: Novelist* (London, 1955).

32. For an analysis of the uses of *genre* criticism in discussion of the cinema, see Stephen Neale, *Genre* (London, 1980).

33. See Claudio Guillen, 'Literature as System', in his *Literature as System: Essays Towards the Theory of Literary History* (Princeton, 1971), pp. 375-419.

34. See, for example, Catherine Belsey, *Critical Practice* (London, 1980), pp. 1-37.

35. Northrop Frye, *Anatomy of Criticism* (Princeton, 1957), *passim*.

36. For a discussion of this point, and a more detailed analysis of mode, see Angus Fletcher, *Allegory: The Theory of a Symbolic Mode* (New York, 1964), pp. 1-23.

37. See Vladimir Propp. *The Morphology of the Folktale*, trans. Laurence Scott, revised Louis A. Wagner (Austin and London, 1968).

38. One of the liveliest attempts at such a synchronic study is Roger Thompson, *Unfit For Modest Ears* (London, 1979), which enumerates the pornographic, bawdy and obscene works appearing in England in the later-seventeenth century. Thompson describes the books very well, but has no method for dealing with their changes over the period, and sees them as static, unchanging entities.

39. A very interesting study, which makes connections between recent Nigerian popular literature and England in the early-eighteenth century is Emmanuel Obiechina, *An African Popular Literature: A Study of Onitsha Market Literature* (Cambridge, 1973).

40. Defoe's distortions of narrative time are dealt with in Paul Alkon, *Defoe and Fictional Time* (Athens, Georgia, 1979).

41. See Belsey, *Critical Practice*, pp. 21-9. Frye's discussion of archetypes is in *Anatomy of Criticism*, pp. 99-112. See also a more recent book by Frye, in which romance is clearly seen as superior, *The Secular Scripture: A Study of the Structure of Romance* (Cambridge, Mass., and London, 1976).

42. Jonathan Culler, *Structuralist Poetics*, p. 136. See also his *The Pursuit of Signs: Semiotics, Literature, Deconstruction* (London, 1981), pp. 7-9.

43. For a discussion of genres as 'mental codes', see Tzvetan Todorov, *The Fantastic: A Structural Approach to a Literary Genre*, trans. Richard Howard (New York, 1975), pp. 3-24.

3 ROBINSON CRUSOE AND ADVENTURE

The early editions of *Robinson Crusoe* were presented as offering a great variety of delights for prospective readers and purchasers. The full title reveals the publisher's concern that all the book's thrills be mentioned, and that likely readers be reassured of the kinds of adventure contained within. If one were to read only that title page, one would assume that the book was another traveller's tale, incorporating some yarns about foreign parts, some interesting bits about solitude, some opportunities for catastrophe and some pirate stuff. Eighteenth-century readers would, thus, be likely to see this new publication as belonging to an authentic kind of voyage literature, rather than to a self-consciously fictitious one, such as *Gulliver's Travels*, or Defoe's early political pamphlet about a journey to the moon, *The Consolidator* (1705). The genre which would most immediately supervise reading, therefore, is the genre of authentic or semi-authentic traveller's tale, and Crusoe's behaviour would be seen through the prism of the behaviour of other travellers.

A great deal of pre-1719 fiction is panoramic and observational. The nominal hero exists only to relate the customs of the lands he rambles through, and his own idiosyncracies are generally of little importance. The interest in such books is largely anthropological, unlike the self-consciously philosophical and ruminative *Candide* and *Rasselas*. One commentator offers a diagrammatic presentation of eighteenth-century travel literature.[1] He asks us to imagine in the centre of the picture the hundreds of genuine travel books written in the period. To the right, we are asked to place the varied imaginary voyages — ranging from the explicitly imaginary, like *Rasselas*, to the use of travel in fictions like *Tom Jones* and *Humphry Clinker*. On the extreme left, we are asked to think of a fascinating conglomerate of texts, ranging from the intermittently mendacious, exaggerating writers such as Chateaubriand to the outright deceivers and inventors, like Defoe. Defoe certainly persisted in trying to deceive his public, and succeeded from time to time. Some people believed *A New Voyage Round the World* (1724) to be genuine; many were taken in by *Captain Singleton* (1720); and there is still some controversy over the reliability of *Robert Drury's Journal* (1729).[2] The question of when Defoe is lying and when he is telling the truth is a vexed and tiresome one, and its answer is of little critical significance. The much more pertinent and interesting question is whether the books were read as true or as false, and which kind of reading they seem to expect.

Robinson Crusoe clearly offers itself as genuine. The title page claims the adventures to be 'written by Himself', and Defoe's name appears nowhere. The references to 'Strange Surprizing Adventures' suggest that though hard to believe, the events narrated are to be taken as true, and the editorial Preface emphasises factuality insistently: 'The Editor believes the thing to be a just History of Fact; neither is there any Appearance of Fiction in it. . .' (p. 1)

All the devices of deception are thus present, but to what extent are they merely conventional utterances? The most frequent explanation of Defoe's avowals of authenticity is that they are a way of getting round the Puritan distaste for fiction. This argument can be applied either to Defoe's own conscience, or, more profitably, to his desire to avoid offending his audience. However, such an argument depends entirely on an implied audience, about whom we know nothing of importance. Were the audience in on the joke? Did they know that such avowals were only part of the grand apparatus of fiction? Or were they credulous, and prepared to accept the book as fact? The answer may lie somewhere in between these two apparently incompatible stances. The strict bifurcation between fiction and non fiction may not be pertinent to the early-eighteenth century. Dr Johnson's definition of 'history', after all, is 'a narration of events and facts delivered with dignity', which would seem to turn the 'history' from being a genre into being a mode. The point is also made by John Clare, in one of his fragments, that fiction could be read as true, with great pleasure. He talks of reading 'sixpenny Romances . . . and great was the pleasure, pain or surprise, increased by allowing them authenticity. . .'[3] It seems likely that unsophisticated readers did not distinguish very carefully between the factual and the fictional. They may have acknowledged a distinction between plainly expository writing, like conduct books, sermons and admonitory pamphlets, and tales, like biographies and autobiographies. These categories themselves would be shifting and slightly unclear, and the strategies of reading would vary — for instance, in which category would people have read the Bible? However, the use of both fictional and non-fictional tales was clearly for diversion, and as long as writers did not draw attention to the implausibility of narration, the use would remain constant.

If this argument about reader-use is acceptable, even as an unprovable hypothesis, it gives the Preface to *Crusoe* an interesting status. The key phrase is 'neither is there any Appearance of Fiction in it', where the word 'Appearance' is tantalisingly ambiguous. It could mean intrusion or semblance. If the former, then the editor is simply assuring the readers that the piece is consistent. If the latter, he is assuring them it is plausible. In either case, the reader is being assured that the book's tone will not disappoint, and that the pretence of factuality will be maintained throughout. The reader is being invited to read the book in a certain way, and to suspend disbelief in order to read the book in the category of the 'marvellous'. Though the whole area of the psychology of readership is very regrettably neglected, it is a required object of study if Defoe is to be properly placed in his culture. By offering his readers such conventional avowals of authenticity, Defoe is simply suggesting a particular kind of use for his book. The appropriate mode of reading, he indicates, is involvement rather than distance.

It is important to emphasise this point, because of the way the book has often been shifted into a different category. The first writer to try this was Defoe himself, in the Preface to the third volume, when he tried to transform the book from being a yarn into being an allegory.[4] If that were true, then the book would have to be read as it is by literary critics, as a remote discourse, wherein the meaning could only be discerned at one remove. Just such a reading was very interestingly given in Luis Bunuel's 1952 film of the book.[5] There is a splendid moment when the imperceptive, rather foolish Crusoe tries to address his God, and only hears an echo of his own voice in return. God, we are to believe, is only Crusoe himself projected onto the landscape. Bunuel makes full use of Crusoe's theological incompetence in his debates with Friday, and so reads the whole book as an ironic analysis of a shallow, hierarchically inclined individual. If this reading were accurate, and consonant with the text's expectations, it would move the book sharply from the left of Adams's suggested diagram to the right. It would also demand that the book announce its ironies to its audience, or that it exist at two levels of reading, the naive and the distanced.

For modern critics, the part of the book which seems most perplexing, where Defoe seems to have given fewest instructions on reading, is Crusoe's relationship with his God. Put broadly, there are two kinds of response to the book's spiritual concerns. First of all, there are those critics who stress Defoe's materialism and his concern with individual self-assertion in a hostile environment. Thus, Ian Watt largely dismisses Defoe's religious concerns; John J. Richetti talks of Crusoe's religious experiences as symptoms of schizophrenia; and Pièrre Macherey refers to Providence in the book as 'a mere screen'.[6] For these writers, Defoe has at best a superficial and conventional interest in religion, which the intelligent reader does well to ignore. Crusoe himself then becomes the object of sceptical analysis, rather than the emotional protagonist of the text.

Opposed to such views are the increasing number of writers who are prepared to take seriously Defoe's commitment to a providential reading of events. M.E. Novak argues such a case on the grounds of Defoe's obvious interest in the theories of Natural Law. Both G.A. Starr and J. Paul Hunter see in all of Defoe's work, and especially in *Crusoe*, a great debt to Puritan habits of thinking, and, more precisely, to the genre of spiritual autobiography.[7] Such critics read the book as an exploration of a life as a religious and spiritual experience, and their view has become the prevailing one. In the words of Pat Rogers, 'the most striking single development in our recent understanding of the novel has lain in the rediscovery of a pervasive spiritual motif'.[8] It remains to be seen, then, whether this discovery is an exhumation of something that Defoe did not need to make obvious, since it was part of his readers' assumptions, or whether it transforms the book into allegory.

There can certainly be little doubt that *Crusoe* invites a providential reading. In the Preface, the editor makes solemn claims for instructiveness and gravity:

> The Story is told with Modesty, with Seriousness, and with a religious Application of Events to the Uses to which wise Men always apply them (*viz.*) to the Instruction of others by this Example, and to justify and honour the Wisdom of Providence in all the Variety of our Circumstances, let them happen how they will. (p. 1)

The Miltonic echo in the words 'justify and honour the Wisdom of Providence' is probably accidental, but it does alert us to a way of reading the whole book. A necessary convention of the first person narrative, as it appears in voyage literature, is that the hero ends in some security. Only by a drift into implausibility or fantasy could the first-person narrator be made to die at the end, or to remain isolated. Thus, the function of Providence in the book is to announce that the mimetic mode will become comic or celebratory by the end. The whole presumption of the narration is that disaster is likely, but that eventual triumph is likelier. Thus the announcement in the Preface that the book will justify Providence serves as a sign to readers, relaxing them into an expectation of a coherent, eventually comic narrative.

However, though this is the eventual strategy of the narrative, the book's tactics are to endanger the hero persistently. Though the book is finally about escape and rescue, it has to be about danger and imprisonment before that. It is here that a distinction may be usefully drawn between the voyage tale and the pirate tale. The voyage tale normally ends with the return to safety of the wanderer, but the pirate tale often ends in execution or murder. In Defoe's *A General History of the Pyrates* (1724), the violent lives of most of the robbers end abruptly by force, and in *Colonel Jack* (1722), rogues are seen to perish at the hands of each other or the law. Only in *Captain Singleton* does Defoe try to wrest a voyage tale from his pirate adventures, by leading his narrator to comfort. Again, the oddity of the benign ending which Singleton recounts may be a result of first-person narrative. *A General History of the Pyrates* is presented in the third person, and so its central figures can be destroyed. Since the narrator cannot be destroyed, Singleton returns at the end to the form of geographical romance which dominated the first half of his book.

In *Crusoe*, the Preface promises that the hero will survive his dangers, through the benignity of Providence, and so the most potent threat is spiritual rather than material. But perhaps it is a mistake to insist on the strict separation of the spiritual and the material in this way. For Defoe's contemporaries, the two were much more closely linked by the instabilities of life. As Christopher Hill puts it:

> We should never forget how insecure life still was. Overseas trade faced the perils of piracy, shipwreck, the hostility of distant powers, scurvy, etc. But life at home was also affected by natural catastrophes, the fires to which wooden buildings were so liable, unstable prices, arbitrary taxation, famine, pestilence, sudden and early deaths. All this with no insurance. . . The margin between success and failure was very narrow: a man might obtain a windfall by, for example, a prudent marriage; but he could be

ruined by factors quite outside his control. It is difficult for us
. . . to recapture the profound emotional instability of our forefathers. Naturally they believed in theories of predestination
(Man's fate is in God's hands, not his own; success justified).
Naturally, they wanted to propitiate this very relevant God —
whether by ceremonies or by virtuous conduct.[9]

Throughout *Crusoe* great emphasis is placed on the narrator's various instabilities, and his use of the idea of Providence is, it seems, simply part of the fabric of his age. Just as it is a mistake to ignore the role of Providence, so too it is misleading to transform it into the theme of the book. Crusoe's relationship with Providence is more casual within the narrative than the Preface would have us believe. However, the function of the Preface is simply to allocate the ensuing narrative to the broad kinds of travel writing with which its prospective audience was already familiar.

In fact, the world through which Crusoe moves is more obviously fraught with dangers than with sources of comfort. Rather like the hostile, unaccommodating world of the picaresque novel, it shows the essential isolation of the central figure, and depicts his struggles to assimilate himself into his world. One commentator has even seen the location of *Crusoe* as being a 'Hobbesian "state of nature", transposed into a social world, atomistic, volatile, where the mere existence of another person is a threat to the self.'[10] In such a world, the sense of being perpetually watched would be much more a source of anxiety and jeopardy than of succour and stability. It is certainly true that when Crusoe does concern himself with the hand of Providence, he is seeking to find pattern and meaning in his existence, as the heroes of spiritual autobiographies did. However, in the fictional world of the voyager, there is much greater emphasis on the observable and anticipated dangers of the world, and at times the handling of Providence seems intrusive and perfunctory. There can be no doubt that selective quotation can make the book's commitment to effective Providence seem very intense, but the unease with which the idea is occasionally handled reveals that Defoe may have been working within the assumptions of his audience, and may have been reacting against their generic expectations. Certainly, any proper articulation of the book must account for Crusoe's anxieties and miseries as well as his occasional outbursts of 'cheerful confidence'.[11]

It must not be forgotten that *Crusoe* combines the voyage tale with a lengthy preliminary section on domestic life. Even here, however, it is possible to see Defoe covertly establishing instabilities in his narrator and in his environment, which make the transition to the travels more coherent. Crusoe tells us that he comes from 'a good Family' (p. 3). His father is originally German, but has for some time been settled in York, and is now retired from trade. He lives quietly with his family. Crusoe identifies himself for us more fully:

> I was called *Robinson Kreutznaer*; but by the usual Corruption of Words in *England*, we are now called, nay we call our selves, and write our name *Crusoe*, and so my Companions always call'd me. (*RC*, p. 3)

Why does Defoe incorporate this seemingly irrelevant detail? It does not do anything to animate the plot, or to forward the action, and might be thought of as simply another of his devices of spurious authentification. The detail is *so* irrelevant that there is no reason for him to lie about it, and so it imparts an air of adventitious plausibility to the beginning of the tale. That is certainly one result of the intrusion, but there are other, complementary explanations. It has been seen as one of those occasions where Defoe's undisciplined creative (or corroborative) skills just ran away with him, leading him to insert an additional fact which carries no thematic weight — another example of what Ian Watt calls Defoe's 'onomastic nonchalance'.[12] More recent scholarship has tried to dredge meaning from the names, under the general assumption that Defoe's names have important labelling functions. After all, Defoe's own change of name, from the artisan Foe to the pseudo-genteel Defoe shows some awareness of the significance of titles. The result in this case has not been very impressive. 'Kreutznaer' translates (roughly) as 'fool of the Cross', which some critics think has relevance to Crusoe's career. It seems unlikely, though, that Defoe would be able to expect his readers to decipher a cryptic German pun, of doubtful relevance.[13]

Even if this particular interpretation of the change of name seems unconvincing, it remains striking that each of Defoe's pseudo-autobiographies is narrated by a character who has his or her name conferred at some point during the tale.[14] In *Captain Singleton*, the narrator is spirited away from home by gypsies at the opening of the tale, and it is they who name him. He describes the process early in his narration:

and this Woman, tho' I was continually dragged about with her, from one Part of the Country to another, yet never let me want for any thing, and I called her Mother; tho' she told me at last, she was not my Mother, but that she had bought me for Twelve Shillings of another Woman, who told her that my name was *Bob Singleton*, not *Robert*, but plain Bob; for it seems they never knew by what name I was Christen'd. (*CS*, p. 2)

The fact that the name is conferred so casually should not detract from its potential significance. Bob is a generic name for any man, as Tom, Dick and Harry are, and Singleton is a title for a 'very foolish silly fellow'.[15] So the radical instability of the narrator's background has left him alone (*Single*ton), innocent and largely unprotected. His early connections are mostly criminal — he tells us that this gypsy mother 'happened in Process of Time to be hang'd' (*CS*, p. 2). The environment he is brought up in is already strange, mostly hostile and offers recurrent jeopardy. In the other tales, the narrator undergoes a similar process of naming, which seems to be a kind of initiation into the *demi-monde*. Roxana is given her name at a dance, and that name is known to only a few characters in her story (*Rox*, p. 174). Moll only gives us a criminal alias (*MF*, p. 7). Colonel Jack never knows his surname, and is named by his nurse (*CJ*, p. 4).

In each of these narratives, the central figure is involuntarily placed in a strange and hostile environment, and has a new name conferred upon him or her. To some extent, that is what happens to Robinson Crusoe as well. The environment of York may not be either hostile or strange, but it is foreign and estranging. It is noticeable that Crusoe refers to the process of change as one of 'Corruption'. The reference to corruption may be casual, but it is not without point. Crusoe reminds his readers that the stability of his domestic life is at best temporary, and that there is something of a history of wandering in his family.

Further and more important references to instability and jeopardy are introduced immediately after this. Crusoe refers to two brothers, whose careers were as violent and erratic as his is to prove to be,

> I had two elder Brothers, one of which was Lieutenant Collonel to an *English* Regiment of Foot in Flanders . . . and was killed at the Battle near *Dunkirk* against the *Spaniards*: What became of

my second Brother I never knew any more than my Father or Mother did know what was become of me. (*RC*, p. 3)

The only parallel occurrence of brothers in Defoe's fiction appears in *Colonel Jack*, where the narrator calls two other characters his brothers (they are actually his nurse's legitimate and illegitimate children), whose careers form an admonitory pattern to his own (*CJ*, pp. 3–5). The implication of stylised presentation of characters is obvious, and is used for resonance and suggestiveness. The introduction of the brothers in *Crusoe* serves to indicate to the readers that outside the domestic security of York, the world is uncertain, hazardous and threatening. Readers are also informed that the Crusoes are adventurers, and that their lives are full of excitement. It is significant that immediately after the quoted passage, Crusoe first mentions his own 'rambling Thoughts' and attributes to them his 'life of Misery' (*RC*, p. 3).

There has been a great deal of speculation about Crusoe's departure from home. It is a voluntary departure, and is given little psychological motivation in the telling, but critics have disagreed greatly about how best to read it. Novak attributes the decision to leave to 'Crusoe's personal characteristics', which he lists as imprudence, lack of a trade, lack of desire to settle, and wanderlust.[16] A different, and more plausible view is given by Starr, who rightly accuses Novak of giving too individualised a portrait of Crusoe. We are actually given very few idiosyncratic features of Crusoe's personality, and it seems much more likely that he leaves home simply because he is a figure in that kind of narrative. Readers coming to *Crusoe* through the genres of travel writing and pirate tales would ask little in the way of psychological padding. For the tale to be effective, the hero has to leave home, and so he does. Apart from the narrative demands, there would be no reason for Defoe to dwell on Crusoe's decision, and it would have been remarkably innovative (and hence probably unpopular) of him to have done so.

Starr's argument, however, is that we should not account for Crusoe's behaviour by referring to his individuality, but by considering the 'wildness that Defoe found characteristic of unregenerate man in general, and of youth in particular'.[17] Starr interprets the departure as a sin, rather than as an act of folly, and he is helped to do this by Crusoe's own remarks. Crusoe himself does not interpret his behaviour as economic self-assertion. He sees himself as having acted 'against the Will, nay the Commands of my Father, and against all the Entreaties and Perswasions of my Mother and other Friends' (*RC*, p. 3). He later laments his decision to leave, and wishes to become 'a true repenting Prodigal' (*RC*, p. 8). It seems perfectly fair, then, to take the departure as a sin, and to align the book to the narratives of repentance and spiritual education. As Starr puts it, 'the sinfulness of the deed consists in its violation of paternal, social, and divine order'.[18] The individual narrative would then be supervised by the recognised pattern of initial sin, followed by a period of punitive wandering, redeemed by providential delivery.

Such a pattern may be consistent with the overall shape of *Crusoe*, but the tale seems to incorporate some features which disrupt the generic pattern. First of all, doubts can be raised about how unequivocally Defoe has made the departure seem sinful. We have already seen, by the references to the dead and the vanished brother, that the social formation of the book is not static and patriarchal. Similarly, Crusoe's partial estrangement in York suggests a more mobile conception of society than Starr suggests. For the deed to be unambiguously seen as sinful, much weight has to be put on the probity of the father's speech. Crusoe is first given a lengthy analysis of the felicities of the 'middle State' (*RC*, p. 4), and its security. Crusoe's father talks of it as 'the best State of the World, the most suited to human Happiness, not exposed to the Miseries and Hardships, the Labour and Sufferings of the mechanick Part of Mankind, and not embarass'd with the Pride, Luxury, Ambition and Envy of the upper Part of Mankind' (*RC*, p. 4). The speech makes use of biblical references, and Crusoe is explicitly warned that God will not bless him if he leaves home. It all ends with the elder Crusoe in tears, weeping for the memory of his dead son.

All this is rhetorically very impressive, and makes use of sermon forms. It implies that what Crusoe seeks to abandon is the social position either enjoyed or envied by readers (the kind of social position which Moll and Singleton and Jack strive so hard to gain), and that such a social position is in itself morally superior to all others. If we are meant to accept the elder Crusoe's position, then Crusoe's departure becomes both an act of folly and of immorality. However, it is possible to read the speech in a less sympathetic way. Ian Watt wholly dismisses the religious overtones:

> the argument between his parents and himself is a debate, not about filial duty or religion, but about whether going or staying is

likely to be the most advantageous course materially: both sides accept the economic argument as primary.[19]

Watt's argument does seem rather reductive and unfair. He seems to suggest that the religious language used, and all the talk of emotional comfort, are only codes for material security, and that both Crusoe and his father are somehow in complicity on the hypocrisy of the stated case. Also, Watt's case is weakened when we remember that what moved old Crusoe was not economic considerations, but the memory of a lost child. So it is not fair simply to translate the speech into material terms, or to suggest that readers were invited so to do.

Yet there are still grounds for reading the speech ironically, though they are slightly oblique. Despite the stringent advocacy of temperance and restraint, the speech is slightly undercut by Crusoe's blithe remark about it taking place in 'his Chamber, where he was confined by the Gout' (*RC*, p. 4). Gout has traditionally, albeit inaccurately, been associated with excess, and particularly with alcoholic excess. Given Defoe's persistent attacks on venery and drunkenness, this very small detail may invite closer inspection.[20] It is corroborated, typologically, by the nationality of Crusoe's father. As a German, he might be thought to fit in with the caricature of Germanic vice which Defoe presented in *The True Born Englishman*:

> *Drunk'ness*, the Darling Favourite of Hell,
> Chose *Germany* to rule; and rules so well,
> No Subjects more obsequiously obey,
> None please so well, or are so pleas'd as they.
> The cunning Artist manages so well,
> He lets them Bow to Heav'n and Drink to Hell.
> If but to Wine and Him they Homage pay,
> He cares not to what Deity they Pray,
> What God they worship most, or in what Way.
> Whether by *Luther*, *Calvin*, or by *Rome*,
> They sail for Heav'n, by Wine he steers them home.[21]

This would certainly be very flimsy evidence from which to construct a picture of Crusoe's father as a lachrymose sot, sentimentally pleading to keep his last remaining son at home. However, though Crusoe calls him a 'wise and grave Man' (*RC*, p. 4), we must be struck by that fact that not one of his sons has paid any attention to him whatsoever.

Since Defoe's skills are always designed to simplify rather than to complicate, he finds difficulty with the conflicting narrative demands of his opening. He is required to signal to his readers that the ensuing tale will be of adventure, wherein the hero's moral state is largely irrelevant. At the same time, he has to engineer Crusoe's departure from home, and to point out his recklessness. The focus is so exclusively on the narrator that we are told almost nothing about the secondary characters — we are given no information whatsoever about what any of the characters looks like, for example. So Defoe's presentation of character is very abrupt and stylised. Crusoe is simply the son who wanders, with little in the way of individuation. Crusoe's father is simply the figure of authority who tries to dissuade him. The hints of individuation in the presentation of Crusoe's father can be explained by the necessity of keeping the narrator morally neutral. Were we to feel strongly a sense of his sin, we would expect more persistent contrition from a voyager, or more ruthlessness from a pirate. By being a kind of compromise between these two figures, Crusoe has to be given only a vestigial moral sense, and so the home which he deserts is only briefly sketched. And the brief sketch itself is not securely wholesome.

Overall, the opening pages reveal a world which is volatile and unpredictable, which offers only fleeting security and recurrent danger. Also, they open up the possibilities of an ironic reading, by providing interesting details which Crusoe himself does not comment upon. He sees his departure as a sin, though we are not fully coerced into accepting this view, and ever after seeks to re-establish a new replica home.[22] The language of contrition reappears when the departure is attended by misfortune. Crusoe casually enlists on a ship from Hull, and when he is frightened by a storm, he understands it as 'the Judgement of Heaven for my wicked leaving my Father's House, and abandoning my Duty' (*RC*, p. 8). However, the severity of Crusoe's understanding is rendered rather silly when the more experienced sailors dismiss the violent weather as 'but a Cap full of Wind' (*RC*, p. 9). A more explicit statement about sin occurs after a second, more severe storm, which frightens even the old salts. In his description of the events themselves, Crusoe is more concerned with the logistics of survival than with salvation, but later he sees the tempest as a providential warning to desist. He even refers to himself as the prodigal son (*RC*, p. 14), and a shipmate's father confirms the providential reading:

> you ought never to go to Sea any more, you ought to take this for a plain and visible Token that you are not a Seafaring Man . . . you see what a Taste Heaven has given you of what you are to expect if you persist . . . if you do not go back, where-ever you go, you will meet with nothing but Disasters and Disappointments. . . (*RC*, p. 15)

Again, an older figure rebukes the rebellious youth, and again uses quasi-biblical analogies, comparing Crusoe to Jonah. Again too, Crusoe ignores the counsel of resignation, and persists in his roaming.

Throughout Defoe's fiction, there is necessarily a tension between respect for Providence and the required hectic flurry of the narrators' lives. Defoe himself never fully opted for either the notion that Providence is in control of events, or the suggestion that life is a process of competitive self-assertion. The most emphatically confused discussions of these ideas occur in *A Journal of the Plague Year* (1722), where the narrator tries to establish that the plague is a providential intervention, and that it can be explained materially. The tension between these leads to passages of very uneasy rationalisation:

> But when I am speaking of the Plague, as a Distemper arising from natural Causes, we must consider it as it really was propagated by natural Means, nor is it all the less a Judgment for its being under the Conduct of human Causes and Effects; for as the divine Power has form'd the whole Scheme of Nature in its Course; so the same Power thinks fit to let his own Actings with Men, whether of Mercy or Judgment, go on in the ordinary Course of Natural Causes, and he is pleased to act by those natural Causes as the ordinary Means; excepting and reserving to himself nevertheless a Power to act in a supernatural way when he sees occasion. (*JPY*, pp. 193–4)

In fact, this theological obtuseness can be seen as purely conventional. H.F., the narrator, has to pay some heed to the theology of his tale, just as Defoe openly did in *Due Preparations for the Plague* (1722), but his main interest lay in the practicalities of the event. The narrator of the *Journal* is actually the most passive of Defoe's narrators, and functions as observer throughout. His individual characterisation is minimal. He remains in London throughout the visitation, and takes few precautions against infection. Strategically, this allows the narration to dwell on the sights and sounds of London, and to rail against the uselessness of medications. Throughout the tale, the reader knows that H.F. will survive, and though he himself may see survival as a providential mercy, the reader knows it to be a narrative requirement of the first person style, and so is not concerned with its importance.

In his periodical writings, Defoe frequently made use of the idea of Providence, as a way of explaining the outcome of history. In his *Review*, Providence was regularly seen as being directly in control of events, and capable of intervention at will:

> tho' I have had a large share of Misfortunes in the world, and no Man more; yet it has pleas'd Providence hitherto, to keep me out of such Hands. (III, 135b)

> *I look up*, and not Examining into *his Ways*, the Sovereignty of whose Providence I adore, I submit with an entire Resignation to whatever happens to me, as being by the immediate direction of that Goodness, and for such wise and glorious Ends, *as however I may not see through*, will, at last, issue in good, even *to me* (Preface, VII)

The implied fatalism of the second quotation is certainly at odds with the aggressiveness of Defoe's narrators, and it is a way of understanding the world entirely at odds with mimetic fiction. Only the self-consciousness and satire of *Candide* could present such stoicism in dramatic terms, and fatalism is certainly not consistent with Defoe's obvious interest in how things work and why they happen.[23] In the *Journal*, fatalism is dismissed as ridiculous and unworkable:

> he proceeded to tell me of the mischievous Consequences which attended the Presumption of the *Turks* and *Mahometans* in *Asia* . . . and how presuming upon their profess'd predestinating Notions, and of every Man's end being predetermin'd and unalterably beforehand decreed, they would go unconcerned into infect'd Places, and converse with infect'd Persons, by which Means they died at the Rate of Ten or Fifteen Thousand a Week, whereas the *Europeans*, or Christian Merchants, who kept themselves retir'd and reserv'd generally escap'd Contagion. (*JPY*, pp. 11-12)

The need for practicality is expressed as a kind of duty, and shows that there is some kind of responsibility on the individual to make every possible effort to survive in hostile circumstances, even when these hostile circumstances are thought of as a 'Judgment'. It is very important to see that H.F. can maintain the two views of the Plague — as judgment and as scientifically interesting phenomenon — within the confines of his narrative. There is no need to see the conflict between those two views as irony, or to see them as being forcibly thrown into confrontation by some implied author. They are simply the two forms of explanation used in so much seventeenth-century writing about illness and natural disaster.

In *Crusoe*, the two forces of Providence and randomness are necessary for the adventures to be formally coherent. Crusoe sets off on his journey through life (a reminder that allegory always lies somewhere behind the literature of travel) in a state of relative innocence, and his experiences are the sources of his enlightenment. He almost detects a full providential patterning in his early experiences, but it is not impressed by it. His awareness of his own 'sin' is presented clearly, but rather perfunctorily, as though the narrative wants to remind us of the prodigal son motif, without making it prominent or effective. As part of his repeated concern with the possibilities of Providential supervision, Crusoe seeks to understand his dreams, and the events which befall him. One of his most interesting discoveries is that his experiences seem to be ordered by the recurrence of significant dates:

> I remember that there was a strange concurrence of Days, in the various Providences which befell me; and which, if I had been superstitiously inclin'd to observe Days as Fatal or Fortunate, I might have had Reason to have looked upon with a great deal of Curiosity.
>
> First I had observed, that the same Day that I broke away from my Father and my Friends . . . the same Day afterwards I was taken by the *Sallee* Man of War, and made a Slave.
>
> The same Day of the Year that I escaped out of the Wreck of that Ship in *Yarmouth* Rodes, that same Day-Year afterwards I made my escape from *Sallee* in the Boat.
>
> The same Day of the Year I was born on (*viz.*) the 30*th* of *September*, that same Day, I had my life so miraculously saved 26 Year after, when I was cast on shore in this Island, so that my

wicked Life, and my solitary Life begun both on a Day. (*RC*, p. 133)

The belief in significant dates, and the use of them to detect providential control, was a widespread feature of seventeenth-century religious writing, and certainly figured in guide literature and spiritual autobiographies.[24] Importantly, though it appears in *Crusoe*, and so seems to offer that narrative as a spiritual instructional text, the narrator sees the practice as superstitious, and denies that it is of much importance. Certainly, if taken as evidence of a pattern in his various life, it is very unconvincing. Given that so many of the other important days of his life (such as the date of his conversion, of his deliverance, and of his first arrival back in England) have no such recurrence, the claim to structure can be ignored by readers as well as by Crusoe himself.[25]

Defoe here was incorporating some features of the religious genres, but restricting their significance. They are present because Crusoe's narrative is compendious, and draws from different genres, not because it really belongs to any one genre. The function of the religious references is to show Crusoe's search for security operating on a spiritual level as well as on a material level, and to show how material insecurity leads to spiritual confusion. In the *Journal*, H.F. talks at some length about the various sharp practices of those who exploited the public's desire for reassurance, and he recounts how with the approach of the plague, 'the People . . . were more addicted to Prophecies, and Astrological Conjurations . . . than ever they were before or since' (*JPY*, p. 21). This reveals Defoe's persistent interest and his audience's interest in the response to jeopardy. In each of his narratives, the central figure feels under severe physical threat (either in a storm, or under sentence of death) and in each case he or she is led into a hasty, shallow repentance, which is never presented as genuine penitence. Defoe seems interested in this as recurrent psychological phenomenon, rather than as a religious problem. It is presented under the general presentation of plausible behaviour, and serves as an occasion for only brief theological concern. So the repentances have a narrative function, in reinforcing psychological plausibility, and carry little serious religious concern. Like the narrator's doubts and fears, they are conventional.

There are very many occasions throughout the book when Crusoe's religious views seem to be at odds with his behaviour, or at least they have been interpreted as so being. This arises from the narrative function of Providence in *Crusoe* (and in the other narratives), as a threat to stability, and another source of jeopardy through which the narrator must pass. When subjected to a great variety of threats, Crusoe relies on practicality rather than on prostration. It is inadequate to attribute this robustness to clumsiness or heavy-handedness on Defoe's part, as though he were ineptly handling the pristine, emergent form of the psychological novel. There certainly are narrative inconsistencies and infelicities to be found — such as the well-known ones of Crusoe swimming naked to his ship, then being said to fill his pockets, or the awkward repetition of events in the narrative and in Crusoe's journal. These clumsinesses cannot be ignored, but they are of a different order from the alleged inconsistency of Crusoe's religious views. The supposed insensitivity is most apparent in Crusoe's treatment of Xury, the slave who helps him escape from his bondage in Sallee. After running away with his help, Crusoe debates whether to throw him into the sea. Eventually, he decides against it, and promises to reward Xury for his kindnesses — '*Xury*, if you will be faithful to me I'll make you a great Man' (*RC*, p. 23). However, the promise is hasty, and is soon forgotten. When the pair reach safety, Crusoe actually sells Xury for some 60 pieces of silver — 20 less than he gets for his boat. So the man who fled from bondage offers his assistant back into bondage. He does, it is true, state some reservations:

> not that I was not willing to let the Captain have him, but I was very loath to sell the poor Boy's Liberty, who had assisted me so faithfully in procuring my own. However, when I let him know my Reason, he own'd it to be just, and offer'd me this Medium, that he would give the Boy an Obligation to set him free in ten Years, if he turn'd Christian; upon this, and *Xury* saying he was willing to go to him, I let the Captain have him. (*RC*, pp. 33–4)

The ease with which Crusoe turns a mercenary act of self-advancement into an act of *largesse* seems disquieting. He does not doubt his right to sell Xury, and only when he remembers how useful a field hand would have been does he think 'I had done wrong in parting with my Boy *Xury*' (*RC*, p. 35). The meaning of 'wrong', however, is that he was mistaken rather than immoral.

This apparent moral imperceptiveness, like Moll's brisk treatment of her children, or Singleton's disquieting repentance, can best be explained in terms of the formal requirements upon the narrative, not immediately in terms of moral ideology. The travel narrative is processional, and cumulative, and so (literally) does not stand on ceremony. By remembering the briskness of the marriage at the end of *Crusoe* or Friday's funeral in the *Farther Adventures*, it becomes plain that Defoe has to find a way of discarding characters who are of no further narrative importance, and of keeping the impetus of the narrative going. Apart from a formal procedure of digression, like the interpolated tale, there are no grounds for maintaining interest in secondary characters in a voyage tale. They must simply be discarded, and Defoe combines Crusoe's need for cash with the narrative's need to jettison Xury. This only seems to be a moral imperceptiveness, or religious inconsistency, if the book is read within moral or religious categories. Reading it as a voyage tale allows for such hastiness, and explains why Defoe does not dwell on what he sees as being irrelevant to his procedure. It may be that his neatness in disposing of Xury invites a moral reading, but it must not dominate the understanding of the necessity of the episode. In a less elegant travel book, Xury would simply have fallen overboard, or dropped dead, and have made his exit from the tale silently. As the episode stands, we are invited simply to follow it, not to set it at a distance for refined moral judgement.

A second episode which shows the over-riding power of narrative requirements is the well-known one of Crusoe coming upon the drawer of money on the wrecked ship.[26] After a compendious list of tools discovered, the narrator comes upon the money, and addresses it:

> I smil'd to myself at the Sight of this money, O Drug! Said I aloud, what art thou good for, Thou art not worth to me, no not the taking off of the ground, one of those Knives is worth all this Heap, I have no Manner of use for thee, e'en remain where thou art, and go to the bottom as a Creature whose Life is not worth saving. (*RC*, p. 57)

Crusoe's point about the paramount importance of immediate utility may be correct here, but his rhetoric is surely grandiose and excessive. There is no reason why he should so loftily spurn a fortunate windfall of this kind. The money is not ill-gotten (as Singleton's is), and so there can be no moral taint involved in keeping it. Crusoe himself seems to become aware of the deficiencies of his first thoughts, for his next remark is 'however, upon second Thoughts, I took it away' (*RC*, p. 57). Admittedly, at this point, he is in greater need of tools than of gold, but there is still nothing to be gained by denouncing and ignoring the gold.

In this episode, Defoe is reinforcing the idea of utility, which is so important to the travel tale. Were the gold to be redundant (as Xury is), it could be dismissed. Crusoe's rhetoric shows that utility is the first criterion of worth in the world of the solitary adventurer, and he simply gets his categories wrong when he first declaims against the money. Earlier in the book, we have seen how volatile the world of the book is, and how wise it is to take stores against disaster. The most direct statement is the remark that 'human Affairs are all subject to Changes and Disasters' (*RC*, p. 36). Interestingly, these words are not spoken by the rather unreflective Crusoe, but by the altruistic and financially prudent Portuguese captain who rescues him. The money might, after all, come in handy, and it would be a mistake to leave it. By this episode, Crusoe seems to learn more about his role as adventurer, and to see that his thinking should be prudential rather than rhetorical.

It is surely misguided to read the episode as ironic. If Crusoe had left home for economic reasons, and found money only when it was of no use to him, then the episode would be dramatically ironic, and its function would be to invite us to see Crusoe as a slightly ridiculous figure. However, Crusoe left home with the conventional voyager's 'wandering Inclination', rather than out of any overt self-assertion or economic quest. In fact, he is well aware that his departure is economically imprudent. Consequently, there is nothing ironic in his discovery of money, and nothing ironic in his decision to take it. Crusoe is acquiring prudence after his initial error in leaving home, and is acquiring the adventurer's adeptness at survival. The money represents a contingency supply, and serves the reader as the promise of farther adventures. In the world of the adventure tale, the adventurer has to learn a prudential view of the world, and the money episode shows only how inappropriate the pause for declamation is in a world which demands hectic and abrupt action.

Crusoe's adventures, and the adventure tale as a genre, are concerned with establishing the dialectic between the hero's control over his destiny and his destiny's control over him. The uncertainties of adventure narrative (of which the travel book is a sub-category) lie in situating the point to which the hero can seize control, and the points at which hazard overcomes him. If *Crusoe* were truly an exploration of the providential view of the world, then the narrator would be wholly in control of his fate — he could ensure comfort merely by the consistent exercise of virtue. When he is first isolated, Crusoe seems to lean towards a providential view of his escape:

> I walk'd about the Shore, lifting up my Hands, and my whole Being, as I may say, wrapt up in the Contemplation of my Deliverance, making a Thousand Gestures and Motions which I cannot describe, reflecting upon all my Comrades that were drown'd, and that there should not be one Soul sav'd but my self; for, as for them, I never saw them afterwards, or any Sign of them, except three of their Hats, one Cap, and two Shoes that were not Fellows. (*RC*, p. 46)

Crusoe's use of the word 'Deliverance' alerts us to his religious understanding of events, and offers a conventional account of escape as a divine intervention in the world. We, of course, know it to be another necessary authorial strategy, and the later part of the passage reinforces the hazardous nature of events. The stubbornly material reminder of the drowned crew emphasises the arbitrariness of fate, and the capriciousness of events within the narrative. So Crusoe's discussion of Providence introduces a further uncertainty into the narrative. Not only does hazard operate, but the degree to which events are guided by a benevolent, controlling Providence is left open to uncertainty. The narrative deliberately diffuses the point to which its narrator is in control of his fate, and so invites the reader to expect surprises every few pages.

At this point in the tale, Providence has been used as a way of keeping Crusoe alive, and his consciousness of it as a moral force is relatively unimportant. This can be seen more clearly by looking at two parallel events in *Crusoe* and *Singleton*, where the respective narrators are shocked by thunder. Thunder, in the same way as storms, could be used as a way of bringing the supernatural into a material narrative. In *Crusoe*, however, the narrator is more concerned with his physical survival than with any understanding of the dramatic event as a warning:

> At the same time it happen'd after I had laid my Scheme for the setting up my Tent and making the Cave, that a Storm of Rain falling from a thick dark Cloud, a sudden Flash of Lightning

happen'd, and after that a great Clap of Thunder, as is naturally the Effect of it; I was not so much surpris'd with the Lightning as I was with a Thought which darted into my Mind as swift as the Lightning itself: O my Powder! My very Heart sunk within me, when I thought, that at one Blast all my Powder might be destroy'd, on which, not my Defence only, but the providing my Food, as I Thought, depended. . . (*RC*, p. 60)

The thunder here becomes a threat of the same order as all others, in that it most obviously threatens Crusoe's material survival, and sets him on to greater precautionary effort. In *Singleton*, however, a similar event is used to effect a necessary narrative transformation.

By the final third of the book, Singleton has become a successful and notorious pirate, and in order to arrive at a suitably celebratory ending, some means has to be found to turn him into a more acceptable voyager figure. Two methods are employed: firstly, the unusual concentration on the secondary character of the pedagogic Quaker William, and secondly the conscience-arousing flash of lightning. Singleton and his shipmates are disturbed by a blast from the skies:

when on a sudden, from a dark Cloud which hover'd over our Heads, came a Flash, or rather Blast of Lightning, which was so terrible, and quiver'd so long among us, that not only I, but all our Men thought the Ship was on Fire. . . As the Blast from the Cloud was so very near us, it was but a few Moments after the Flash, that the terriblest Clap of Thunder followed that was ever heard by Mortals. (*CS*, p. 194)

Singleton's sense of jeopardy is initially physical, but it leads to some spiritual torment eventually. The ensuing fear brings him to consider his dangerous condition:

and this was the first Time that I can say I began to feel the Effects of that Horrour which I know since much more of, upon the just reflection of my former Life. I thought my self doom'd by Heaven to sink that Moment into eternal Destruction. . . (*CS*, p. 195)[27]

The reference to sinking invites a combination of the physical and spiritual peril, for Singleton is in danger of sinking in both senses. His possible damnation is brought abruptly to mind by the lightning, and the narrative uses such an abrupt dramatic device to ensure a celebratory ending, without having to dwell on psychological change.

Crusoe's response to the lightning flash occurs much earlier in his narrative, and so has a different function. He sees its danger as purely physical and material, and makes no references to any spiritual dimension: 'I was nothing near so anxious about my own Danger, tho' had the Powder took Fire, I had never known who had hurt me. (*RC*, p. 60) Crusoe here avoids the religious rhetoric of the money episode, and Defoe does not use the episode to effect any great narrative change. Since the present business of the narrative is to offer an inventory of threats, and to maintain interest by surprise and sudden intrusions of jeopardy, there is no need to invoke Providence here. Providence in Defoe operates primarily as a rhetorical device, convenient for the presentation of change, and for the tying up of narratives. Whether he genuinely believed in its efficacy or not is a question of little importance. The important question is to identify the narrative functions of the concept of Providence, and the degree of intensity with which it is employed seems to vary with the extent to which the narrator has to be transformed.

One pattern which recurs throughout this narrative is Crusoe's customary acceptance of a non-providential, material explanation for events when one is available. Always the supernatural is tested, and almost invariably dispelled in favour of a more verifiable solution. In several episodes, Crusoe seems to be examining the supernatural, in the way that the narrator of *Mrs. Veal* did, as for example in the episode of the sprouting of green barley on the island. The incident has clear biblical parallels (which the narrative does not point out), and Crusoe's first reaction is to interpret the event as a providential blessing:

> It is impossible to express the Astonishment and Confusion of my Thoughts on this Occasion; I had hitherto acted upon no religious Foundation at all, indeed I had very few Notions of Religion in my Head, or had entertain'd any Sense of any Thing that had befallen me, otherwise than as a Chance, or, as we lightly say, what pleases God; without so much as enquiring into the End of Providence in these Things, or his Order in governing the World. . . (*RC*, p. 78)

Crusoe's understanding of the barley as a divine intervention entirely for his own benefit may well be seen as 'both arrogant and naive'.[28] The very abrupt change from the Crusoe who is concerned wholly with survival to the elegant sermoniser seems needless and superfluous to the narrative at this point. Were it to be taken seriously, it would bring in the principle of celebration very early in the book, and make the later adventures much less involving. Were we to feel that Crusoe was confidently under God's stewardship, we would be unable to be excited by his dangers, for we would know of his safety.

Defoe seems aware of such dangers, and changes the significance of the episode immediately afterwards. Crusoe begins to think about the whole business, and remembers the real cause:

> at last it occur'd to my Thoughts, that I had shook a Bag of Chickens Meat out in that Place, and then the Wonder began to cease; and I must confess, my religious Thankfulness to God's Providence began to abate too... (*RC*, p. 78)

The dispersal of the supernatural explanation in favour of a slightly disappointing, prosaic cause looks decisive. However, the episode is not yet closed, and Crusoe has another outbreak of revisionism:

> for it really was the Work of Providence as to me, that should order and appoint, that 10 or 12 Grains of Corn should remain unspoil'd, (when the Rats had destroy'd all the rest,) as if it had been dropt from Heaven... (*RC*, p. 79)

Crusoe's initial belief in the direct intervention of God has been moderated to a more orthodox belief in God's mysterious but indirectly efficient workings. In the words of G.A. Starr, Crusoe moves from seeing God as a 'first cause' to seeing him as a 'second cause'.[29] We may remember that the same transition is visible in H.F.'s discussions of the Plague (*JPY*, pp. 193-4). However, the rhetorical significance of the discussion outweighs its theological implications.

It is very important to see the way the book puts these two possible explanations, the spiritual and the material, on almost equal footings. The hesitations and switherings prevent any one view from destroying the credibility of the other. Whereas in *Singleton*, the supernatural was used to effect changes in conditions, in *Crusoe* it is described as a possible condition itself. In any narrative, there are two separate kinds of episode. There are those which describe states of stability and instability, and those which effect changes between states. In reading *Crusoe*, the reader is left uncertain as to whether any given state is one of stability, if it is providential and safe, or instability, if it is material and dangerous. Changes between these states are dramatically effected by the reliance on hazard (material) and the intrusion of guidance (Providence). The reader is never able to decide which of the two explanations is required, and so is able to read in a state of suspense throughout. In this way, *Crusoe* falls into the genre of the fantastic. As Tzvetan Todorov puts it:

> The fantastic . . . lasts only as long as a certain hesitation: a hesitation common to reader and character, who must decide whether or not what they perceive derives from 'reality' as it exists in the common opinion. At the story's end, the reader makes a decision even if the character does not; he opts for one solution or the other, and thereby emerges from the fantastic. If he decides that the laws of reality remain intact and permit an explanation of the phenomena described, we say that the work belongs to another genre: the uncanny. If on the contrary, he decides that new laws of nature must be entertained to account for the phenomena, we enter the genre of the marvellous.[30]

Crusoe's hesitation, which becomes the reader's hesitation, oscillates between the uncanny and the marvellous, without ever being able to decide between them.

It is worth pointing out that Defoe had very little wholly materialist fiction to draw upon. The predominant supervisory genres of the spiritual autobiography and the voyage narrative both saw the hand of Providence as operative, and so both presented their experiences in the category of the uncanny. The other traditions of dealing with the supernatural, such as the pamphlet accounts of ghosts or bizarre happenings, enter the category of the marvellous. What is strikingly innovative about *Crusoe* is the way it invites generic readings, but moves further towards the fantastic. Since there are very few materialist genres available (the Spanish picaresque may be the only important one), Defoe uses the pirate tale to incorporate the dangers and surprises that his narrative needs. His narrative then becomes generically compendious, and keeps its readers uncertain about firm strategies of reading. Part of the attraction of Defoe, in terms of popular fiction, is that his texts accommodate a great range of genres, even when explicitly set within one particular form, and so reading any of his narratives involves a process of rich and varied popular allusiveness, and a wide-ranging supervision.

Even with the book's participation in the fantastic, Crusoe tries to force his experience into the category of the marvellous by emphasising the mysterious yet certain presence of God. When he falls ill on his island, and begins to think on his death, he sees his past life as a pattern of punishment for sin:

> thro' all the Variety of Miseries that had to this Day befallen me, I never had so much as one Thought of it being the Hand of God, or that it was a just Punishment for my Sin; my rebellious Behaviour against my Father, or my present Sins which were great; or so much as a Punishment for the general Course of my wicked Life. (*RC*, p. 88)

Crusoe is clearly inviting us to read the book as a spiritual tale here, but it is significant that when he does so, he is being retrospectively inaccurate. Consideration that his experiences could be punishment for sin *had* taken place earlier — on his first sea voyage, on his being washed ashore, and on his finding the barley growing. His new view of punishment is more firmly and persistenly held, but it still fails to articulate the experiences which his narrative encompasses. As readers, we are beginning to doubt Crusoe's privileged insight into his own experience, and the possibilities of an ironic conception of his character are at least being opened up.

However, he does emphasise very strongly his turning to religion. When he begins to seek conversion, he makes use of a convention which sought God's hand in apparent randomness, by selecting a biblical passage at random and taking it as a text. Such selection was a Puritan convention which recognised the surrender of the individual will to providential guidance.[31] The consequent conversion is expressed soberly, and that may be why so many commentators have found trouble in giving it its proper position within the narrative. For instance, Defoe's most reliable biographer dismisses Crusoe's religious remarks as 'boggy stretches of moralising'.[32] Similarly, Ian Watt refers to 'the relative impotence of religion in Defoe's novels'.[33] Yet if we look at Crusoe's own account, we see that he places his religious observances at the top of his list of daily priorities. Crusoe announces his daily routine as follows:

> *First*, my Duty to God, and the Reading of the Scriptures, which I constantly set apart some time for thrice every Day. *Secondly*, The going Abroad with my Gun for Food, which generally took me up three Hours in every Morning, when it did not Rain. *Thirdly*, The ordering, curing, preserving, and cooking what I had killed or catch'd for my supply. . . (*RC*, p. 114)

So in Crusoe's own recollection, his religious duties came before everything else.

Even if this passage is very striking, we still get to encounter very little of Crusoe's religion. Much more narrative time is occupied by the second and third activities, which allow greater variety of recitation. The reason for this method of narration lies in the vital distinction between Crusoe's life and his *Life*. His report of his own activities is stylised and conventionalised, and need not be exhaustive or complete. The narrative is designed to interest and involve the reader by means of its variety, and so there is little to be gained be recounting an event which occured every day. The fictional and generic demands of the book mean that Crusoe's religious experiences are announced, but not developed. The Crusoe of the narration has to be an active and aggressive figure of practicality. He also has to provide announcements which seem to contradict this personality, like 'My Mind being entirely composed by resigning to the Will of God, and throwing my self wholly upon the Disposal of his Providence' (*RC*, p. 135). The narrative function of such announcements is to keep the tale in the category, very broadly, of the comic, since they ensure our implicit confidence in Crusoe's deliverance. Also, they serve to give the possibility of sudden reversal (as in *Singleton*) and attempt to render strokes of chance and arbitrary happenings plausible. So the function of the providential references in the book is to signal the overall category of the narration to the reader, and to allow readers to remain involved in the blow-by-blow events of the tale. Any attempt to ask whether Crusoe is *really* religious or not is irrelevant, since it seems to postulate a Crusoe existing around or outside the narration, and assumes that the narrative tells us about Crusoe the individual. Since the book's main source of meaning is its continuousness, any such question becomes meaningless.

Crusoe's God is thus a narrative assumption, which needs only to be referred to now and again to maintain his role as overseer, guaranteeing a comfortable conclusion. The book, then, explores practicality, within a religious context, and the references to God are not fully meaningful or informative. It is because they assign the book to the category of the marvellous (at the end), that they seem to be so unrelated to Crusoe's own conduct. As one critic puts it, 'a possible shortcoming in . . . theologically oriented studies is . . . their failure to account adequately if at all for the abundant textual evidence that Crusoe's conversion fails to affect sweeping changes in his character and values.'[34] Even Crusoe himself seems to keep forgetting about his conversion, and still sees himself existing in a random world of adventure. As he says revealingly at one point, '. . . by meer Accident (I would say, if I did not see abundant Reason to ascribe all such Things now to Providence)' (*RC*, p. 176). Crusoe's central narration remains stubbornly material, though Defoe seems to be making efforts to relocate the book into a different genre. There may well be a 'pervasive spiritual motif' in the text, but it remains latent, and serves only to prepare the narration for its satisfactory conclusion, and to allow adventuring to continue without fatally imperilling the narrator.

The book's gestures towards a spiritual overview are continually thwarted by Crusoe's own material sensibility. When he feels threatened, his worst fear is death, not damnation. On finding the footprint on the shore, he reveals his priorities again:

> Then terrible Thoughts rack'd my Imagination about their having found my Boat, and that there were People here; and that if so, I should certainly have them come again in greater Numbers and devour me; and that if it should happen so that they should not find me, yet they would find my Enclosure, destroy all my Corn, carry away all my Flock of tame Goats, and I should perish at last for meer Want. (*RC*, p. 155)

The pathos of Crusoe's plight is well rendered by the catalogue of destruction he imagines, and by the wonderfully childlike fear of being eaten. The narrative here is designed to convey immediate reactions, not considered ones, and the sense of deferred disclosure which the adventure tale requires means that any more considered interventions must be kept to a minimum. The whole pretence of the narration is that the narrator does not know what will happen next, and for the excitement of jeopardy to be conveyed successfully, the safe, reflective Crusoe must avoid reassuring us of any overall plan. But the book also demands that Crusoe survive, and so he reminds us occasionally that, though he cannot make full sense of his life, he must believe it to be coherent:

> Such is the uneven State of human Life . . . I consider'd that this was the Station of Life the infinitely wise and good Providence of God had determin'd for me, that as I could not foresee what the end of Divine Wisdom might be in all this, so I was not to dispute his Sovereignty. . . (*RC*, pp. 156-7)

Crusoe is never held to doubt God's sovereignty, but uses it only as an assumption which makes his narration coherent, and often ignores it in specific recollections.

Crusoe's meditations begin to reveal the conflict between the requirements of the adventure tale and the coherence of formal narrative. The adventure tale requires a phenomenological approach, where the readers can never discern what the next event will be, or how the narrator is to escape from his various plights. More formal narrative, especially in the first person, requires some principle of organisation. Defoe's tactic is to claim that there is some principle of organisation in the adventures themselves, though its revelation is continuously deferred. This leads to hesitation in the reader (and in Crusoe) about how best to understand individual events. For a good example of this hesitation, it is worth looking at the episode of the figure in the cave. Crusoe comes across a cave on his island, and, on looking in, sees 'two broad shining Eyes of some Creature, whether Devil or Man I knew not, which twinkled like two Stars' (*RC*, p. 177). The possibility that the figure is the Devil himself is allowed by narration's references to Providence, and so the providential intrusions increase the scope of adventure. Crusoe tries to combat his terror by reminding himself that 'the Power and Presence of God was every where, and was able to protect me' (*RC*, pp, 177-8). When the scary figure is seen to be an old dying goat, Crusoe passes no comment. The episode is turned to no moral end, and remains a case where the Devil has been introduced as another threat, rather gratuitously brought in and discarded. As Pierre Macherey puts it:

> The exorcism does not even necessarily pass through the moment of interpretation: the 'story' itself puts the devil to flight; it was a cannibal, an old goat . . . and Providence is quickly forgotten.[35]

The narrative (or 'story') has to rout the Devil, in order that the process of equilibrium and disequilibrium may continue. The ease with which Providence is invoked and then ignored is equally seen when Crusoe hears a ghostly voice crying '*Poor* Robin Crusoe, *Where are you*? *Where have you been*? *How came you here*' (*RC*, p. 143). Once Crusoe realises that he is only hearing his parrot, he quickly forgets the portentousness of the message. In neither of these episodes does the providential suggestion in any way supervene the narrative requirement of pace and surprise, and the hints at religious interpretation seem only conventional.

It is very important to notice that neither occasion is pressed into irony. There is no evidence that the providential reading exists as an ironic sub-text or pretext, inviting us to assess Crusoe's limitations. We are told of Crusoe's fears and his weaknesses as part of the fabric of the tale, not as a theme, to be removed from the tale and assessed. In *Moll* to a certain extent, and in *Roxana* extensively, the narrator's deficiencies are indicated, and we are invited to withdraw from them. In *Crusoe*, however, the headlong nature of the recitation invites only involvement on such occasions.

The conflict between practicality and spirituality is vividly presented in the episode of Friday and the cannibals. When Crusoe first comes across the footprint, he takes it as frightening evidence of the Devil. Yet once he has had time to think of it, he takes it to be the work of 'some more dangerous Creature' (*RC*, p. 155). If Crusoe's conversion is thought to be a psychological phenomenon, rather than a rhetorical premise, then such a remark is incoherent. There could be no *more* dangerous creature than the Devil. Nonetheless, he still offers some discussion of Providence (*RC*, pp. 156-7). Again, his response to jeopardy involves rather pompous pieces of sermonising, allied to a grim and effective practicality. Crusoe both reviews his spiritual condition and improves his fortifications, showing the way Defoe draws on a variety of popular genres in his narrative. It can be argued that all Defoe's narrators respond to danger in this oddly dual way, but such a duality should not be used to dismiss either the spirituality or the practicality as sham or inappropriate.[36]

Crusoe's narrative offers no overt recognition of a conflict between his religious prostrations and his robustness. The dichotomy is in fact a recurrent feature of Defoe's writing, and appears as early as 1697:

> MAN is the worst of all God's Creatures to shift for himself; no other Animal is ever starv'd to Death; Nature without has provided them both Food and Cloaths; and Nature within has plac'd an Instinct that never fails to direct them to proper means for a supply; but Man must *Work or Starve, Slave or Dye*; he has indeed Reason given him to direct him, and few who follow the Dictates of that Reason come to such unhappy Exigencies; but when by the Errors of a Man's Youth he has reduc'd himself to such a Degree of Distress, as to be absolutely without Three Things, *Money, Friends*, and *Health*, he dies in a Ditch, or in some worse Place, *an Hospital*.[37]

The view presented here is that of the adventure tale, wherein the narrator or hero effects the transition from disequilibrium to equilibrium by his own efforts. There is no sense of an over-riding Providence working, and the analysis seems to be entirely secular. The later privations, as in *Crusoe*, are the result of 'Errors' rather than sin, and they can be combatted by reason rather than prayer. It is only when translating this view of humanity into fiction that some overall religious view must be added. For a fiction to be coherent, there must be seen to be some principle operative, which makes the transitions comprehensible. If there were not one, then the range of possible consequences of any event would be infinite, and the narrative would be incoherently discontinuous or fragmentary. In the adventure tale, the principle of coherence can be overlooked, if the narrative is purely linear (i.e. A happened, then B happened, then C happened . . . without any connection being suggested beyond the chronological). However, in a popular fiction like *Crusoe*, the element of overall design and control is necessary, for the book's generic categorisation to be possible. Defoe incorporates Providence to facilitate reading, by allowing the book at least partial residence within the category of the spiritual autobiography. As an adventure tale, it adopts the rather contrary view of randomness and sensation, and does not seek coherence. For this reason, it need not end, and sequels become possible. By incorporating the spiritual dimension, Defoe adds another thrill to the adventure, but gives it some rudimentary shape as well, even if it is a shape which does not fully fit the book as it stands.

Of the three necessities mentioned above, money, friends and health, Crusoe has only the last in any great measure. He has some money, but it is of little immediate use to him, and he is in a position where it is not vital. Friendship, however, is more important in this book, with the appearance of Man Friday. Friday's arrival on the island is heralded by a dream prognostication, which seems to offer it as a providential blessing (*RC*, p. 198). The dream proves to be accurate, so disrupting the linear chronology of the strict adventure tale, and Crusoe is given the opportunity to secure Friday's allegiance by saving his life. The most intriguing point about the handling of Friday is that, despite Crusoe's repeated outcries about his lack of companions on his island, he never treats Friday as anything more than a servant. It has been argued that Crusoe is perfectly entitled to treat Friday as a slave, since he has saved and spared his life.[38] However, it is still surprising that the allegedly repentant Crusoe thinks so obviously in terms of ruling rather than of serving. Earlier in the tale, he talked lightheartedly of his 'subjects':

> there was my Majesty, the Prince and Lord of the whole Island; I had the Lives of all my Subjects at my absolute Command. I would hang, draw, give Liberty, and take it away, and no Rebels among all my Subjects. (*RC*, p. 148)

There is a small joke here about the way rulers behave, but the main levity in the passage lies in the fact that Crusoe's 'Subjects' are a parrot, a dog and two cats.

It could be suggested that *Crusoe* is aligned with Defoe's many publications which deal with the problems of social order, and that its presentation of benign sovereignty fits in with Defoe's anti-Jacobitism. But even if this were true, it would not help to provide a coherent reading of the treatment of Friday. Defoe, as we have seen, published many pieces on the proper behaviour of masters towards servants, and Crusoe's treatment of Friday fits in broadly with these recommendations. However, other elements are introduced. Firstly, Friday presents himself as a willing slave:

> At last he lays his Head flat upon the Ground, close to my Foot, and sets my other Foot upon his Head, as he had done before; and after this, made all the Signs to me of Subjection, Servitude, and Submission imaginable, to let me know, how he would serve me as long as he liv'd. (*RC*, p. 206)

This is presented as a colourful travel episode, rather than as an event to be related to the psychology of the narrator. Crusoe serves merely to recount the episode, and makes no mention of the parallel with Xury, or his own desire for companionship. Crusoe here is only partly individuated, and his main function is that of reporter. There is certainly no overt irony in his omission, or in what might appear to be forgetfulness, for his change of function from participant to observer disrupts the continuity of his character.

Crusoe's first act towards his new servant is the most explicit of all acts of ownership, that of naming. Crusoe does not attempt to ask for Friday's name, he confers one upon him:

> in a little Time I began to speak to him, and teach him to speak to me; and first, I made him know his Name should be *Friday*, which was the Day I sav'd his Life; I call'd him so for the Memory of the Time; I likewise taught him to say *Master*, and then let him know, that was to be my Name. (*RC*, p. 206)

At no point does Crusoe find anything strange about the power he so crudely exercises over Friday. Even when he likens Friday to a son (*RC*, p. 209), he thinks of filial bonds as binding, and forgets that a son can run away from his father, even off to sea if he wishes. The relationship is never one of equals, but of kindly master and simple, loyal servant. Again, the reason why the relationship takes this form lies not in the elusive psychology of Crusoe, but in the conventional form of the fiction. In travel tales, the place of secondary characters is relatively minor, and the tale is dominated entirely by its narrator. The personalities of figures encountered have to be subservient to the dominance of the narrator, for the tale to be told, and so Defoe has no resources from which to establish a more fully individuated secondary character. The typology from which he draws his fiction casts natives as either ferocious heathens or simple savages, and in order to establish *rapport* with his audience, Defoe has to work within the limits of his typology. He simply cannot present Friday as a reliable companion to Crusoe, because that would transgress the accepted patterns of his narrative.

Crusoe's treatment of Friday is self-conceived as kindly and humane, but on closer inspection it can be shown to rely on the traveller's values of self-assertion and survival. In his tracts about the treatment of servants, Defoe does advocate a measure of kindliness. However, he recommends it on the basis of its promotion of efficiency, rather than on any altruistic basis. He suspects that if you treat servants badly, they will work badly, and that if you treat servants well, they will work happily harder. Such a paternalist view can be seen, too, in *Colonel Jack*, when Jack is in charge of the slaves on a West Indian plantation. He has behaved kindly towards a slave called Mouchat, and when faced with a doubtful slave owner, Jack defends his own conduct:

> It may be true, Sir, that there may be found here and there a *Negro* of a senceless, stupid, sordid Disposition; perfectly untractable, undocile, and incapable of due Impressions. . . But, Sir, if such a Refractory, undocile Fellow comes in our Way, he must be dealt with, first, by the smooth Ways, to try him; then the violent Ways, to break his Temper . . . and if this was done, I doubt not, you should have all your Plantation carried on, and your Work done, and not a *Negro* or a Servant upon it, but what would not only Work for you, but even Die for you. . . (*CJ*, pp. 145-6)

Jack's argument is designed to promote efficiency, for which purpose he sees gentleness as more effective than strength. In *Colonel Jack*, such a self-serving economic view of charity evokes no surprise, for the narrator does not pretend to be anything other than a businessman. In *Crusoe*, the parallels between the treatment of Xury and Friday are disquieting, if Crusoe's religious conversion is thought to be effective.

The reason that he treats Friday, after his conversion, in the same way that he treated Xury, before the conversion, lies in the static presentation of character in travel narrative. The traveller is by definition robust and fairly resilient. He is to report events which happen to him, but cannot be profoundly changed by them, within the narrative requirements of coherence. Were the traveller to start to change his personality, the whole pose of retrospective narration becomes highly problematic. The narrative is linear, but is required to make some gestures towards conclusion. So Crusoe's conversion is just another event which happens to him, and which leaves him intact and solid, at the linear level of narrative. At a deeper level, it is used to signal conclusion and shape to readers, and to offer a reading category. So, for Defoe's various purposes, it is possible, indeed it is inevitable, that Crusoe both undergoes a conversion, and that conversion has little obvious effect on him. He is, after all, the robust reciter of events, and has to remain relatively single and uncomplicated for our attention to be properly focused on the adventures.

Only rarely is it possible to detect authorial playfulness in the revelation of the narrator's robustness. Crusoe is frequently presented as rather coarse and insensitive, as for instance, when he gives the score card of casualties in his skirmish with the cannibals:

3 Kill'd at our First Shot from the Tree.
2 Kill'd at the next Shot.
2 Kill'd by *Friday* in the Boat.
2 Kill'd by *Ditto*, of those at first wounded.
1 Kill'd by *Ditto*, in the Wood.
3 Kill'd by the *Spaniard*.
4 Kill'd, being found dropp'd here and there. . .
4 Escap'd in the Boat. . .
21 In all. (*RC*, p. 237)

This callous recital of 17 deaths is presented without any missionary zeal. It is simply another colourful adventure to be encompassed by the narrative, just like Crusoe's conversion. We can see Crusoe as imperceptive here, and turn that into a moral property, but it is more likely that he is a narrative figure who only makes such comments as the headlong report requires. Again, he does not make any great effort to make his narrative psychologically coherent — Friday's joyous reunion with his father is not accompanied by any thoughts of family from Crusoe (*RC*, p. 238). Crusoe's attitude towards the natives is consistently that they are part of the hostility of the environment, and so must be conquered. Parallel views can be found in Defoe's other major travel narrative, *Captain Singleton*. There, the Captain and his men attack some natives, killing 37 of them, including 3 women. The Captain's only announced regret is that 'there was no great Spoil to be got' (*CS*, p. 77).[40] It is such episodes which lead one commentator to find in Defoe 'a genuine sympathy with the poor and the oppressed — of his own race, at any rate'.[41]

The process of the narrative is thus continuously opportunist, both for Crusoe and for Defoe. Crusoe seeks to impose himself upon his environment, and to take advantage of everything that comes his way. So too, at times, Defoe takes advantage of the opportunities for irony which his static narrator gives him. As a solid convert, Crusoe feels compelled to lecture his new servant on Christian ethics. However, his attempts to explain are very clumsy and confused, and Friday's naive questions render him helpless. Apart from one gratuitous swipe at the 'Priestcraft' involved in

Friday's religion, Crusoe takes no serious interest in his servant's views. Yet his inability to answer fairly simple questions shows his failure to grasp the basis of his own religion. The length to which he takes his evasiveness and insecurity (he spends about three pages praying for guidance, *RC*, pp. 217-19) prevents the episode toppling over into any savage, anti-Crusoe ironies, but it does show Defoe's awareness of the deficiencies of his narrator.

This incident is not treated with the fierce irony of, say, Gulliver's unwitting revelations to the King of Brobdingnag, but it does reveal a degree of planned incompetence in Crusoe. At no other point does Defoe indicate any such distancing, and most of the time we are asked to see Crusoe's religion as a component in his adventuring. It comes in useful in the *Farther Adventures*, where Crusoe actually blows up a Tartar idol, Cham-Chi-Tonga, where his religious sensibility and his robustness in adventure are combined (*FA*, pp. 183-8). So though irony is possibly present in one episode, it fails to overcome the dominant mode of mimesis, or the implied role of naive involvement with the narrative.

From this point onwards, the book sees no need to refer further to Crusoe's religion, and provides a catalogue of more and more adventures. The only significant references to Crusoe's religion in the later parts of the narrative are Crusoe's remarks about allowing 'Liberty of Conscience' to his three subjects who have the varied religions of Protestant, Papist and cannibal (*RC*, p. 241). In fact, he offers them only a limited freedom, for he does not let the cannibal eat anyone. The dominant concern with survival is made obvious when Crusoe leaves the island, and offers the stranded mutineers some advice. He presents the island to them as a hostile, dangerous environment, only to be rendered accommodating by great physical effort. He provides much practical advice — how to manage goats, how to make bread, how to fortify a dwelling place. However, he offers them no spiritual guidance whatsoever. He does not mention repentance, and fails to remember God's Providence. So if there is a 'pervasive spiritual motif' hidden in the book, its overt appearances are sporadic and only noticeable in the first half of the tale.

It is not necessary to dabble in psychology and suggest that Crusoe himself has become less penitent as the book continues. Any attempt to do so would turn the book into a psychological study of its narrator, and it is clearly more conventional and static than that, not to mention more jumbled. More inconsistencies could be pointed out, both in plotting and in characterisation.[42] It is significant, too, that Defoe's most characteristic stylistic device should be the approximating phrase, which allows a certain rough and ready quality to the whole narrative.[43] These last devices indicate a degree of controlled uncertainty in the presentation of material; their purpose being to allow the book to remain as fiction, while presenting itself as fact. The fact that there are such inconsistencies, and such absence of precision, indicates a degree of uncertainty in Crusoe's world. This too is a necessary assumption of the travel narrative, which depends so entirely on the possibility of surprise and sudden change. The world of *Crusoe* cannot, then, be wholly assimilated to the world of the spiritual autobiography, though that world is referred to, but must be seen as predominantly the world of the capriciously fated traveller.

After Crusoe has left the island, the narrative rambles on for a while in a linear fashion, and draws to a close in a leisurely way. Crusoe finds out about his family, who are mostly dead, and discovers that the survivors have forgotten about him — another indication of the lack of family pattern in the whole narrative. He discovers, also, that his money has been working for him during his isolation, and that he has unwittingly become a rather wealthy man. All this takes place without much in the way of reflection, and without much emphasis on the miraculous or providential change which has taken place in his fortunes. The reason for such omissions cannot be the desire for brevity or the haste to conclude, for there is a lengthy, unassimilated episode where Friday is chased up a tree by a bear. It seems as though the book's ending will be contrived without the reliance on a benign, securing Providence, except for one small religious intrusion — 'I had some little Scruple in my Mind about Religion' (*RC*, p. 287). However, Crusoe's concern is denominational. His disquiet is aroused by the recollection that he called himself a Papist all the while he was in Brazil, and now he wishes he had not, since 'it might not be the best Religion to die with' (*RC*, p. 287). Even religion, then, becomes absorbed into the narrative's concern with securing comfort and with finality.

Crusoe's scruples are fairly weak, and do not detain him for very long. He seems more concerned with ecumenical tidiness, than with the state of his eternal soul:

> As I had entertain'd some Doubts about the *Roman* Religion, even while I was abroad, especially in my State of Solitude; so I knew there was no going to the *Brasils* for me . . . unless I

resolv'd to embrace the *Roman* Catholick Religion, without any Reserve; unless on the other Hand, I resolv'd to be a Sacrifice to my Principles, to be a Martyr for Religion, and die in the Inquisition; so I resolv'd to stay at Home. . . (*RC*, p. 303)

Crusoe is clearly not the stuff of which martyrs are made, and any fervent emotions, religious or other, are quelled by the narrative's move towards stable closure. Crusoe's earlier fervent desire to convert heathens and sceptics has no further narrative purpose, and has to be eliminated in favour of a more tolerant acceptance of calm.

As Crusoe comes to sum up his experiences, he stresses their diffuseness rather than any hidden principle of organisation within them. His most direct summary offers no religious sentiments at all:

thus I have given the first Part of a Life of Fortune and Adventure, a Life of Providence's Checquer-Work, of a Variety which the World will seldom be able to shew the like of. . . (*RC*, p. 304)

The suggestion of 'Providence's Checquer-Work' seems a purely conventional way of trying to incorporate some religious plan into a narrative which requires variety and fortune. Crusoe as narrator seems to have abandoned the sophisticated theological argument about 'second causes' in favour of a less strict view of natural phenomena. He now sees them as a 'Variety', rather than as a pattern or shape. The book then ends indeterminately, neither fully stable, nor wholly volatile. Crusoe marries 'not either to my Disadvantage or Dissatisfaction' (*RC*, p. 303), has three children and becomes a widower, all in less than one whole sentence. There is no need to dwell on such matters, for they merely form the preamble to another voyage, a return to the island to inspect its progress. The concluding remarks, then, form a kind of advertisement for the *Farther Adventures*, which appeared the following year.

The narrative, then, neither opens nor closes in stability, and each of these relative instabilities can be seen as necessary features of travel literature, whose main concern is volatility. Crusoe, by the conclusion (or suspension) of his tale, has ceased to see a pattern in his adventures, and does not offer his life as a didactic pattern for others. No longer does he offer an analysis in terms of sin and the hard road to salvation, and he certainly does not see his new status as a reward for repentance. When he comes to expand on these final remarks at the opening of the *Farther Adventures*, he thinks of himself not as subservient to God, and responsible for all his own actions, but rather as the helpless victim of a kind of ruling passion. He refers to 'the strong inclination I had to go abroad again, which hung about me like a chronical Distemper' (*FA*, p. 112). Yet he does make some references to Providence, as the source of the reversals which his narrative depends on — 'But in the Middle of all this Felicity, one Blow from unforeseen Providence unhing'd me at once' (*FA*, p. 116). The event referred to here is his wife's death, passed over so casually at the end of *Crusoe*. So Providence is used as a narrative agent again, useful for providing sudden reversals (as in *Singleton*, or the *Plague Year*), rather than as a fully represented spiritual force.

There are a number of such references throughout the *Farther Adventures*, but they neither amount to a theological idea, nor to a principle of coherence within the tale.[44] The function of Providence in the two parts of *Crusoe* seems to be twofold. First of all, it can be used neatly to provide catastrophes, which then need no further explanation. Secondly, it provides some vestigial cohesion during the narrative, which offers some sense that the process is more than simply linear. The hesitation the reader is forced to feel over the role of Providence mirrors the voyager's own state of anxiety and instability, and invites him to read the narrative within the category of the fantastic. Only once or twice are there any more fully committed presentations of Providence within the narratives, as when Will Atkins says, 'whenever we come to look back upon our Lives, the Sins against our indulgent Parents are certainly the first that touch us' (*FA*, III, 44). Crusoe thinks this to be true of his own case, but he has not made much mention of it before. The remark is best understood as just another aside in a rambling and discursive narrative, which does not seek single-mindedness, or the persistent emergence of any one theme. The main direction of Defoe's two Crusoe narratives is towards adventure only, and adventure is a compendious principle around which to present a narrative. It is significant that we leave Crusoe knowing more exactly what he has earned from his travels (£3475 17s 3d) than what he has learned from them.

The overall narrative of the Crusoe books is widespread and compendious. It is very tempting, but unfair and misguided, to try to extract one theme from the books, and by this one theme typify them. Most recently, the idea that the books owe much to the genres of spiritual autobiography and confessional tale has been translated into the view that the books *are* spiritual autobiographies or confessional tales. Such a view privileges certain episodes over others, and the narrative does not invite such selectivity. In the travel tale, all the events have the same status, and none is selected for more particular attention. Defoe's procedure is essentially to provide a linear string of events, which readers are invited to read as diversionary travel literature. There is little attempt to individuate the narrator, whose existence lies within the conventional role of the traveller, and there is no reason to read the book as anything other than a narrative which fits loosely into a number of genres. Its predominant mode is certainly mimesis, in that our credulity is demanded. We need not believe the events presented, but we must read them as though we did. There are very rare signs of a move towards the ironic mode, but they are not persistent. The use of Providence in the book is mainly to provide a vestigial coherence, and a promise of a partly comic conclusion. By being published as a book, rather than as a serial, *Crusoe* offers the reader some kind of contract of closure — the reader will always be aware of how near the end of the book he is, simply by the bulk of pages left to read. Providence is used to ensure that this conclusion is possible, and can therefore, disrupt the linear pattern of events. However, it is in fact only another event, of no more importance than any other one, and so the narrative is able to restart without trouble.

Defoe relies on a very crude psychology for his narrator, since that is all that the travel book requires. The narrator must be impelled to travel, somehow or other, and he must be in a fit state to produce reliable reports of his experiences. Defoe, then, avoids excessive individuation for Crusoe, so that he may offer reports which are acceptably general. The strategies of the narrative are imperialistic, in that Crusoe is out to subdue the places and people he meets, and in that the narrative seeks to encompass and inventory them, rendering them its exclusive property. In this way, Crusoe's conversion, about which there has been so much comment, is just another event which has narrative importance, but which he can subdue and keep in control. It does not remove the book from the category of travel literature, but serves to allow the narrative to proceed continuously. The devices of the narrative are best understood conventionally and generically. Crusoe behaves as he does not through the promptings of any unrevealed psychology, but because that is how the narrators of travel literature behaved in the book's time. Overall, it is a narrative which avoids irony, which seeks to enthrall and which offers a delight in factuality and novelty. It seeks to achieve its aims by working within the conventionalised language of early-eighteenth-century popular fiction, in which voyagers behaved in certain stylised ways. The novelty of *Crusoe* lies in its reserved compendiousness, and in its range of generic references. By isolating the narrator, Defoe was able to concentrate, to the limit of the reader's attention, on survival and hardship. As the book progresses, a greater interest is shown in logistics than in salvation, and sufficiently idiosyncratic situations are provided to retain that interest.

The central enterprise of the first two parts of *Robinson Crusoe* is, thus, to extend a tension between mobility and stability, between jeopardy and security. I said in the opening chapter that the notion of peril was central to all of Defoe's fiction, as it was central to all popular adventure tales. In *Crusoe*, that jeopardy arises from a volatile world, fraught with the dangers of tempest and hostile natives, wild animals and shipwrecks. It is explored by means of the robust central figure, whose own 'wandering Inclination' is the biggest of the hazards he has to face. The oscillation between adventure and prudence throughout the tale mirrors Defoe's own career, and without having to postulate anything as precise as allegory, the two figures of author and creation share a sense of the world's obduracy. When Crusoe spends so long making a boat that he cannot get to sea, or when he is first sold into slavery, the book is offering little fables of the vanity of human wishes. But when it shows us Crusoe successfully building his fortifications, or learning home economics, it is offering a more positive understanding of the human capacity to make sense of the world. That thin line between success and failure was the location of much of Defoe's own career as a political figure and as a man of business, and it was the invigorating effect of popular fiction to defamiliarise the repetitive patterns of everyday existence.

Defoe, more than any other popular author of his time, attended to the mixed, see-sawing understanding of life that his readers must have known so well. In a dynamic society, some could rise quickly, but others could fall just as rapidly. Man's attempt to seek as much security as possible in that dangerous world is latent throughout *Crusoe*, but in *Moll Flanders* it becomes even more prominent.

Notes

1. See P.G. Adams, *Travelers and Travel Liars 1660-1800* (Berkeley and Los Angeles, 1962), pp. 2-5.
2. For a discussion of Defoe's hand in this book, and of possible sources, see two pieces by John Robert Moore, *Defoe in the Pillory and Other Studies* (Bloomington, 1939) and *Defoe's Sources for Robert Drury's Journal* (Bloomington, 1943).
3. The passage is quoted from Edmund Blunden, *Sketches in the Life of John Clare* (London, 1931), pp. 50-2. It is discussed in Margaret Spufford, *Small Books and Pleasant Histories: Popular Fiction and its Readership in Seventeenth-Century England* (London, 1981), pp. 3-4. It may be worth pointing out that Clare mentions *Crusoe* as one of the earliest books he became familiar with.
4. *Serious Reflections During The Life and Surprising Adventures of Robinson Crusoe, With His Vision of the Angelick World* (1720), in *Romances and Narratives by Daniel Defoe*, G.A. Aitken (ed.), 16 vols, (London, 1895), III p. 101.
5. Bunuel himself seems to have disclaimed this film. He is quoted as saying, '. . . it is a commercial film . . . the book never interested me. . .'. See Francisco Aranda, *Luis Bunuel: A Critical Autobiography*, translated by David Robinson, (London, 1975), pp. 156-9.
6. See *The Rise of the Novel*, pp. 78-85; *Defoe's Narratives*, p. 42; and Pierre Macherey, *A Theory of Literary Production* (1966), translated by Geoffrey Wall (London, 1978), pp. 240-9.
7. M.E. Novak, *Defoe and the Nature of Man*, pp. 22-65; Hunter, *The Reluctant Pilgrim*, passim; Starr, *Defoe and Spiritual Autobiography* and *Defoe and Casuistry*. See also William H. Harewood, 'Religion and Invention in *Robinson Crusoe*', *EC*, XIV (1964), pp. 339-51; and Martin J. Greif, 'The Conversion of Robinson Crusoe', *SEL*, VI (1966), pp. 551-74.
8. Pat Rogers, *Robinson Crusoe*, (London, 1979), p. 51.
9. Christopher Hill, *The Pelican Economic History of Britain Volume Two: Reformation to Industrial Revolution* (Harmondsworth, 1969), pp. 109-10.
10. Homer O. Brown, 'The Displaced Self in the Novels of Daniel Defoe', *ELH*, XXXVIII (1971), p. 566.
11. David Blewett, *Defoe's Art of Fiction* (Toronto, 1979), p. 55. Blewett places very great stress on Crusoe's resilience, and may neglect the book's emphasis on danger and volatility,
12. Ian Watt, *The Rise of the Novel*, p. 109. See also Watt's 'The Naming of Characters in Defoe, Richardson and Fielding', *RES*, XXV (1949), 322-38.
13. See Hunter, *The Reluctant Pilgrim*, p. 154n. Hunter also sees a significance in the Anglicised name, comparing it with Timothy Cruso, a classmate of Defoe, and later a well-known author of 'guide' literature. See also Blewett, *Defoe's Art of Fiction*, p. 23n.
14. This point is made by Homer O. Brown, *The Displaced Self*, pp. 562-3.
15. See Eric Partridge, *The Penguin Dictionary of Historical Slang* (Harmondsworth, 1972), pp. 91, 845.
16. M.E. Novak, *Economics and the Fiction of Daniel Defoe* (Berkeley and Los Angeles, 1962), p. 32.
17. G.A. Starr, *Defoe and Spiritual Autobiography*, p. 77.
18. Ibid., p. 82.
19. Ian Watt, *The Rise of the Novel*, p. 67.
20. Many examples of Defoe's condemnation of excess are quoted by Hans H. Andersen, 'The Paradox of Trade and Morality in Defoe', *MP*, XXXIX (1941), pp. 22-47. Crusoe himself gets drunk after his first voyage and forgets his brief repentance (*RC*, p. 9). In *Colonel Jack*, the hero's drunkenness is the cause of his transportation to the West Indies (*CJ*, pp. 109-11), where he meets his first wife, who

is broken by alcoholism (*CJ*, p. 240). The recurrent concern with alcohol and its evils is a strong dissenting tradition, and would not need to be made explicit in the books. It could also be used by Defoe as a convenient way to effect very abrupt transitions in the tales.

21. *The True Born Englishman* (1701), in Boulton, p. 57.
22. See Pat Rogers, 'Crusoe's Home', *EC*, XXIV (1974), pp. 375-90.
23. For a discussion of this point, and for further examples of Defoe referring to Providence, see M.E. Novak, *Defoe and the Nature of Man*, p. 6.
24. See Keith Thomas, *Religion and the Decline of Magic* (1971, Penguin edn., Hardmondsworth, 1973), pp. 735-45.
25. There is another slight inaccuracy in Crusoe's remarks here — he is 27 when he reaches the island, not 26.
26. The famous passage has been extensively and variously analysed. For a summary of the argument, see Pat Rogers, *Robinson Crusoe*, pp. 80-2.
27. For a similar anecdote, where a blast of lightning brings a notorious atheist to his senses, see *Serious Reflections*, Aitken (ed.), III, p. 298.
28. This incident is discussed by Hunter, *The Reluctant Pilgrim*, pp. 149-51; and by Starr, *Defoe and Spiritual Autobiography*, p. 194. See also Greif, 'The Conversion of Robinson Crusoe', p. 565.
29. Starr, *Defoe and Spiritual Autobiography*, p. 195.
30. See Tzvetan Todorov, *The Fantastic: A Structural Theory of a Literature Genre* (1970), translated by Richard Howard (New York, 1975), p. 41.
31. See Hunter, *The Reluctant Pilgrim*, pp. 158-60; Starr, *Defoe and Spiritual Autobiography*, pp. 103-6. Just such a random selection of text is used by H.F. to find his justification for staying in London throughout the plague (*JPY*, pp. 12-13), and so shows that Defoe was aware of how such a convention could be used to provide very abrupt, yet plausible, motivation for odd behaviour.
32. James Sutherland, *Defoe* (London, 1937), p. 239.
33. *The Rise of the Novel*, p. 84. Cp. 'Though a religious element enters all his principal sources for *Robinson Crusoe*, he goes much beyond them', A.W. Secord, *Studies in the Narrative Method of Defoe* (Illinois, 1924), p. 239.
34. E. Anthony James, *Daniel Defoe's Many Voices* (Amsterdam, 1972), p. 166n.
35. *A Theory of Literary Production*, p. 243.
36. See the discussion of this point in James, *Daniel Defoe's Many Voices*, pp. 143-54.
37. Daniel Defoe, *An Essay Upon Projects* (1967), in Boulton, p. 24.
38. See M.E. Novak, *Defoe and the Nature of Man*, p. 52.
39. Crusoe's act of naming is discussed by Hans W. Hausermann, in his 'Aspects of Life and Thought in *Robinson Crusoe*', *RES* XI (1935), p. 449.
40. Elsewhere in *Singleton*, the Captain and his band perform outrages like setting fire to some Indians in a tree, with a similar lack of qualm. It is worth noting, too, that when they enslave a dignified African prince, the first thing they teach him to say is, 'Yes, Sir' (*CS*, p. 60).
41. David Skilton, *The English Novel: Defoe to the Victorians* (London, 1977), p. 16.
42. See James, *Daniel Defoe's Many Voices*, pp. 27, 36-7, 192n, 231.
43. See Arthur Sherbo, *Studies in the Eighteenth Century Novel (Michigan, 1969)*, pp. 155-65; G.A. Starr, 'Defoe's Prose Style: 1. The Language of Interpretation', *MP*, LXXI (1974), 277-94; Pat Rogers, *Robinson Crusoe*, pp. 119-25.
44. See *FA*, II, 150, 160, 166, 221; III, 4, 13, 18, 25, 34, 38, 40, 80, 142.

4 MOLL FLANDERS, CRIME AND COMFORT

In recent years, historians such as Christopher Hill, Keith Thomas, E.P. Thompson and Robert W. Malcolmson have explored the various sub-cultures of late-seventeenth-century life, and so have partially laid open the habits of thought of the prospective contemporary audience for Defoe's fiction. The importance of their work has not only been to lessen the hold of the patrician view of the eighteenth century as an age of exclusive elegance, but also to allow new ways of talking about the low life of the period. In much earlier scholarship, there was a tacit (and sometimes an announced) assumption that low life was only interesting as a kind of background, against which the most interesting figures reacted. Low life was often taken to be synonymous with criminal and vagabond cultures, and the literature of low life was often held to be the literature of various kinds of delinquency. What the recent historians have achieved is the destruction of such an assumption, and the re-creation of the view that low life was diverse and manifold, as capable of variety and complexity as high life, and as multifarious in its views and opinions as any other culture.

The rediscovery of the richness and variety of eighteenth-century low life has very important consequences for the reading of its fiction. Firstly, it is necessary, when dealing with the area of crime fiction, to try to imagine the various possible attitudes towards crime, from which the fiction would draw its resources. The criminal would have been as he (or she) has always been, capable of arousing fear, envy, horror, self-righteousness or pity. His (or her) life story could be presented as a warning, as a pattern of divine intervention, or as an economic homily. The fictional modes employed might be comedy, irony, or tragedy. The numerous possibilities were clearly conventionalised into those which overtly tried to warn their readers against criminals (understood as a different, threatening class), and those which offered a prurient, even racy account of how criminals lived. Of course, some books which seemingly offered themselves in the first category would more properly be read in the second, but the two species of presentation are discernible. The Elizabethan cony-catching pamphlets are perhaps the purest members of the first class. For example, Robert Greene's *A*

Notable Discovery of Cozenage (1591) was addressed to 'Young Gentlemen, Marchants, Apprentices, Farmers, and plain Countrymen', and offered to help and advise them:

> my younger yeeres had uncertaine thoughtes, but now my ripe daies cals on to repentant deedes... The odde mad-caps I have been mate too, not as a companion, but as a spie to have an insight into their knaveries, that seeing their traines I might eschew their snares: those mad fellowes I learned at last to loath, by their owne graceless villenies, and what I saw in them to their confusion, I can forewarne in others to my countreis commodity.[1]

Greene was then addressing himself to working people, to prevent others taking advantage of their honesty and simplicity. The audience as conceived here was simple, fair and honest, and rather naive. The subjects of the tale were presented as evil, cruel and avaricious, and were seen as a threat.

When the audience was not conceived of as unfailingly honest, the criminal could be given a more sympathetic treatment, as in *Volpone*. An important strategy in the fostering of criminal fiction, was for the audience to be conceived of as impressionable, and for criminals to be thought of as in some degree the victims of circumstance. If the collapse into a life of crime could be seen as hapless and involuntary, then the audience could simultaneously enjoy the fact that their lives were honest, but that the criminal was a recognisably similar figure to themselves. Criminal fiction gains its meaning from its place within a range of similar fiction, such as voyage fiction or scandalous tales, but also from the way it can draw upon the audience's sense of what crime is.[2] Thus, the criminal life could offer itself as a double example — as showing the kind of life to be avoided at all costs, yet as showing also some commendable self-examination and even repentance. This second possibility relies greatly on first-person narration, and is much more obviously a feature of early-eighteenth-century criminal fiction than of earlier works. Even Bunyan's *The Life and Death of Mr Badman* (1680) keeps the central figure at bay, by presenting its narrative in the form of a dialogue between Mr Wiseman and Mr Attentive. Bunyan recognises the danger of the evil criminal becoming sympathetic, and strives to prevent him from taking over the reader's attention as anything other than a moral example. The inevitable ambivalence which arises when an evil, dynamic figure is at the centre of a narrative is nullified by Bunyan's procedures of distancing.

In *Crusoe*, we saw that Defoe's procedures were designed to involve the reader, rather than to keep him isolated and private. In *Moll Flanders*, Defoe's combination of the criminal tale, the female adventure and the repentance story, all presented in the first person, raises different sorts of narrative problems. By involving the reader, as he always did, Defoe was immediately offering a prurient tale rather than an admonitory one. Moll was to be perceived as a character not remarkably different from the reader, or those of the reader's acquaintance, and the book is clearly not designed to warn us against the likes of Moll. But there is greater individuation of character here than there was in *Crusoe*, and the ambivalence which arises with the criminal as heroine is a persistent feature of the narrative.

Any articulation of *Moll Flanders* must begin with the reader's relationship with the narrator, and it is this issue which has dominated critical discussion of the book. The possibility of irony in *Crusoe* was raised in the preceding chapter, but no overall ironic strategy was detected. In the case of *Moll*, it is a much more vexed question. In *The Rise of the Novel*, Ian Watt offered a subtle distinction which seems to rule out the reading of the book in the ironic mode — '*Moll Flanders* is undoubtedly an ironic object, but it is not a work of irony' (p. 135).[3] Against this view of the book's haphazardness, it is possible to put Dorothy Van Ghent's remark that the book is 'a coherent and significant work of art' in the way it presents 'a complex system of ironies or counterstresses'.[4] The way of expressing the issue offered by Van Ghent seems to remove *Moll* from popular literature, and to offer her a place at the high table. Were there to be such persistent irony, then it would be possible to do this, but it would make *Moll* a remarkably uncharacteristic Defoe text. The controversy as stated in these two views does seem to raise rather unanswerable questions about the degree of control Defoe exercised over his material. Do the 'ironies' simply represent inconsistencies and a rather unfeeling temperament? Or are they a deliberately laid strategy, which no eighteenth-century reader seemed able to detect? Again, the terms of debate seem far too polarised, and the whole question seems to demand too much decisiveness and consistency of Defoe. Such decisiveness is not a feature of popular literature, which feels free to be as inconsistent and diffuse as it wants, and would not be a full articulation of the complex feelings raised by the twin issues of crime and femininity. Similarly to *Crusoe*, where neither the idea of Providence or the idea of randomness was singly sufficient to articulate the narrative, in *Moll*, too, the reader is required to hesitate. The book is never simply ironic or mimetic, but flits between these two modes, depending on the specific generic supervision in given episodes.

The title page of *Moll* again offers a rich variety of generic references. Moll's life will offer a 'continu'd Variety', including the saleable adventures of prostitution, incest, theft, transportation, wealth and penitence. The bizarre conglomeration of adventures is a fairly accurate summary of the book's contents, and indicates just how cluttered are its pages. More importantly, it also indicates the varied categories of reading required, and, as with *Crusoe*, these do not always seem compatible. How is the scurrilous whoring to be made compatible with the penitence? And how is incest to be made comfortable in the same book as honesty? These questions are perhaps the product of a reading which is trained to seek unity and consistency above variety, to find some partly concealed plan. In Defoe's fiction, the principle of accumulation or compendiousness overrules the aesthetic niceties of unity, and his narrative invites reading as sequence rather than as a purposive development. Variety is not only the most immediate feature of Moll's life, it is also the first principle of Defoe's fiction. The fact that these varied events happen within a chronology, to the same character, should not blind us to their phenomenological status, as sporadic or separate adventures.

Moll Flanders first engages its readers in a Preface, wherein the 'Editor' offers a summary of the book, and tries to make it seem educative and grave. Again, similarly to *Crusoe*, the Preface is best seen as a series of instructions in how to read the ensuing narrative, partly misleading, and it should not be taken as a proper description of that narrative. In the Preface, the book is presented *as though* it were consistently moral or pious, when in fact it is no such thing. By presenting it in this way, the editor can invite the reader to participate in judgements, even when the narrative does not fully support these judgements. Defoe seems closest to admitting the tactical role of the prefaces in *Colonel Jack*, where he says:

> this Work needs a *Preface* less than any that ever went before it; the pleasant and delightful Part speaks for itself; the useful and instructive Part is so large, and capable of so many

Improvements, that it would imploy a Book, large as it self, to make Improvements suitable to the vast Variety of the Subject. (*CJ*, p. 1)

Defoe is suggesting that the extant text of *Colonel Jack* has a great deal of potential improvements in it, but that it is largely up to the reader to draw these inferences. In the text as it stands, the emphasis is on variety, rather than on coherence, and the aim is to be 'pleasant and delightful'. So too in *Moll*, the Preface serves to get the necessary moral flummery out of the way, by allowing it much importance, but leaving it in the hands of the reader. The reader is being alerted to the moralising potential of the text, but simultaneously being offered a text with little actual moral content.

Defoe's prefaces regularly perform this tactical function, and only very rarely offer a convincing description of the work in hand. In *Memoirs of a Cavalier*, he offers a catalogue of the various delights to follow, speculates about the identity of the author (who is, of course, Defoe himself), and hints heavily about the possibilities of a sequel:

for how do we know but that this Author might carry it on, and have another Part finished which might not fall into the same Hands, or may still remain with some of his Family. . . Nor is it very improbable, but that if any such farther part is in being, the publishing these Two Parts may occasion the Proprietors of the Third to let the World see it. . .[5]

In other words, an elaborate game of bluff and entreaty is going on between reader and author, where the various proprieties are going on, and the diplomatic exchanges are taking place. The subdued meaning is that the editor is not fully in control of his material, but is at the mercy not only of his narrators (after all, he cannot alter what they say very much), but also of manuscript owners and eventually readers. This is much more than a device of authentication, and has to be seen as one of Defoe's ways of partially disclaiming responsibility for his work. He confers upon the reader the role of properly categorising the latent text, and invites the reader to draw the proper conclusions.

In other prefaces, he tried to emphasise the separate, irredeemable state of his books. In the Preface to *The True Born Englishman*, he talked of his poem as though it were some event over which he had only vestigial control:

> I may venture to foretell, That I shall be Cavil'd at about my *Mean Stile*, *Rough Verse*, and *Incorrect Language*; Things I might indeed have taken more care in. But the Book is Printed; and tho I see some Faults, 'tis too late to mend them.[6]

The book had rapidly been swallowed up by events, and like his narrators, Defoe had little time for self-recrimination about the past. The pressure of time and the urgency of events bring about error, and there was little Defoe could do to alter things. Elsewhere, on the other hand, he used the prefaces to indulge in some kind of revisionism. In the preface to the *Serious Reflections*, he referred back to *Crusoe*, and tried to alter the category of its reading. He makes the strange claim that 'the story, though allegorical, is also historical', and boasts that 'there is a man alive, and well known too, the actions of whose life, are the just subject of these volumes'. But even this implausible assertion is best seen as a way of disclaiming responsibility for the events of the narrative. Defoe was not responsible for them, as they had to follow the contours of someone else's life, he argued. In all these cases, we are being asked to take the text as an autonomous entity, which Defoe offers as a product. His role is not that of fabricator (in any sense of that word), but that of manager or purveyor. Even this alone would lead us away from seeing the text as some kind of repository in which Defoe as author inscribed meaning. Whether he knew it or not, Defoe's prefaces present a theory of reader-centred meaning which is much more relevant to the understanding of popular fiction than any author-centred theory.

The Preface to *Moll* does offer a number of instructions in how we should understand the narrator. The editor makes the conventionally required distinction between novels and genuine histories, placing *Moll* forcefully in the latter category. Similarly to the avowals of authenticity in *Crusoe*, this is to be taken as an instruction that we should read the book *as though* it were genuine. However, the editor then goes further to suggest his own limitations when he talks of the alterations he has been required to make to his original manuscript. He has had to alter the style of several passages, since his source is rather too bouncy for 'one grown Penitent and Humble' (*MF*, p. 1). To make the book less prurient, certain very vicious parts have been omitted. The editor quietly admits that 'there cannot be the same Life, the same Brightness and Beauty, in relating the penitent Part, as is in the criminal Part' (*MF*, p. 2), which serves to place the book in the category of criminal *exposé* rather than that of repentance tale. As a further tactic of disavowal, the editor puts the blame for his relocation of the narrative not on himself, or even on Moll, but on 'the Gust and Palate of the Reader' (*MF*, p. 2). The book has, then, been refined in the process of publication, but the editor is at the mercy of his readers' whims. Defoe is striving to present himself as a pure, hard-working editor, rather than as the reprehensible vendor of filth. He himself feels his product to be wholesome, but his readers may find crude uses for it.

He even goes so far as to announce that the book has an organising principle, and states it flatly:

> THROUGHOUT the infinite Variety of this Book, this Fundamental is most strictly adhered to; there is not a wicked Action in any Part of it, but is first or last rendered Unhappy and Unfortunate: There is not a superlative Villain brought upon the Stage, but either he is brought to an unhappy End, or brought to be a Penitent: There is not an ill Thing mention'd, but it is condemn'd, even in the Relation, nor a vertuous just Thing, but it carries its Praise along with it. . . (*MF*, p. 3)

Any reading of the book, however cursory, must find this statement to be grossly inaccurate and misleading. Moll's wickedness does not, it is true, lead to complete calmness, but she does succeed in living off the spoils of incest and crime with as little qualm as Singleton. The editor himself offers the possibility of doubt, when he admits that Moll's penitence was temporary:

> where she liv'd it seems, to be very old; but was not so extraordinary a Penitent, as she was at first; it seems only that she always spoke with Abhorrence of her former Life, and of every Part of it. (*MF*, p. 5)

Again, this allows the possibilities of doubt to creep in, but it is very misleading. When Moll recounts her past life, she does not evince shame; she reveals glee, gusto and verve.

The Preface, taken as a whole, sets the book adrift from its presenter. The material seems to be beyond control, and there is little he seems to feel he can do to ensure that readers adopt the proper attitudes to what happens in the narrative. The central conflict of the book makes any general statement about it, even by its author, very difficult. That conflict is Moll's combination of 'a zest for criminal ingenuity and a taste for moral preachment'.[7] Such a conflict seems to be a feature of Moll's psychology, but it might be better seen as a feature of the audience's reading procedures. *Moll* seems to seek categorisation in the zestful criminal genre as well as in the penitence tale genre, and such conflicting appeals leave little possibility of cohesion and unity. The narrative reaches beyond the limits of its narrator, into a wider categorisation, and that invites problems when talking about the book as the product of its narrator. Any reading which fully personalises Moll, and tries to make her a consistent character, will fall into difficulties or distortions. Moll has to be seen as a conventional device for the stringing together of various kinds of adventures, though Defoe does make some very interesting gestures in the way of individuation.

The Preface thus offers a religious categorisation of the narrative, which the narrative does not accept. When Moll herself introduces the narrative, she sees herself in an economic and social environment, but not in a religious one. She begins by reminding us of her criminal origins, and gives us only a criminal's alias for her name:

> MY True Name is so well known in the Records, or Registers at *Newgate*, and in the *Old-Baily*, and there are some Things of such Consequence still depending there, relating to my particular Conduct, that it is not to be expected I should set my Name, or the Account of my Family to this Work. . . (*MF*, p. 7)

The device of concealed identity is a necessary tactic in the genre of criminal fiction, as a procedure of authentication, and as a provisional guarantee of plausibility. The criminal is still so heavily entangled in his or her world, that it would be dangerous to reveal all, and so the tale itself becomes a covert, furtive act, thus validating its criminality. In Moll's case, the pseudonym serves to emphasise how violent and estranging her background is. Her social world is seen to be very volatile and wholly material, despite the rhetorical flourishes about Providence or the Devil. Obviously, her world is even more dangerous than Crusoe's, whether in the comfort of York or on the island. Crusoe is rarely faced with the variety of threats with which Moll has to cope. At the opening of the narrative,

Moll is already isolated, and so whereas Crusoe had the luxury of being able to act on impulse or inclination, Moll is immediately forced into ensuring her own survival.

Moll opens her account by telling us how sordid her background was. However, as is so typical of the book, she quickly moves on to discuss a rather more hygienic state of affairs.[8] After the age of three, she was raised by a kindly nurse, who instilled in her some rudimentary religious sense. Moll remembers being taught three things, and the order in which she recites them is reminiscent of the order of priority in Crusoe's daily calendar:

> BUT that which was worth all the rest, she bred them up very Religiously, being herself a very sober pious Woman. (2.) Very Housewifly and Clean, and, (3.) Very Mannerly, and with good Behaviour. . . (*MF*, p. 10)

The religious education is mentioned, but it is seen as a useful social accomplishment, rather than as any private spiritual boon. Moll herself sees this early training in purely social terms — 'we were brought up as Mannerly and Genteely, as if we had been at the Dancing School' (*MF*, p. 10). The role of religion in the book, then, seems to be as something which genteel people have leisure to accomplish. Moll's persistent desire to be genteel is expressed overtly, and in the rather spurious gentility of her account, and her references to religion are best seen as part of her later, restrospective achievement of mannerly social position.

At the beginning of the book, however, Moll's vestigial sense of gentility leads her only to misery. When she discovers she is most likely to be put into service, she is horrified and deeply distressed. Her distress is shared by her 'good Motherly Nurse' (*MF*, p. 11), and disrupts the very brief domestic stability they have enjoyed. Moll's horror at the idea of being a servant is never fully explained in the novel, and it is presented for a variety of procedural reasons. First of all, it shows early on the abrupt emotional reactions which she presents throughout, and which are used to effect the violent transitions in the narrative. Secondly, it shows the impediments which surround Moll's search for social mobility. Her very naive belief that she can move rapidly through the social ranks by working as a spinner is first seen as comic, but soon makes everyone weep at its folly. The introduction of an episode where Moll mistakes a prostitute for just the kind of 'Gentlewoman' she herself wishes to become is used as dramatic irony, and as an indication that in her world, appearances are never to be trusted.

In *Crusoe*, we saw that only Crusoe's father had any sense that society was benign and hierarchical, and that he alone saw it as stable. Even that stability was slightly undercut by the sly ironies in the presentation of his speech, and Crusoe's own career relied much more on the volatility of sudden transition than on any sense of shape or pattern. In *Moll*, society is turbulent and violent throughout. Moll's early days are actually spent in a relatively cloistered environment, since she lives in Colchester, which Defoe thought of as more enlightened and humane than some other places.[9] However, the spectre of Newgate has already been established, as the place of her birth, and as her most likely destiny. So the career we watch is seen as a recurrent series of scrapes, which increase the danger of her return to Newgate, and from which she seems always to escape. The characteristic procedure of the adventure tale, whether it be the voyage or criminal kind, is to place its central figure in danger, and to make his or her escape as unlikely as possible. Moll's references to Newgate offer the danger, and her early education offers the means of escape. If there is a principle of organisation uniting Moll's very diffuse adventures, it is the way her desire to be a gentlewoman reappears persistently. Sometimes it leads her to avoid telling us things which a more haphazard narrative would be pleased to include — there are many popular tales which are much more sexually explicit than *Moll*, for instance — and at other times this concern leads to Moll's rather over-eager attempt to make her behaviour seem respectable.

Defoe used such a concern with gentility in a similar way in *Colonel Jack*. In Jack's tale, the narrator is typically unsure of his origins, but relies on local legend to confirm his belief that he is the offspring of a 'Man of Quality' and a 'Gentlewoman', put out to a nurse to remove his (unmarried?) parents from 'the Importunities that usually attend the Misfortune of having a Child to keep that should not be seen or heard of' (*CJ*, p. 3). Jack goes on to recount how his father is thought to have laid down only one stipulation concerning his child's education:

> if I liv'd to come to any bigness, capable to understand the meaning of it, she should always take care to bid me *remember, that I was a Gentleman*, and this was all the Education he would desire of her for me, for he did not doubt, he said, but that sometime or

other the very hint would inspire me with Thoughts suitable to my Birth, and that I would certainly act like a Gentleman, if I believed myself to be so. (*CJ*, p. 3)

Jack's belief that he is a gentleman does in fact serve as a moral restraint upon him, by ruling out certain crimes as beneath his dignity. He feels impelled, for example, to make restitution when he finds he has robbed some one worse off than himself. Moll's sense of being genteel does not act in such a moral way, as it does not actually prevent her from doing anything. It does, however, prevent her narrative from incorporating everything she claims to have done, out of a sense of modesty and decorum. So whereas gentility in *Colonel Jack* is used as a moral property, to make the hero's actions coherent, it features in Moll as a barrier to full revelation, and so acts as a rhetorical restraint. In each case, it serves as the traditional single motive found in so much popular fiction. Character is reduced to a single notion of what it ought to be, and the main impulse of the book is towards the deferred gratification of that wish. In *Moll*, readers are presented with two schematised possibilities — Newgate and gentility. We know that Moll is likely to end up either in one or having achieved the other, and the process of the narrative is the oscillation between them, in the search for a comic resolution.

In the early part of the narrative, Moll's desire for gentility is seen as eccentric, and it makes her something of a celebrity. She is taken up, for a while, by the Mayor of Colchester and his daughters, largely as a novel plaything. During this period, Moll defines what she means by gentility, which is 'to be able to get my Bread by my own Work' (*MF*, p. 13). When she offers an example of what she means by this, we are forced to see the ironic innocence of her desire. She mentions someone who fulfils her requirements, and though this person is a lacemender (a menial enough activity), she is also a bawd of some kind. The interesting part is when Moll says, 'I insisted she was a Gentlewoman, and I would be such a Gentlewoman as that' (*MF*, p. 14). This is one of the very few overt ironic statements in Defoe's fiction, and its ironies are varied and fairly complex. First of all, there is the unwitting revelation of the paucity of Moll's conception of security, when her paragon is seen to be a lacemender. Secondly, there is the further irony in that this person is actually not a gentlewoman, but someone involved in prostitution. And thirdly, there is the irony that Moll does indeed turn out to be just such a gentlewoman, though she cannot at that time realise the accuracy of her prediction.[10]

The complexity of the irony makes it seem a deliberate part of the narrative, designed to alert us to Moll's possibilities. However, though it seems vivid and obvious to readers, the retrospective Moll offers to comment on its appropriateness. This is very different from, and perhaps more subtle than, the episodes in the other narratives when just such an ironic prediction is heavily underlined by the narrator. In *Colonel Jack*, the fates of Jack's two 'brothers' provide him with the opportunity to make rather weighty and solemn moral comments about himself. In *Crusoe*, the narrator makes an exact prediction of his eventual fate:

> In this manner I used to look upon my Condition with the utmost Regret. I had no body to converse with but now and then this Neighbour; no Work to be done, but by the Labour of my Hands; and I used to say, I liv'd just like a man cast away upon some desolate Island, that had no body there but himself. (*RC*, p. 35)

Had Crusoe said nothing further, then this episode would have been a direct parallel to Moll's unwitting prediction. But Crusoe goes on to reflect, and in doing so brings out the essential difference in genre between the two books:

> But how just has it been, and how should all Men reflect, that when they compare their present Conditions with others that are worse, Heaven may oblige them to make the Exchange, and be convinc'd of their former Felicity by their Experience. (*RC*, p. 35)

Crusoe's narrative is inviting a reading within the category of the cautionary tale, and this is one of the episodes where a meaning is drawn out of the action, and dangled before the reader.

In a narrative which has fewer pretentions to admonition, no such moralising is appropriate. In *Captain Singleton*, there is a similar piece of prolepsis when the narrator's likely fate is pictured for him by a companion:

> he came to me, takes me by the Hand, and looking into the Palm of my Hand, and into my Face too, very gravely, My Lad, *says he*, thou art born to do a World of Mischief: thou hast

commenced Pyrate very young, but have a Care for the Gallows, young Man; have a Care I say, for thou wilt be an eminent Thief. (*CS*, p. 25)[11]

Singleton's response is merely laughter, and he does not dwell upon either the accuracy or the portentousness of the prediction. His narrative is quite clearly an adventure tale, wherein the connection between events is chronological only. He makes no effort to discern any pattern within his life, and the narrative, thus, does not require the presence of irony. His adventures are of such a hectic, diffuse kind, that there is neither the need nor the desirability of reflection.

So too in *Moll*, the narrative does not seek to present itself as a retrospective revelation of the workings of Providence. The irony presented here is dramatic, but has little significance for the overall categorisation of the tale. It is simply another piece of rhetorical opportunism on Defoe's part, cheerfully adding irony to the various zestful delights of the criminal tale. Only very rarely are readers invited to distance themselves from the narrator in any ironic way. The implied procedure of reading is once again unmediated involvement, and even a reader who seeks to be remote from the text finds himself or herself being dragged along by it — as G.A. Starr puts it, 'sympathy keeps breaking in, and our ironic detachment — along with Defoe's — is tempered by imaginative identification'.[12] One method of supporting this sympathy is Defoe's use of Moll's partial (and rather selective) innocence. When the narrative reveals more than the narrator does, our sense of detachment is reinforced, but only rarely does Defoe allow that to be obvious. The more frequent tactic is to force Moll to relate her events in the most immediate, least reflective of ways. Her retrospective stance is rarely made effective, and much of the book could just as well be presented in the present tense.

The main process of the narrative is Moll's convoluted and twisting search for comfort and security. She originally, and innocently, sees the path to stability lying in her own honest efforts as a worker, but, as one critic puts it, 'what Moll will have to learn to do in the course of her narrative is to relinquish this middle-class dream of honest and self-sufficient survival'.[13] It is very interesting that, whereas *Crusoe* showed the possibilities of self-sufficiency, *Moll* shows the impossibilities. Moll lives in a social world, and her attempts to secure stability are disrupted as much by her relationships with other people as by accident or chance. Of course, it may be tempting to see her presentation of this as an attempt at excusing herself, but her character is never as fully motivated and understood as that would require. Whatever the case, the agency of her disillusionment is her romantic life, and the book balances the tale of Moll the criminal adventuress with the Moll who presents herself as the helpless victim of uncontrollable desires. In the later half of the book, these two tales seem rather at odds with one another, but there is little conflict in the earlier part.

Moll's first romantic encounter is with the elder brother of the family she is living with, and it is described in such a way as to allocate the tale to the group of romances about rakes and innocent serving wenches. Moll has already been established as a simple, rather gullible girl, and the seducer is introduced characteristically and conventionally as a rake:

> a gay Gentleman that knew the Town, as well as the Country, and tho' he had Levity enough to do an ill natur'd thing, yet had too much Judgment of things to pay too dear for his pleasures; he began with that unhappy Snare to all Women, (*viz.*) taking Notice upon all Occasions how pretty I was. . . (*MF*, p. 9)

The endangering feature here, presented as familiar to all readers of this sort of fiction, is Moll's innocent vanity. The whole episode is presented without dramatic impetus, as though it is recognised by readers as inevitable, and it is understood in purely conventional terms. Moll affirms 'my Vanity was the Cause of it' (*MF*, p. 19), and the whole episode has a rather stylised, impersonal appearance to it. The most important thing about it is not the loss of Moll's virginity, which she is characteristically coy about, but the awakening of insight that it produces. At one point, Moll overhears a conversation between her future seducer and his sister, in which he praises Moll's merits. The sister replies in a very worldly and disdainful way:

> I wonder at you Brother, *says the Sister; Betty* wants but one Thing, but she had as good want every Thing, for the Market is against our Sex just now; and if a young Woman have Beauty, Birth, Breeding, Wit, Sense, Manners, Modesty, and all these to an Extream; yet if she have not Money, she's no Body, she had as good want them all, for nothing but Money now recommends a Woman. . . (*MF*, p. 20)

The sister's sense of the supremacy of money, anticipating Roxana, is largely confirmed by the events of the tale, but Moll never comes fully to this cynical view. Readers are being alerted to the cynicism of the tale's world, but, very interestingly, the narrator does not participate in this all but universal sourness of view. Moll's innocence is damaged by her encounter with the rakish elder brother, but it is never fully dispersed. Defoe uses it to keep the book out of the category of pornography, where the heroine is as cynical as everyone else, and yet he is able to incorporate crime and promiscuity into a largely blithe narrative.

In fact, the issue of love and money was a recurrent theme throughout Defoe's non fiction, as well as appearing in *Colonel Jack*, *Captain Singleton* and, dominantly, in *Roxana*. It figures prominently in *Religious Courtship* and *The Complete English Gentleman*, and some critics have suggested that Defoe himself was heavily involved in discussing such matters when haggling over the dowry of his daughter Sophia.[14] It would be possible to present the conflict between love and money in any fictional mode, and in non fiction, it appears often as tragedy — brief tales are given of foolish lovers, whose impecunity drives them to grief. However, in *Moll* it is kept in the comic mode by Moll's undying innocence. One critic claims that the book shows Moll's education in the ways of the world — 'she learns that charm, wit, grace, and beauty are insufficient assets to the gentle world, but that diamonds are a girl's best friend'.[15] No doubt this view accurately represents the social world of the narrative, but Moll herself never becomes fully hardened to it as so many writers suggest. In the early part of the novel, she seems uncertain about her role, and makes very few recriminations of herself or others. She seems to accept the seducer's behaviour as being the way of the world, and her own innocence as being equally involuntary. The behaviour of the younger brother, who falls in love with her, at least maintains the possibility of conduct motivated by something other than money, and it helps to maintain Moll's naivety for a surprisingly long time.

Though Moll does recognise the power of economic necessity, it is by no means the only force which motivates her conduct or impedes her progress towards comfort. As her first seduction is completed, and the seducer gives her more and more money, Moll paradoxically announces her own culpability in the affair. She does not see the opportunity for her own self-advancement, and becomes in effect a willing, self-castigating accomplice to his scheme. Eventually, when he gives her a hundred guineas, she says, 'I made no more Resistance to him, but let him do just what he pleas'd; and as often as he pleas'd'.[16] The money she receives is not understood by Moll as a bribe, but as an earnest of his sincerity, and as a confirmation of his good faith. Despite the financial reward, she does not seem to realise, even retrospectively, that her body and charms are marketable assets, though she is tacitly engaged in selling them. She sees the loss of virginity as closing down her economic options, rather than as opening them up, as it were — '. . . for from this Day, being forsaken of my Vertue, and my Modesty, I had nothing of Value left to recommend me, either to God's Blessing, or Man's Assistance' (*MF*, p. 29). It is clear that Moll is not scheming to entrap the elder brother, and that she still clings to the foolish notion that virtue is more saleable than vice. Even in retrospect, she does not qualify her view that love is a source of jeopardy rather than comfort, and that it enfeebles her pursuit of stability.

It is at this point that the narrative is complicated by the younger brother Robin's announcement of his love for Moll. Obviously, this serves to involve her in a grim dilemma, in which her emotional security is at odds with her financial stability. Is she to accept the love of Robin, which may entail his being cut off from his family, and rendered destitute? Or is she to stay secretly with the elder brother, and enjoy a covert but profitable affair? For a ruthless narrator, like the narrators of the Spanish picaresque novels, there would be no dilemma. The affair with the elder brother could continue while the marriage to Robin was contracted and carried out. Moll's situation is rendered complex, not by moral qualms, but by her irrational sense of attachment. Her individuality, which is made much greater than Crusoe's, is expressed by her emotional idiosyncracies, and this aligns her to the romance heroines of Aphra Behn rather than to the criminal narrators. She even goes so far as to say to the elder brother, 'I had much rather, since it is come to that unhappy Length, be your Whore than your Brother's Wife' (*MF*, p. 40). Her distresses cause her to fall ill, and she is diagnosed by the physicians to be 'IN LOVE' (*MF*, p. 42). She still seems to maintain a romantic conception of her affair, though the reader is surely invited to see it as a purely carnal and financial matter on the part of the seducer, who is clearly prepared to pay to get her off his hands. Eventually, she accepts his ending of the affair, and marries Robin. Since this alliance is neither romantic nor criminal, it does not appear in the narrative, and has as little force as Crusoe's marriage.

We are told only that for five years they 'liv'd very agreeably together', until Robin dies, leaving Moll 'a Widow with about 1200L. in my Pocket' (*MF*, p. 58).

All in all, this whole episode serves to bring into the novel the powerful force which Moll later refers to as '*that Cheat call'd* LOVE' (*MF*, p. 60). Moll's view of romantic attachment is initially very unusual in context, and only gradually becomes sour. Defoe's professed views were rather different, and they too can be seen as idiosyncratic. In the context of contemporary debate, Defoe's arguments about romantic love, and its relation to matrimony, can be seen as fairly liberal. However, he still saw that the danger of romantic attachment was that it was often merely a screen for sexual desire, and that marriage based on sexual attraction 'brings madness, desperation, ruin of families, disgrace, self-murders, killings of bastards, etc.'.[17] Moll herself never develops any coherent attitude or policy towards her dilemma, and that is one of the ways she is rendered individual, distinct from conventional heroines and from Defoe himself. When describing her early sexual conduct, the retrospective Moll makes very few reflections, as though some of her illusions remain intact. In the Preface, the 'Editor' excuses this part of the book by claiming that it 'has so many happy Turns given to expose the Crime, and warn all whose Circumstances are adapted to it, of the ruinous End of such Things, and the foolish Thoughtless and abhorr'd Conduct of both the Parties' (*MF*, p. 2). Though the editor points out the moral lesson to be drawn, Moll does not, and the narrative does not seem to invite any such solemn reading. Moll's comments are very limited and never seem as strict as the editor would have us believe. Though she may recognise the shoddiness of the elder brother's behaviour in 'shifting off his Whore into his Brothers Arms for a Wife' (*MF*, p. 58), she retains her blinding affection for him. She may retrospectively acknowledge that love is a cheat, but she seems helpless to prevent it, and her condemnation affects her behaviour negligibly.

Significantly, Moll does not interpret her treatment as a cruelty, and she does not become hardened against the world as the *pícaro* does. Love is understood as the area of Moll's life most subject to hazard, and it has the narrative function that the weather has in *Crusoe*. The tempests which disrupt the narrative in *Crusoe* are actual; in *Moll*, they are metaphorical, but nonetheless effective as agents of disruption. Moll may fall in love at anytime, though she does become much more self-assured as the book progresses, and there are the attendant hazards of children and illness. Yet though this area of her life is the most subject to chance, it is the area where Moll's moral scruples are most active. If the book presents itself as divided into criminal adventures on the one hand, and romantic interludes on the other, Moll saves her piety for the latter, and even there it actually does very little.[18] In her criminal adventures, her self-reproach is infrequent and perfunctory, though there may be some signs of the pattern of overreaching apparent to the reader. Only in her romantic adventures does she offer any descriptions of evil, or show genuine repugnance or abhorrence, although in that area of her life she seems least responsible for her own behaviour. It may be suggested that what emerges in the narrative is a picture of what Lawrence Stone calls 'the growth of affective individualism', placed within the context of a society which is hostile to such individualism, and within a narrative which relies more heavily on conventions and types.

Moll's self-assurance and calculation increase rapidly after the first marriage, and become the motivating forces for her second wedding. As she puts it, 'I was resolv'd now to be Married, or Nothing, and to be well Married, or not at all' (*MF*, p. 60). However, even within the self-imposed limits of caution and prudence, Moll is characteristically impulsive and excessive in the way she treats her husband's money, and in the way she thinks of love. She learns that life in London is very different from life in the relatively rural Colchester, a fact which was already apparent to the reader in the fast behaviour of the elder brother:

> I was not to expect at *London*, what I had found in the Country; that Marriages were here the Consequences of politick Schemes, for forming Interests and carrying on Business, and that LOVE had no Share, or but very little in the Matter... (*MF*, p. 67)

Though Moll does come to accept the general truth that 'Money only made a Woman agreeable' (*MF*, p. 67), and that good looks and wit were good properties in a mistress, not in a wife, she still thinks of herself as an exception. Certainly, none of her marriages really deserves to be called a 'politick Scheme'. They all may start from that idea, but they are soon changed by foolishness or affection. She is persistently impolitic in spending money so easily, and especially so in paying attention to her feelings for her Lancashire husband, the fellow criminal, Jemmy. They extent to which her dealings are dominated by calculation may be surprisingly less than she herself believes. One critic claims that 'Moll has to set aside many feelings and attitudes which she cannot afford. . . Moll lives a life crowded with event and absolutely bare of feeling'.[19] While it is clearly the case that Moll's life is congested, it is surely a mistake to think of her as devoid of feeling. There are even a number of occasions when feeling wins out over prudence, such as the incest and abortion episodes, and these typify her affairs more than does cynical calculation.

The very important episode concerning her unwitting incest is one of those instances of rediscovered family that appear throughout Defoe's fiction. The reunion between Friday and his father, Jack's rediscovery of his wife in Virginia, and Roxana's furtive reunion with her daughter are all used as central plotting devices in their respective tales. There are a number of these events in *Moll*, notably the meeting of Moll and her highwayman husband in Newgate, but the most important one is her discovery that she has inadvertently married her own brother. The event is her third marriage, and before entering it, Moll has satisfied herself that her spouse is after more than just her cash, Moll then briskly arranges the financial matters, and on this occasion, talks very little about romance. After they have settled in the husband's plantation in Virginia, Moll spends sometime with his mother, whom she realises with horror to be her own mother. Moll's first reactions are very dramatic and powerful:

> I WAS now the most unhappy of all Women in the World: O had the Story never been told me, all had been well; it had been no Crime to have lain with my Husband, since as to his being my Relation, I had known nothing of it. . . (*MF*, p. 88)

Were she *only* to be concerned with financial security or comfort, she could accept this accident reasonably calmly, and could tolerate the living arrangements. But Moll repeatedly asserts that her position is somehow deeply repugnant to 'Nature'. Though she cannot be held in any way responsible for this state, which is the result of pure chance (and, on a narrative level, rather implausibly abrupt chance), she still suffers extreme guilt and shame. This alone would indicate that her life is not 'bare of feeling', though the feelings may seem to be histrionically expressed.

Moll's secrecy about her incestuous marriage lasts a startling three years, a period of time more suitable to the fairy tale than to the realistic report. The truth eventually slips out in a quarrel, and her brother/husband is shocked into serious illness. One critic sees in this illness a parallel to Moll's own sickness before her partly incestuous marriage to Robin.[20] Indeed, the two episodes can be presented as closely related — Moll's illness is interpreted as a kind of punishment for her deceptive marriage to Robin. Certainly, Moll herself has thought of the earlier marriage as incestuous, since she thought of Robin's brother while lying with Robin. There is a long casuistical tradition in which lustful thoughts are no less evil than lustful deeds.[21] Of course, Moll herself makes no mention of any parallel between the two episodes, but that alone does not rule out its validity. Defoe could be said to be surreptitiously unifying his narrative by giving the reader a more coherent view of events than the narrator has, and so turning the narrator into an ironically myopic figure. Such a procedure would be wholly outside the realm of popular fiction, but it is still a possibility. However, the basis for such an analysis of the book's hidden structure is rather unconvincing.

The episode with Robin and the later marriage are only very loosely and chronologically related. Moll's three years of reticence has no parallel with her earlier, brisk behaviour, and generally the incest episode stands on its own, obtruding from rather than cohering with the rest of the tale. *Moll* is, of course, not the only eighteenth-century narrative to encompass incest — it appears, fleetingly, in *Tom Jones* and elsewhere — and Stone's book makes it clear that the whole subject was obviously under widespread discussion. Given the congested accommodation in which most people lived, and the lack of social mobility, acts of incest must have been frequent, though almost always covert. However, the idiosyncratic thing about the episode in *Moll* is the extent to which the narrator's revulsion is developed. Moll describes her feelings acutely and at some length:

> I was really alienated from him in the Consequence of these Things; indeed I mortally hated him as a Husband, and it was impossible to remove that riveted Aversion I had to him; *at the same time* it being an unlawful incestuous living added to that Aversion; and tho' I had no great concern about it in point of Conscience, yet every thing added to make Cohabiting with him the most nauseous thing to me in the World; and I think verily it was come to such a height, that I could almost as willingly have

embrac'd a Dog, as have let him offer any thing of that kind to me, for which Reason I could not bear the thoughts of coming between the Sheets with him. . . (*MF*, p. 98)

It is made clear here that the revulsion is not simply a kind of moral condemnation ('. . . I had no great concern about it in point of Conscience'), but a kind of irrational, personal revulsion. The very graphic image of the dog enhances the power of Moll's remarks, which do not seem to fit easily into her otherwise rather blithe personality.

The horror which incest holds for Moll is reinforced by her lover's reaction to the discovery. He is so disturbed that he makes two attempts at suicide, and eventually falls into a consumption. This would indicate that Moll is not the only one to feel such powerful reactions, and gives the episode an eerie, frighteningly sombre effect. Yet the reaction is certainly given great dramatic force, by being so much greater than the audience might be likely to expect. M.E. Novak has shown that the condemnation of incest here is much stricter than would be likely from any of the theorists of Natural Law, from whom Defoe drew so much.[22] The theorist Pufendorf, for instance, accepted that some countries might sanction incest, and that any European revulsion at it might only be the result of ingrained custom. Even the customs of the time were much less severe than Moll's reaction might lead us to believe. Lawrence Stone describes the legal position:

> the punishments meted out by Church courts in cases of incest in Elizabethan England were surprisingly lenient, and there is no reason to think that sodomy and bestiality were more repugnant to popular standards of morality than breaking of the laws of incest, which must have been common in those overcrowded houses where adolescent children were still at home. . .[23]

If this was known to be true of Elizabethan courts, it is likely to have been the case in the 1650s, when, by the chronology of the tale, Moll's actions are alleged to have occurred. Bearing all these facts in mind, Moll's reaction to the incestuous marriage is highly dramatic, and unrepresentative of the way incest was treated in other popular discourses.

The episode serves in the tale to introduce a more thorough delineation of a character's responses to hardship. In *Crusoe*, the narrator's responses to privation were stylised and conventional. In *Moll*, much more of the narrative is taken up in presenting how things felt, and in rendering them immediate. To some extent, this makes *Moll* much more a book about character and development, though the development it portrays is fairly rudimentary. But Moll herself certainly has more than a conventionally unifying function. She is provided with qualities of individuality which keep the book's generic categorisation at bay. Because Moll is somewhat volatile and unpredictable, readers are unable to assimilate the full process of the narrative in advance, and so Defoe is able to move from the criminal tale, to the confessional or romantic tale, without having to change the conventional attributes to his narrator.

Another example of Moll's individuality can be seen in the way she responds to children. Much has previously been made of her rather casual attitude to them, though Stone has shown how common her type of 'fostering-out' was, and though they are understood best as mere narrative props.[24] After all, the narrators of *Moll*, *Colonel Jack* and *Captain Singleton* are all originally children discarded by their parents. However, it is worthy of note that Moll has curiously strict views about abortion. At one point, she is likely to bear a rather inconvenient child:

> my Apprehensions were really that I should Miscarry; I should not say Apprehensions, for indeed I would have been glad to miscarry, but I cou'd never be brought to entertain so much as a thought of endeavouring to Miscarry, or of taking anything to make me Miscarry, I abhorr'd, I say so much as the thought of it. (*MF*, p. 161)[25]

Seen in terms exclusively of self-interest and policy, Moll would be well advised to seek abortion. Her rejection of that recourse seems both irrational and fundamental, but not the result of deliberate thought. She rejects both abortion and incest on emotional, instinctive feelings of repugnance, not on the basis of some ethical code.

So far, then, Moll has been given a sporadically individuated characterisation, with eccentricities and idiosyncracies of viewpoint which cannot simply be explained as forgetfulness on the part of the author. Her motivation stems episodically from her sense of gentility, from her desire for economic self-sufficiency and from love. As such, it is much more varied than Crusoe's repeated 'wandering Inclination', and his fears of death. Moll's behaviour is not made coherent (or even presented *as* coherent) by any series of references to the shaping hand of Providence. Nor does her criminal career fit into any obvious pattern of punishment or reward. The intensity of her emotional reactions makes Moll a much more complex character than Crusoe, and allows the narrative a greater flexibility than the more schematic presentation of the earlier tale. Crusoe's emotions were often presented, but only on occasions of guilt or loneliness, which could always potentially correspond to a providential reading.[26] Moll's emotions are much more extensive and varied than those of her generic predecessors, like Lindamira, and they certainly rely a lot less on the alleged promptings of supernatural intrusion. Even her conscience does not seem to be a very important factor (despite the attention drawn to it by the Preface), and her emotions are largely spontaneous and unpredictable.

In her criminal adventures, Moll fits more readily into the acknowledged fictional patterns of her predecessors. The narrative occasionally takes on the pattern of the confessional tale, with the apparently penitent Moll expressing conventional disapproval of the former conduct with which her narrative is actually trying to entertain us. She sees most of her thieving as voluntary, and so has to see herself as culpable, though throughout the presentation of this part of her life there is a great deal of elision and equivocation. She believes that her earliest crimes arose from necessity, and, therefore, that they are conventionally acceptable. They serve to warn the reader that anyone can be driven to such extremes, and to remove the taint of prurience from reading by fitting the thefts into an admonitory pattern. She is aware that theft can sometimes be acceptable as an alternative to starvation, but even this rudimentary moral point is presented imperceptively and sporadically.

Necessity is offered as an exculpatory plea on a number of occasions. Moll deceives most of her suitors about her true financial position, for instance, and offers the excuse that such deviousness is necessary for an unprotected woman in a hostile world. The degree to which Moll is genuinely in jeopardy, and the degree to which she is a predator in her own right, are kept uncertain throughout the narrative. However, Moll's view is that such crookedness is necessary, and if it is necessary, then it is morally excusable. Such a view is consonant with Natural Law theory, and appears throughout Defoe's fiction.[27] Her reliance on necessity as a plea of justification is most prominent when she is in difficulties, and when she is discussing her affairs with a banker:

> I was now a loose unguided Creature, and had no Help, no Assistance, no Guide for my Conduct: I knew what I aim'd at, and what I wanted, but knew nothing to pursue the End by direct Means; I wanted to be plac'd in a settled State of Living, and had I happen'd to meet with a good sober Husband, I should have been as faithful and true a Wife as Virtue it self cou'd have form'd: If I had been otherwise, the Vice came in always at the Door of Necessity, not at the Door of Inclination... (*MF*, pp. 128-9)

If this position were plausible, then Moll would always be in the clear, and the fact that it sounds so much like arrant self-justification may turn the narrative more towards irony when Moll is being reflective. Moll's attempts to excuse her lapses are never fully convincing. Her greatest criminal excesses arise much more from the fear of eventual or impending poverty than from immediate or imminent poverty. She steals in advance of necessity, in case necessity comes along, which is as morally incoherent as retaliating before provocation.

Though we need not fall for Moll's interpretation of her own life, we are still invited to follow the events avidly, in an involved way. In the narrative, as opposed to Moll's moral interjections, the theme of exculpatory necessity recurs. The banker describes his estranged wife as 'a Whore not by Necessity, which is the common Bait of your Sex, but by Inclination, and for the Sake of Vice' (*MF*, p. 135). Moll's acceptance of this tale helps her justify her own behaviour, and she does consistently approach other people's behaviour in very simple graphic terms — acting from necessity is excusable, but acting viciously from inclination is reprehensible and intolerable. It is noticeable that this view of inclination is very different from Crusoe's where it was partly an exculpatory factor in itself. However, even this very simple moral view within the tale, which is the kind of graphic morality necessary for the functioning of popular fiction, is disrupted whenever emotional attachment intrudes. She never applies her standards to the elder brother in Colchester, to her mother, or to Jemmy, and so the narrative, it seems, takes only a fitful and crude interest in the moral status of its events.

Moll's first criminal acts occur after her banker husband has died, leaving her very poor. She is led to quote a remark which becomes familiar in this book, as well as in *Colonel Jack* and *Roxana*, 'Give me not Poverty lest I steal' (*MF*, p. 191).[28] Another familiar tactic is her attribution of her criminal inclinations to the Devil's promptings.[29] Certainly, this is the first time in the narrative that Moll offers a supernatural intervention, and it does seem to happen at a disquietingly convenient time:

> THIS was the Bait, and the Devil who I said laid the Snare, as readily prompted me, as if he had spoke, for I remember, and shall never forget it, 'twas like a Voice spoken to me over my Shoulder, take the Bundle; be quick; do it this Moment. . . (*MF*, p. 191)

Moll's dramatic presentation of her own state is less conventional than Crusoe's and more aware of itself as a piece of imaginative reconstruction. The use of a sly 'as if' renders the account dramatic, and yet makes it also appear as though Moll is the victim rather than the aggressor here. As a presentation of the supernatural, it should not be taken seriously. Even in *Crusoe*, the talk of predictions, dreams, 'secret hints' and so on, was never fully sustained or coherent, but it was persistent enough to become an integral part of the narrative, and to assist in its generic categorisation as sporadically a spiritual autobiography. In *Moll*, the reference is too isolated for this, and serves to concentrate attention on the drama of the moment, rather than on any overall plan.

Moll's life of crime is by now established, and in this respect the narrative becomes somewhat uneasy. The mode of presentation is never simple or single, and many passages offer ironic possibilities, as well as admonitory ones. In the famous episode where Moll justifies, or attempts to justify, the theft of a child's necklace, the variety of modes is obvious. If we accept the Natural Law background to the tale, then stealing from someone worse off than yourself is clearly wicked.[30] However, Moll retrospectively tries to make the theft into an act of rough charity and benevolence, in a charmingly flagrant piece of rationalisation:

> Poverty, as I have said, harden'd my Heart, and my own Necessities made me regardless of any thing: The last Affair left no great Concern upon me, for as I did the poor Child no harm, I only said to my self, I had given the Parents a just Reproof for their Negligence in leaving the poor little Lamb to come home by it self, and it would teach them to take more Care of it another time. . . (*MF*, p. 194).

Once she has cast herself in the role of protector of innocent children, Moll is captivated by the notion. The child's mother obviously suffers from 'Vanity', and the maid whom Moll supposes to have been looking after the child becomes 'a careless Jade . . . taken up perhaps with some Fellow that had met her by the way' (*MF*, p. 195). This kind of expansive opportunism is typical of Moll's presentation of her criminal life. The quickness of thought, and recognisable consistency of character, is very much more pronounced than it ever was with Crusoe. Defoe makes use of the opportunities of the criminal narrative to incorporate comic capers, and to establish a consistently self-seeking character for his narrator.

So both Moll's career as a thief, and as an autobiographer are best characterised by spontaneity and opportunism. Rather than being carefully planned and organised by Moll, both careers are erratic, wayward and skilful in the exploitation of opportunity. It is possible to think of Moll psychologically, unlike Crusoe, and to see her as consistently impulsive, cunning and volatile. Consequently, Moll's narration is much less stable than Crusoe's, and she seeks to encompass even more forms and modes than he did. The various conflicts and discrepancies in *Crusoe* could not be explained by the character of the narrator, but they can be more readily explained that way in *Moll*. Moll consistently offers us *her* view of the world, rather than simply being used to present a generically competent view of the world.

Such an argument comes close to claiming that the book is consistently ironic, and that reading it depends on the reader's sceptical aloofness from the narrator. However, there is no need to make the book quite as consistent in viewpoint as that. When discussing the episode of the child's necklace, and a later outrage where Moll takes advantage of a drunken gentleman (for his own good, as she says), Dorothy Van Ghent came to this conclusion:

> We are left with two possibilities. Either *Moll Flanders* is a collection of scandal-sheet anecdotes naively patched together with the platitudes that form the morality of an impoverished soul (Defoe's), a 'sincere' soul but a confused and degraded one; or *Moll Flanders* is a great novel, coherent in structure, unified and given shape by a complex system of ironies.[31]

What Van Ghent might mean by a 'complex system of ironies' is not clear, and the alternative views she suggests are surely not the only possibilities of articulating the text. It seems fairer to suggest that the book is a collection of anecdotes, some of which would find a home in scandal-sheets (why not?), but that the characteristics of its narrator give it the kind of shape it has. At times, too, an ironic reading is made possible by the tension between what Moll tells us, and what we can deduce from her omissions and distortions. However, the book is too eclectic to be understood as consistently ironic or consistently mimetic. Its modes are various, as are its genres, and the sole consistency lies in the emergent character of the narrator.

The self-serving nature of Moll's narration can be seen by looking at the way she refers to the supernatural. In *Crusoe*, the narrator had nothing to gain by invoking Providence, only an increase in guilt, and yet another threat, so his references to it were not self-serving. However, Moll's use of the plea of necessity, and her supernatural motives, becomes much less convincing as the tale progresses:

> THUS the Devil who began, by the help of an irresistable Poverty, to push me into this Wickedness, brought me on to a height beyond the common Rate, even when my Necessities were not so great, or the prospect of my Misery so terrifying; for I had now got into a little Vein of Work, and as I was not at a loss to handle my Needle, it was very probable, as my Acquaintance came in, I might have got my Bread honestly enough. . . (*MF*, p. 202)

The return of the ideal of working diligently at a small skill is only cursory, and Moll returns to grand acts of theft. There is some sense here of the limits of excusable behaviour, as there is in the incest and abortion episodes, and, in a much more dramatic way, in *Roxana*. However, the most important thing about the passage is the way it signals to the reader that Moll is now exactly the kind of gentlewoman she wished to be at the very beginning. Moll herself does not draw any parallels, and this may indicate a larger organisation of irony than is often apparent. The references to the Devil as the force which prevents her from attaining this sought-after quiet life seem highly unconvincing and conventional, but show Moll herself trying to fit her criminal behaviour into a recognised generic pattern. She wants to present herself as the paradigm of the good person locked in combat with the Devil, losing temporarily, but winning finally. Our recognition that her behaviour does not fully accord with this pattern is strengthened if we are familiar with the popular genres in which it is apparent, such as the confessional tale, and the spiritual autobiography.

The book is entering into a kind of ironic parody of these popular genres, by laying great emphasis on Moll's reticence, and her partial disclosures. In the overt, stated interpretation of her life, Moll moves from childish innocence, into poverty, justifiable theft and unjustifiable theft, before finally being rewarded for her penitence. Clearly, if it is possible to have doubts about any stage in this process, it is possible to doubt the probity of her penitence. Like the early storm repentances of Crusoe, it seems very much in the penitent's interests, and to be motivated entirely by fear. It occurs after Moll has returned to Newgate, and is haunted by her fate.[32] She has been caught red-handed in the act of theft, and has been condemned to death. Her tutor in crime, too, has been condemned to die in prison, and the combination of shocks and frights brings Moll round to a kind of temporary penitence. She had been provided with further admonitory examples — like the arrest of two colleagues (*MF*, p. 209), or the sight of a thief being given over to 'the Rage of the Street' (*MF*, p. 212). Even in court, when she was seeking damages for her wrongful arrest, her earlier bravado prevailed. The significant date of Christmas Day, on which she was arrested, passed without comment. After all these warnings, more apparent to the trained reader of confessional tales than to the narrator, she finds herself in Newgate. In M.E. Novak's view, these episodes are most properly seen as unnoticed examples of stealthy Providence. In discussing Moll's behaviour after her first casual attempt at repentance, at the fire, he says, 'it is suggestive of divine Providence that the next time Moll attempts to steal at a fire, she is struck and almost killed by a mattress which is thrown from a window'.[33] However, the possible providential pattern before her capture is not mentioned by Moll herself, and seems only fortuitous.

Moll's subsequent 'conversion' is made to seem easy and brief, and it has no effect at all on her behaviour. In the oppressive atmosphere of the prison, she feels what she takes to be stirrings of remorse and abhorrence for her past life. The sight of Jemmy, also imprisoned, makes her feel irrationally responsible for his fate. There is no need for this, and it seems like emotional indulgence. Jemmy was, after all, a confirmed and notorious highwayman before meeting Moll, and he had simply returned to his old occupation. Once again, we are not obliged to accept Moll's understanding of events, and the brief possibility of irony is again present. She is still under sentence of death, and the language she uses to express her contrition makes it all seem very self-interested:

> He visited me again the next Morning, and went on with his Method of explaining the Terms of Divine Mercy, which according to him consisted of nothing more than that of being sincerely desirous of it, and willing to accept it; only a sincere Regret for, and hatred of those things I had done which render'd me so just an Object of divine Vengeance . . . I was cover'd with Shame and Tears for things past, and yet had at the same time a secret surprizing Joy at the Prospect of being a true Penitent, and obtaining the Comfort of a Penitent, I mean the hope of being forgiven. . . (*MF*, pp. 288-9)

The paradoxical simultaneous occurrence of shame and joy is typical of the moment of conversion, as represented in Defoe.[34] However, Moll seems to get the shame out of the way fairly quickly, and to get on with the joy as soon as possible. She seems struck by 'Divine Mercy' as a kind of bargain, and her references to its 'Terms' makes the idea of a transaction more apparent. This stress on the convenience of penitence, and on its cheapness, must make it seem like just another violent transition in the narrative, rather than the ultimate, important one.

Moll's conversion seems as naive and impulsive as all her earlier behaviour. Its self-interest is much more apparent to readers than to her. When she tells it, she is not trying to deceive us into thinking it to be more serious than it really was. Rather, she is consistently expressing her eagerness and whimsicality, which she thinks of as earnestness and conviction. This curious kind of persistent innocence is one of the book's most interesting features, and one which moves it out of the adventure category into the character study, at least in parts. The innocence is apparent not only in the conversion scenes, but also in the passages of self-justification, such as the theft of the child's necklace. Moll is emphatically not trying to put one over on us, or to get away with things she believes to be wrong — she simply believes anything that strikes her at any moment. Her most idiosyncratic feature as a criminal narrator is her lack of guile, and her credulity, which is a kind of unworldliness very much at odds with her aggressive criminality. Rather as some people may be tone deaf or colour blind, Moll seems to be morally insensitive to her own behaviour, and to remain somehow remote from its implications. This allows her to change with great speed and agility, and yet also to avoid cynicism and hypocrisy. She understands events spontaneously and irrationally, as in the abortion scene, and never finds an overall view of herself. Though it would be very wrong to think of her as an *ingenue*, she does seem to lack any wholehearted calculation, and retains a freshness and spontaneity to the end.

Such openness to change can be seen in the way Moll eventually does get out of Newgate. Her more worldly fellow prisoners advise her that bribery is the way to secure freedom, and Moll is convinced. It takes little argument to get her to see that lining pockets is a more reliable and immediate way of having her sentence commuted than prayer. As her tutor says, 'did you ever know one in your Life that was Transported, and had a Hundred Pound in his Pocket' (*MF*, p. 294). Moll's ready acceptance of this advice shows the degree to which her conversion is simultaneously genuine and self-seeking. It is adopted as the best way to escape hardship, and as such, it is seen to be a full, if not a profound, emotional experience. It cannot be seen as a moral experience, since it is dispersed as soon as an easier, or quicker, avenue to escape is revealed.

It seems, then, as though Moll's conversion might be wholly genuine as long as it lasts, for Moll is entirely convinced by it. The fact that she does not retrospectively assess its impermanence is very interesting, and shows us something about the conventionality of the narrative posture. At this point in the tale, Moll has not only bribed her way to a reprieve from the gallows, she has also gained a kind of conditional pardon. Though she takes no direct part in the bribery herself, she is certainly prepared to accept the intercessions of others on her behalf, and does not inquire at all closely into their methods. It would be inappropriate to see this as hypocrisy, because of Moll's suddenness of emotion. It may appear inconsistent at first, but once Moll is seen to be volatile and persistently changeable, it seems an appropriate thing for her to do. We are not being invited to respond to this shift morally, but to accept it dramatically as one of the urgent transitions on which popular narrative is organised. These transitions are not deeply laid within the text, but arise suddenly, without premeditation.

Moll's penitence soon passes, and no memory of it lingers. The advantage of her abruptness is that it renders the past null and void, and Moll only exercises her memory as narrator, not as character. Once she has secured her release from Newgate, there are no vestiges of penitence left. When she sets up home in Virginia, she is perfectly prepared to live from the earnings of her criminal life, and even when she is reminded of her bigamous and incestuous state, she does not feel the need to do anything about it. Her money ensures a good trip to Virginia, and by bribing the ship's captain, Moll and Jemmy are allowed their freedom very readily. At this point, stable and secure, Moll reminds us of her alleged purpose in writing her autobiography:

> AS the publishing this Account of my Life, is for the sake of the just Moral of every part of it, and for Instruction, Caution, Warning and Improvement to every Reader. . . (*MF*, p. 326)

But would every reader be instructed, cautioned, warned and improved by the narrative? The demands seem very great, and do not seem to accord with the narrative as it stands. The reader is likely to have been enthralled and entertained, as readers of popular fiction are entitled to be, but no other major endeavour has been noticeable. Popular narrative has the dual function of reminding you what the world is actually like, while allowing it not to be effective for a while. In *Moll*, the world is seen to be wholly mercenary and fairly vicious, as it is in *Crusoe*, but the pontentially disastrous consequences of that violence are kept at bay by the conventional structure. *Moll* becomes a comic narrative, because of the self-preserving romantic innocence of the protagonist, and because that innocence is allowed to triumph.

Most critics who have tried to see the book as unified or cohesive have seen it as a consistent search, organised by the characteristics of the heroine. Terence Martin, for instance, sees Moll's desire to be a gentlewoman as the central feature of the text. Moll first tries to secure her status by marriage. When this fails, she turns to crime, and when crime fails she turns to penitence.[35] Martin's case depends on the number of references to be found in the narrative to gentility and to a kind of speculation about a hidden structure which depends on Moll's own character. If his argument is acceptable, the main part of the narrative becomes an ironic examination of the meaning of gentility in a material society. Moll achieves what she desires, and in the process, readers come to see the shabby reality of gentility. However, Martin's argument becomes rather distorted when he overemphasises the degree of singleness of purpose to be found in the book. The ironies of Moll's quest are granted, and her character gives the book its consistency, but it never becomes fully unified or cohesive. Martin pays very little attention to the incest episode, which obtrudes from his scheme, and he deals only sketchily with her penitence. The penitence could certainly be accommodated to an ironic reading of the text, but the incest episode does not seem to fit. Again, as in *Crusoe*, Defoe is adopting the popular standard of compendiousness, rather than the polite standard of single-mindedness. The book simply does not present itself as a linear process of any kind — 'Moll's progress is not simply from fear to moral stupidity to repentance. Such a bald moral summary neglects the actual strategies of the narrative. . .'[36] In *Crusoe, Colonel Jack, Captain Singleton* and *A Journal of the Plague Year*, the redemptive process is only one of several dramatic threads, and is not necessarily superior to the others. In *Moll*, it is offered by the editor as dominant, but the narrative itself is capable of various interpretations, diffuse and lacking in singleness of purpose.

What really prevents a full ironic rendering of the narrative is certainly the odd incest episode. Indeed, it seems as though that episode thwarts *any* reading of the book as a single, linear enterprise. Even Novak's persuasive view of the book as a dramatised presentation of the ideas of Natural Law has to be emended to encompass Moll's inappropriate horror. Similarly, few of the other writers who see the narrative as unified (Van Ghent, Martin, Koonce, Michie) offer much analysis of that topic; and Brook's view that it is the most important episode in the book is surely incompatible with a full reading of the variousness of the narrative. The most plausible view of the event is that it shows the opportunism of Defoe's procedure. Having by accident or design (it does not really matter which) come to present the character of Moll, Defoe offers her adventures in as wide a range of circumstances as his genres will allow. Just as in *The English Rogue*, where Meriton Latroon is allowed to have all manner of adventures, so Defoe's heroine is only restricted by the peculiarities of her situation. By giving her this strange series of irrational scruples, Defoe allows her to be unpredictable, and so incorporates another interesting uncertainty into his drama. Meriton Latroon, like Crusoe to some extent, is only a convenient foil for adventures, and is given only the most rudimentary characterisation. So too with the heroes and heroines of criminal tales, jest books and the like. The central figure of *Long Meg of Westminster*, for instance, is only individuated by her physique and the nature of her adventures. Defoe promises comic adventures in the title, with its references to 'Fortunes and Misfortunes', but he complicates and enhances these by making his heroine capable of idiosyncratic reactions. By making Moll capable of sentimentality, as when she kisses the ground her son has travelled over, Defoe effects a kind of compromise between the criminal tale and the romance. The predominantly comic mode (announced immediately by the breezy first person narration) allows the adventures to continue indeterminately, with the category of ending being comfortably assured. So no abrupt penitence is required to effect the ending, only a kind of accommodation and assimilation of Moll into a family group.

By stressing the popular genres in which *Moll* partly participates, and by stressing the incorporation into her character of coyness, a certain prudishness and some sentimentality, the book becomes both comic and partly heroic. It celebrates the way its heroine survives intact throughout hardship, and offers her adventures as a source of comfort and satisfaction. By trying to wrest the book into the sensitive, even rather desiccated world of polite literature, critics can transform its robustness into a kind of hard insensitivity, and so distort the book's vitality. As Denis Donoghue argues:

> What Defoe says about life, in *Moll Flanders*, is true, as far as it goes, but the book is based upon a set of terms which ignores two-thirds of human existence; these terms cancel all aspects of human consciousness to which the analogies of trade are irrelevant. . . As a result, the book cannot conceive of human action as genial, charitable, or selfless; hence it cannot survive comparison with a novel like *Portrait of a Lady* in which the enabling vision of life is wide, generous, answerable to human possibility.[37]

Donoghue's case seems to be based entirely on a strange view of literature, and on a category mistake in treating Defoe. If you believe, as he seems to, that worthwhile literature has to say something about 'life', and that it has to have a vision which is to be 'wide, generous, answerable to human possibility', then only very few books should be allowable reading or considered seriously. All popular fiction, all journalism and a great deal of ineffective polite literature has to be discarded, in favour of a select canon of great books. The purpose of studying these books becomes one of minute but perceptible moral improvement in the reader. This is clearly not a workable view for a literary historian, interested in the kinds of book which people have read, and why they have found them worth their attention. And only the literary historian of that kind will be able to make any sense of Defoe. Comparing *Moll Flanders* to *Portrait of a Lady* is a worthless and foolish exercise. What is it meant to reveal? The books are obviously different, and offer wholly different kinds of satisfaction. They presume utterly different kinds of reader, and utterly different kinds of reading. *Moll* can easily be made to appear mercenary and squalid by the comparison, but it is unfair.

As well as these reservations about Donoghue's whole procedure, there are two obvious points of disagreement between his position and mine. First of all, it is mistaken to amalgamate Defoe's views and Moll's, since there are obvious attempts at irony, and obvious attempts to make Moll an autonomous character. Secondly by stressing Moll's proneness to 'that Cheat call'd LOVE', and its importance in the narrative, it is possible to see something present other than the mercenary. However, the interest of the book does not lie in avoiding the mercenary. There is, after all, no reason why stories should not be wholly mercenary. But the main interest in the story is the way it exists within a system of genres, and the way it offers variants of these genres, some innovative, some not. The genres which foresee any reading of *Moll* would be the criminal tale, the confessional, the romantic adventure and perhaps the extended jest book. The narrative is unique, however, in the way it begins to establish a character for its narrator, and to base all its events on the cumulative revelation of that character.

As yet, Defoe's fiction is still very monist in its presentation of character. Secondary characters have only a fleeting existence, and the narrative goes beyond egoism to the point of solipsism. In *Crusoe*, the characters of his father, Xury, Friday and the others were presented in a stylised and casual way. In *Moll*, the narrator's various lovers are only lightly sketched (indeed, some are not even mentioned as anything other than components of a total), and only Jemmy and the criminal tutor are given any extensive role. Important characters such as Moll's mother and brother, and Robin, are only very briefly in existence within the tale. So both books have formally presented the adventures of one character, to whom all others are subordinate. The world in which they move has had little room or time for emotional ties of any kind, except with Moll's more serious alliances. In Defoe's final fiction, he went on to dramatise the conflicts which arise from such egoism, and managed to incorporate other people into his narrative. The problem of how to treat others in a hostile world does not arise within the confines of *Crusoe* or *Moll*, but it is fundamental to *Roxana*. The genre of the voyage tale, to which *Crusoe* largely belonged, had no opportunities to deal with matrimony or children. The urgency of the criminal tale in *Moll* meant that such events were of little narrative interest, and could be jettisoned. In *Roxana*, Defoe went on to treat the various social problems of matrimony and courtship, and showed the extent to which the narrator could subdue all ties in favour of self-assertion.

In *Crusoe*, Defoe exploited the possibilities of the adventure tale to present a linear, digressive narrative, based on a simple sense of the protagonist's motivating psychology. In *Moll*, the handling of a supposed internal world is firmer, and the narrator's individual personality becomes more prominent. In neither fiction are public events discussed. Crusoe shows us no interest in affairs of state. Despite being away from England for most of his adult life, he asks no questions about public affairs. Moll, too, seems remarkably remote from the affairs of the day. If we take seriously her offered date of composition, 1683, she must have lived through the Civil War, the Restoration, the Plague and the Great Fire, yet none of these events enters her tale. The supervisory genre of the criminal tale does not demand such omission, and Defoe's concentration on Moll's domestic and amatory life is one of the ways that his fiction begins to emerge from its generic classification. By situating the tale at the intersection of romance and crime, drawing on notions of femininity and money, Defoe is able to concentrate on the idiosyncratic nature of his heroine. The public issues concerned with private lives, such as the need for money or the dangers of imprisonment, are clearly handled. In *Roxana*, the private side of the narrator and her public life are put most interestingly in tension, and that allows Defoe greater room to explore her psychology.

It is in his handling of psychological notions like guilt and misery that Defoe moves beyond contemporary generic classification. That process is fleetingly present in Crusoe's terror, or in his yearnings. It is more conspicuous in Moll's capacity to fall in love. In the first case, Defoe keeps within the limits of the castaway story, and in the second, he puts the whole issue in doubt by putting Moll's protestations of emotional softness alongside her financial cunning. In *Roxana*, however, the examination of public and private life is much more purposeful, and takes the tale beyond the limits of the scandalous disclosure. The move towards a more thorough handling of character, less reliant on typology or convention, makes Roxana more congenial to modern readers, but we should not overlook the vestigial traces of older forms which Defoe retained.

Moll Flanders, then, can be fitted into Defoe's career by showing its further move away from public issues. Remarkably, Defoe dealt with crime and legislation in that fiction from the point of view of its effects. Unlike his earlier treatments of these issues, the political implications are largely ignored, and Defoe can be seen to be increasing his attention to states of mind and personal involvement. The vicariousness of Moll's experiences is offered to readers without the usual sense of mission — there are no concealed projects in *Moll Flanders*, no hidden purpose. By showing us the conflicts of an upwardly mobile woman in a competitive world, Defoe involves us in his social vision, but he asks us to concentrate on Moll, not on anyone else. Moll is less typical than Defoe's earlier characters, and less polemically employed. In the move to *Roxana*, Defoe found a way to consolidate both his private and his public concerns, and that makes it the most complex of his fictions. However widely read *Crusoe* might have been, and however popular *Moll* has subsequently become, it is *Roxana* which shows Defoe's fiction at its most exciting.

Notes

1. Robert Greene, *A Notable Discovery of Coosnage* (1591), G.B. Harrison (ed.) (London, 1923), pp. 7-8.
2. Some suggestive comparisons between the criminal in fiction and the criminal as presented at Tyburn and elsewhere are offered by Lennard J. Davis, 'Wicked Actions and Feigned Words: Criminals, Criminality, and the Early English Novel', in *Rethinking History: Time, Myth, and Writing* (Yale French Studies, 59), pp. 106-18. For a broader analysis of eighteenth-century thinking about crime, see Douglas Hay, Peter Linebaugh, John G. Rule, E.P. Thompson and Cal Winslow, *Albion's Fatal Tree: Crime and Society in Eighteenth Century England* (London, 1975). The best collection of the crime fiction of the period is Spiro Peterson (ed.), *The Counterfeit Lady Unveiled and Other Criminal Fiction of Seventeenth Century England* (New York, 1961).
3. See also Watt's, 'The Recent Critical Fortunes of *Moll Flanders*', *Eighteenth-Century Studies*, I (1967), pp. 109-26.
4. Dorothy Van Ghent, *The English Novel: Form and Function* (New York, 1953), p. 36.
5. Daniel Defoe, *Memoirs of a Cavalier* (1720), James T. Boulton (ed.) (Oxford, 1978), p. 4.
6. See Boulton, p. 53.

7. Howard L. Koonce, 'Moll's Muddle: Defoe's Use of Irony in *Moll Flanders*', *ELH*, XXX (1963), p. 379. Koonce puts forward a very interesting view of the conflicts within the narrative, but sensible and proper doubts have been raised by Pat Rogers, 'Moll's Memory', *English*, XXIV (1975), pp. 67-72. There is some interesting consideration of this issue in M.E. Novak, 'Defoe's "Indifferent Monitor": The Complexity of *Moll Flanders*', *Eighteenth-Century Studies*, III (1969), pp. 351-65.

8. As will be shown later, one of the most idiosyncratic things about *Moll* is the way it hastens over both criminal and sexual misdeeds. Compared with, *The English Rogue* or *Fanny Hill*, Moll's tale is remarkably inexplicit and oblique.

9. In his *Tour*, Defoe remarks that Colchester has 'two CHARITY SCHOOLS set up . . . and carried on by a generous subscription, with very good success' (p. 33).

10. There has been a great deal of debate about Defoe's use of irony, most of it unilluminating, and stuck in the rigid categories of irony used by Henry James and subsequent writers. The best contributions are two papers by M.E. Novak, 'Defoe's Use of Irony', in *The Uses of Irony: Papers on Defoe and Swift Read at a Clark Library Seminar, 2 April, 1966* (Los Angeles, 1966) and 'Conscious Irony in *Moll Flanders*: Facts and Problems', *College English*, XXVI (1964), pp. 198-204.

11. Crusoe also receives a very similar warning, which he too ignores. He does, however, retrospectively recognises its accuracy in a way that Singleton never tries to. See *RC*, p. 15.

12. *Defoe and Casuistry*, p. 114.

13. John J. Richetti, *Defoe's Narratives* (Oxford, 1975), p. 99.

14. See G.A. Starr's edition of *Moll*, p. 363.

15. R.R. Columbus, 'Conscious Artistry in *Moll Flanders*', *SEL*, III (1963), p. 420. There must be some doubt about how many of these qualities Moll displays in the first place. What evidence is there for her grace?

16. Moll's discussion of sex is always couched in such coy, evasive locutions, which are very different from the way sex is treated in popular pornographic fiction, or in the analogous picaresque novel. The issue is discussed by Robert Alter, *Rogue's Progress: Studies in the Picaresque Novel* (Cambridge, Mass., 1964), p. 38. The pornographic fiction of the later-seventeenth century is well documented in Roger Thompson, *Unfit For Modest Ears* (London, 1979).

17. The quotation comes from a long debate on this topic, in which Defoe's contributions are summarised. See Lawrence Stone, *The Family, Sex and Marriage in England 1500-1800* (Abriged and revised edn, Harmondsworth, 1979), pp. 149-216.

18. William Bowman Piper, in his '*Moll Flanders* as a Structure of Topics', *SEL*, IX (1969), pp. 489-502, suggests a tripartite division of the book into sexual adventures, adventures in theft and Virginia adventures. For the purposes of the present generic approach, the Virginia sections can be further subdivided into sexual (like the incest episode), or criminal (like the transportation).

19. Dennis Donoghue, 'The Values of *Moll Flanders*', *Sewanee Review*, LXXI (1963), pp. 287-303.

20. Douglas Brooks, '*Moll Flanders*: An Interpretation', *EC*, XIX (1969), pp. 46-59. See also the more fulsome treatment in his *Number and Pattern in the Eighteenth-Century Novel* (London, 1973).

21. See G.A. Starr, *Defoe and Casuistry*, pp. 123, 134-5.

22. *Defoe and the Nature of Man*, pp. 108-10.

23. Stone, *The Family, Sex and Marriage*, p. 309.

24. Ibid., pp. 267-99.

25. Moll's plight must have been very common, when contraception was so rudimentary. Examples of the kinds of potion which are available to those less squeamish than Moll are given by Stone, *The Family, Sex and Marriage*, p. 266.

26. See Benjamin Boyce, 'The Question of Emotion in Defoe', *SP*, L (1953), pp. 44-58.

27. See 'The Problem of Necessity in Defoe's Fiction', in *Defoe and the Nature of Man*, Chapter III.

28. G.A. Starr refers to five other allusions to this proverb in other works by Defoe. See *Defoe and Spiritual Autobiography*, p. 78n.

29. Starr refers to Defoe's *Political History of the Devil* for a parallel passage (*MF*, p. 191n), and the whole episode can be compared with the benign supernatural interventions in *Crusoe* and *Singleton*.

30. An episode of this kind occurs in *Colonel Jack*, and it is Jack's realisation that it is a despicable crime that serves to bring him to his senses.

31. *The English Novel: Form and Function*, p. 42.

32. It is possible to make too much of the symbolic nature of Newgate, and to forget that it serves as a genuine, rather than as a symbolic, threat to Moll. Arnold Kettle's claim that it is 'an eighteenth-century *huis clos*' seems strained, if we remember the actual jeopardy Moll is under in Newgate. See Kettle, 'In Defence of *Moll Flanders*', *Of Books and Humankind*, John Butt (ed.) (London, 1964).

33. *Defoe and the Nature of Man*, p. 79.

34. See G.A. Starr, *MF*, p. 289n.

35. Terence Martin, 'The Unity of *Moll Flanders*', *MLQ*, XXII (1961), pp. 115-24. For similar arguments, see Koonce, 'Moll's Muddle', and J.A. Michie, 'The Unity of *Moll Flanders*', in *Knaves and Swindlers: Essays on the Picaresque Novel in Europe*, C.J. Whitbourn (ed.) (London, 1974), pp. 75-93.

36. John J. Richetti, *Defoe's Narratives*, p. 139.

5 *ROXANA,* SCANDAL AND TRAGEDY

In the earlier discussions of *Crusoe* and *Moll*, it has become apparent that neither book achieved complete thematic organisation or concentration. *Crusoe* was as compendious and episodic as adventure tales most appropriately were, and could not be articulated by the appearance and development of themes. Such themes as could be discovered were the assumptions behind the narrative, and were not foregrounded. *Moll,* too, was digressive, even if its digressions were made more coherent by the flitting, opportunist narrator. By developing the character of the *raconteuse,* Defoe gave his tale a kind of consistency, and foregrounded her idiosyncracies much more than Crusoe's. Defoe's last major extended fiction, *Roxana, The Fortunate Mistress* (1724), is significantly different from all the earlier narratives, and deserves to be seen as his most successful tale in terms of internal organisation and structural coherence. It is certainly the most unified of Defoe's narratives, with the sustained and persistent examination of its central figure. The concentration on the fascinating figure of Roxana herself removes the book partly from its supervisory genres, and allows it to be articulated more as an autonomous text.

However, despite its greater accessibility to conventionally text-centred methods of literary criticism, *Roxana* was for a long time relatively overlooked. For instance, Ian Watt barely mentions it in *The Rise of the Novel.* He recognises that it is in some ways different from the other narratives — '*Colonel Jacque, Roxana* and *A Journal of the Plague Year* all have some excellencies unrivalled elsewhere' (p. 98) — but he does not specify these 'excellencies' and confines his discussion to *Moll* and *Crusoe.* The relative neglect of *Roxana* is symptomatic of a wider neglect of the scandal fiction of the early-eighteenth century, which has survived less well than the adventure tales or the criminal yarns. Since it belongs to a group of tales now largely forgotten and irrecoverable, *Roxana* has become dislocated, and it suffers from the special reverence and oversight as *Amelia* and *Sir Charles Grandison.*[1]

Some of the reasons for this partial neglect are historical. As well as the irretrievability of the scandal tales, the problem of the text of *Roxana* is important. For most of the nineteenth century, the edition of the book with the widest circulation contained a spurious and flaccid continuation of the narrative, which some critics took to be the genuine article.[2] Later, in the early-twentieth century, the book was seen as too seedy for critical analysis, because of its morbid and distasteful subject matter.[3] Only recently has the book found a responsive public, perhaps because of the appeal of its discussion of womanhood, insanity and promiscuity, and it has only in the last 20 years begun to have an effect on the overall assessment of Defoe's work.

The most obvious difference between this late book and the earlier narratives is the immediate announcement of its greater gravity. In very broad terms, it is possible to see the earlier narratives as comic, in their celebration of the resilience of their narrators and their emphasis on survival and accommodation. *Roxana*, on the other hand, offers itself much more seriously as an admonitory tale, and touches on tragedy. The full title does not disclose the mode of the tale, but stresses the social mobility it contains: *The Fortunate Mistress; or, a History of the life and vast variety of fortunes of Mademoiselle de Beleau, afterwards called the Countess de Wintselsheim in Germany being the person known by the name of the Lady Roxana in the time of Charles II*. The title then promises a 'vast variety of fortunes', and offers readers a social and geographic tour. The categorisation offered is within the broad grouping of scandalous tales, with the title echoing the combination of social elevation and intrigue that such tales relied upon. Readers are also being promised something of the erotic-pathetic genre specialised in by Mrs Haywood, with novels such as *Idalia: or, the Unfortunate Mistress* (1723), *Lasselia: or, the Self-Abandon'd* (1723), and *The Injur'd Husband: or, the Mistaken Resentment* (1723). The similarity of these titles to Defoe's would have alerted prospective readers to the inclusion of erotic adventures, which seemed popular at the time. Also, Defoe's references to the court of Charles II draw on the other scandalous tradition of the 'secret history', where revelations (or allegations) of misdeeds in high places were presented in a veiled way, relying on the reader's acumen to spot the true identities of the participants. The best-known writer of these tales was Mary de la Rivière Manley, whose Tory propaganda in the last years of Queen Anne was extremely influential. Her two most successful works were *The Secret History of Queen Zarah, and the Zarazians* (1705) and *Secret Memoirs and Manners of several Persons of Quality, of both Sexes. From the New Atalantis, an island in the Mediter-*

ranean (1709), which were both controversial books, much more stringent in their polemic than any of Aphra Behn's romances or anything similar. Defoe's narrative, then, looks like a combination of these two forms, the secret history and the erotic novella, and entices readers by combining categories in a novel way.[4]

The title page, with its allusiveness, reassures readers that they are dealing with a recognisable type of fiction, dealing with dirty deeds in politics and wedlock, and invites purchase by its combination of different popular types. The title can be construed in two different ways, however, and shows the wider possibilities which Defoe actually explored. The word 'Fortunate' could refer to the narrator's good luck in maintaining her deceptions for so long, or it could ironically indicate the way her fortune catches up with her at the end.[5] So the possibility of a graver rendering of scandal is at least hinted at. The title also offers compendiousness, like all of Defoe's full titles, and stresses Roxana's 'vast variety of fortunes'. Here, too, the word 'fortunes' is ambivalent. It could refer to her various stations in life, some enviable, others not, or it could more prosaically refer to her differing financial states throughout her career. It is worth remembering that the title page offers generic categorisation only, and makes no indication of mode of presentation.

The increased gravity of presentation is what makes this book autonomous from its genres, and it is introduced by the editor's stress on the authenticity of his tale. After the title page has provisionally categorised the book with Manley and Haywood, the Preface seeks to withdraw from that commitment:

> this *Story* differs from most of the Modern Performances of this Kind, tho' some of them have met with a very good Reception in the World: *I say*, It differs from them in this Great and Essential Article, *Namely*, That the Foundation of This is laid in Truth of *Fact*; and so the Story is not a Story, but a History. (*Rox*, p. 1)

The distinction between fact and fiction is conventional enough, and repeats the earlier protestations in the Prefaces to *Crusoe* and *Moll*. In this case, it aligns the book more towards the secret histories of Manley than the erotic novellas of Haywood, but it even seeks to deny that category as much as possible. The sneering reference to 'Modern Performances of this Kind' is dismissive, and seeks to establish the work under review as special. It does this by establishing a context of reference, and then remarking on the tale's emergence from this context. Difference is declared by a greater reliance on verisimilitude than in Manley or Haywood, and by subduing the romance element prominent in their works and in Defoe's own earlier pieces.

The illusion of verisimilitude is fostered by Defoe's characteristic methods. The author is suitably precise about names, dates and places, and incorporates seemingly irrelevant details as a form of corroboration. Also, the editor claims to have privileged knowledge of certain participants. He claims to be 'particularly acquainted' with Roxana's first husband, and with her father, and so offers his personal guarantee that the tale will not transgress the bounds of realism and slip into fantasy or allegory. The main reason for this is to implicate the narrator in the seemingly inevitable train of events. We see that her career is doomed, unless something extraordinary were to happen, and the prosaic, precise editor serves as an assurance that nothing outrageous to the rules of verisimilitude will be tolerated. The supernatural will certainly play a less powerful role in Roxana's tale than in the earlier ones, and the reader will be invited to dwell on the meaning of events, not simply to follow them along naively. The reader is invited to adopt a more remote perspective on Roxana's deeds than on Crusoe's or Moll's, and greater consideration seems to be required. Since the heroine herself is conscious of the implications of her career, the reader is prevented from the simpler naive involvement of the earlier yarns. Whereas Moll and Crusoe were sufficiently similar to the books' implied addressees to allow identification with them, Roxana is sufficiently different from the implied readers to introduce more strongly the possibility of irony, and to demand evaluative distance.

In neither *Crusoe* nor *Moll* was a coherent moral overview of the tale offered. Nor was there any fully sustained, consistent view of the harshness of the world. The nature of the two narratives presupposed a partly hostile environment, against which the narrator had to strive; but at the same time, the tone of the narration offered a compensatory benignity which kept the tales essentially comic. The horizon of expectation offered to readers did not cover the possibility of grim *dénouments*. In *Roxana*, the act of retrospection is much more important to the narrative, and introduces to it a consistent view of the past. The double time scheme of the tale is especially interesting. Despite the allegation that it is set in the time of Charles II, the internal evidence is that it is set in a Georgian court. Readers are thus invited to see parallels between the licentious Caroline world and their own monarch, in a manner reminiscent of the secret histories of Mrs Manley. By being set both in the earlier and the near-contemporary period, Roxana's tale operates as a political critique as well as a personal confession.[6]

The political element should not be forgotten, but the retrospective view is most powerfully presented as a grim confessional. Rather than being a racy *exposé* of universal corruption, the tale concentrates its energies on an intense presentation of its narrator's sense of guilt and shame. The editorial comments ask readers to direct their attention more towards Roxana than towards her surroundings:

> It is true, she met with unexpected Success in all her wicked Courses; but even in the highest Elevations of her Prosperity, she makes frequent Acknowledgements, That the Pleasure of her Wickedness was not worth the Repentance; and that all the Satisfaction she had, all the Joy in the View of her Prosperity, no, nor all her Wealth she rowl'd in; the Gayety of her Appearance; the Equipages, and the Honours, she was attended with, cou'd quiet her Mind, abate the reproaches of her Conscience, or procure her an Hour's Sleep, when just Reflections kept her waking. (*Rox*, p. 2)

The implied sobriety of view, and the requested concentration on the narrator, are more integral to the subsequent narrative than are the usual distractions offered by Defoe's prefaces, and show the book's rejection of the complacent poses of Crusoe and Moll. Crusoe was able to look back over his wandering life with satisfaction and complacency, confident that his eventual comfort vindicated his earlier waywardness. He described his eventual position as one of 'complicated good Fortune' (*RC*, p. 304), and even when his retrospection became distressed or anxious, it never became ponderous or solemn. Moll's ending is equally felicitous, and her final words, after explaining her incestuous marriage to her current husband, are, 'all these little Difficulties were made easy, and we liv'd together with the greatest Kindness and Comfort imaginable' (*MF*, p. 342). It is too easy to labour Moll's light-heartedness, for there would be little she could do to effect restitution to those she has mistreated. But still, her blitheness seems very complacent, and serves to satisfy the reader's desire for closure, without the dramatic disruptions of climax.

In Defoe's linear narratives, the non-climactic closure is most frequent. I have already quoted the final words of *A Journal of the Plague Year*, which offer a kind of *coda* in which the central theme of survival is redefined:

> *A dreadful Plague in* London *was,*
>   *In the Year Sixty Five,*
> *Which swept an Hundred Thousand Souls*
>   *Away; Yet I alive!* (*JPY*, p. 248)

The epigrammatic summary of the tale is possible because the events have reached their natural conclusion. When that pre-ordained shape is unavailable, Defoe's narratives finish with a hiatus, the narrator arresting at some point before the point from which he or she is narrating. The gap between the point of arrest of the narrative, and the point of narration, is exploited to make Crusoe's *Farther Adventures* possible, and to permit the ironic disavowal in the Preface to *Moll*. Otherwise, it remains silent, for various reasons. In *Captain Singleton*, the narrator is discrete about his whereabouts at the point of storytelling, for reasons of security, and his farewell is singularly complacent and bland:

> And now, having so plainly told you, that I am come to *England*, after I have so boldly own'd what Life I led abroad, 'tis Time to leave off, and say no more for the present, lest some should be willing to inquire to nicely after
>
> *Your Old Friend*,
>   CAPTAIN BOB (*CS*, p. 277)

There are no signs of the remorseful ex-pirate here, and the captain's criminal career, which has energetically sustained the second half of the narrative, is not disparaged. Bob's only concern is that he might be discovered, but even the occasion of the publication of his memoirs continues his delight in adventure, by being a piece of *bravura* self-advertisement. There is no sense of climax here, only of cessation.

A more complex piece of final retrospection is seen in the ending of *Colonel Jack*, where the narrator draws an interesting distinction between the available varieties of penitence. This is worth quoting in full, for its relevance to the closure of *Roxana*:

> I had, *as I said*, leisure to reflect, and to repent, to call to mind things pass'd, and with a just Detestation, learn as *Job* says, *to abhor my self in Dust and Ashes.*
> IT is with this Temper that I have written my Story, I would have all that design to read it, prepare to do so with the Temper of Penitents; and remember with how much Advantage they may make their penitent Reflections at Home, under the merciful Dispositions of Providence in Peace, Plenty, and Ease, rather than Abroad under the Discipline of a Transported Criminal as my Wife and my Tutor, or under the Miseries and Distresses of a Shipwreck'd Wanderer . . . or in Exile, however favourably circumstanciated as mine, in absence from my Family, and for some time in no probable View of ever seeing them any more.
> SUCH *I say*, may repent with Advantage, but how few are there that seriously look in, till their way is hedg'd up, and they have no other way to look? (*CJ*, pp. 308-9)

There are at least two points of major importance here. One is the colonel's emphasis upon the hectic lives and hazardous circumstances of all Defoe's narrators — circumstances which make immediate survival more important than leisured retrospection. Their lives are constantly imperilled, by physical hazards, and the danger of damnation usually seems a very remote concern. In keeping with the linear forms of popular fiction, Defoe's narratives concentrate a lot more on what will happen next than on what might happen eventually. The second point is that the colonel's notion of being 'hedg'd up' is rare in Defoe's fiction, where the narrators are normally offered a way out of their jeopardies, without major psychological disturbance. In the main narratives, the participants are eventually placed in a position sufficiently secure to allow a leisurely penitence, if appropriate. Such urgent repentances as they make, in storms or in prisons, are fitful, remaining part of the volatile dramatic fabric of the books. Eventual repentance is always a possibility, but it is not presented as a climax, only as a method of arresting a headlong narrative. In *Roxana* alone, the sense of retrospection is made much more prominent, and Roxana's evaluation of her own life, while seemingly 'hedg'd in', is foregrounded in her narrative.

Only in his last major work of fiction did Defoe seek to exploit the dramatic possibilities of a cumulative rather than a serial life, and in doing so he explored the pessimism at which Jack only hinted. The ending of *Roxana* leaves the narrator bereft, in rather cryptically described circumstances, after a sustained revelation of a corrupt, volatile world. Her view of her life is dark and bitter, full of self-recrimination and self-distrust. In terms of contemporary popular fiction, this persistent accusation is very unusual, as it figures rarely even in criminal autobiography or final confessions. Defoe avoids making Roxana a defiant figure, and fits her more into the moral world of the Spanish picaresque novel, where survival is all. The ending of one such narrative, Quevedo's *El Buscon* (1626, translated into English in 1707), shows a more resigned version of Roxana's hopelessness and despair:

> and therefore with the Advice of my Doxy *Grajales*, I resolved to go to the *West-Indies*, taking her along with me to try whether I could meet with better Fortune in another Country, but it prov'd worse; for they never mend their Condition, who only change places without mending their Life and Manners.[7]

This very stark and grim ending is not a feature of English fiction of the period, which is either broadly admonitory (often in the form of irony), or eulogistic (as with Deloney), or comic (as with Defoe's other narratives). So *Roxana* seems to be presented within a mode which was not fully familiar to its prospective readers, though it is generically secure. The narrative's constant emphasis on instability and corruption is in itself unsettling and subversive of a calm, leisurely reading, and may serve to break down the readers' expectations of mode.

At the beginning of *Roxana*, the narrator's background is again shown to be unstable. Like Crusoe, her family is of foreign descent, but in her case, we are told why they came to England. They were forced to flee the persecution of the Protestants, and arrived in England in 1683.[8] What makes Roxana immediately different from the other characters, though, is the financially comfortable background into which she fits, and the polite training which it gives her. Her early education is much more extended than, say, Moll's, and is designed to make her suited for a genteel life of quality:

> I was (*speaking of myself as about Fourteen Years of Age*) tall, and very well made, sharp as a Hawk in Matters of common

Knowledge; quick and smart in Discourse; apt to be Satyrical; full of Repartee, and a little too forward in Conversation; or as we call it in *English*, BOLD, tho' perfectly Modest in my Behaviour. Being *French* Born, I danc'd, *as some say*, naturally, lov'd it extremely, and sung well also, and so well, that, *as you shall hear*, it was afterwards some Advantage to me: with all these Things, I wanted neither Wit, Beauty, or Money. In this Manner I set out into the World, having all the Advantages that any Young Woman cou'd desire, to recommend me to others, and form a Prospect of happy Living to myself. (*Rox*, pp. 6–7)

Of course, as can be gleaned even from the tenor of the narrative, this 'happy Living' never arrives. Despite all of Roxana's social, economic and personal advantages, she suffers the sorriest fate of all of Defoe's narrators.

The book proceeds by following a pattern of deferred disaster, whereas the earlier books offered a pattern of deferred gratification. Elsewhere, Defoe remarks on the rare surprise engendered by persons of good, stable backgrounds, and personal promise, who turn to a life of wickedness. In his account of the notorious pirate, Major Stede Bonnet, in *A General History of the Pyrates*, Defoe entices his readers to be puzzled by the reasons which drive such a man to evil:

The Major was a Gentleman of good Reputation in the *Barbadoes*, was Master of a Plentiful Fortune, and had the Advantage of a liberal Education. He had the least Temptation of any Man to follow such a Course of Life, from the Condition of his Circumstances. It was very surprizing to every one, to hear of the Major's Enterprize, in the Island where he liv'd; and as he was generally esteem'd and honour'd, before he broke out into open Acts of Pyracy, so he was afterwards rather pity'd than condemned, by those that were acquainted with him, believing that his Humour of going a Pyrating, proceeded from a Disorder in his Mind.[9]

The idea of the stylised motivation of an unexamined disorder of the mind recalls the equally unexplained 'wandering Inclination' of Crusoe. Both can be seen as rather perplexed, and tentative attempts to provide explanations for odd behaviour, though perfectly competent within the conventions of the discourse. The description of Bonnet goes slightly further, and offers some explicitness by claiming that his disorder was brought about by 'some Discomforts he found in a married State' (ibid.). This splendidly casual remark, which could apply to almost every protagonist in European fiction, seems nearer to the motivating experience offered in *Roxana*.

It has already been establish in the narrative, by means of the enforced flight from France, that sudden strokes of misfortune are capable of disturbing the most sedate of lives, and disturbing them both violently and catastrophically. Roxana is, thus, always presented to the reader as potentially ready to be overwhelmed by chance turns of fortune. It is apparent, too, from a reading of Defoe's pieces on the infamous criminals Jack Sheppard and Jonathan Wild, that the figure of the corrupting gentlewoman, who has fallen on hard times, was an acknowledged convention in popular crime writing of the time. In the narrative of *The Fortunate Mistress*, to use the appropriate longer title, Roxana starts from a position of social advantage, but is soon brought to destitution, and is made to suffer at the hands of fortune. Her main problem, as she interprets her life, is that she was arranged in marriage to an eligible suitor, who transpired to be a fool, and who connived in the loss of both her money and her status. The problem which readers see, and Roxana seems not to, is that her self-image as a lady of quality does not vanish with her money, and she cannot reconcile her understanding of her status to her actual circumstances. The narrative then goes on to reveal the usefulness of Roxana's genteel training in a world which is revealed to be mercenary and competitive. Like *Moll*, this tale shows a world in which status and money are not synonymous at first, but which are seen to be mutually reliant, in Defoe's characteristic Whig manner.

In the mercenary world, where attributes are assessed in terms of their usefulness or marketability, Roxana's attainments are of little use. By being deprived of a realistic sense of trade and economy, and by having so few marketable skills, Roxana has only her native wit and wiles to rely on. When stripped of her wealth, these abilities fit her only for a life of deception and persistent fraud. In Defoe's discussions of trade, which I presented earlier, the trading life was seen as the most honourable and honest one. There is a passage in *The Complete English Tradesman* (1725), where the mercantile life is explicitly contrasted with the kind of behaviour that Roxana excells in:

> Trade is not a ball, where people appear in masque, and act a part

to make sport; where they strive to seem what they really are not, and to think themselves best dressed when they are least known. But 'tis a plain visible scene of honest life, shown best in its native appearance, without disguise; supported by prudence and frugality...[10]

This defence of the integrity of trade is couched in language which is very hostile to Roxana. The references to masks and disguise describe the later career of Roxana, and are used by Defoe to mount an attack on frivolity. For the Tory satirists, like Pope, one of the major sources of irritation in contemporary society was the development of a monied class of tradespeople, who did not have the social accomplishments to match their new status. In the *Dunciad*, Pope assaults the unlearned and barbarous new classes. However, for a moderate like Defoe, the relation of money and social status was less clear, and in *Roxana*, he analyses the pretentions to status of someone without honest money to support it. The genteel life of masques and dalliance is presented as deceptive and fraudulent throughout this narrative, and Defoe uses his narrator to reveal the hollowness of the sham. By being trained as she is, and being rootless, Roxana has no recourse but deceptions, and so the book functions as a defence of the activities of its tradespeople readership. For most potential readers of Defoe, trade was invested with the power to defend its supporters against the world's uncertainties. For that audience, then, *The Fortunate Mistress* would function as a cautionary tale, but not as an admonitory one. It would reveal the spuriousness of a different way of living, and tacitly invigorate the values of the readership. Roxana herself would become the appropriate object of pity, rather than of moral outrage or contempt, and the narrative would operate at the level of persistently vicarious suffering.

To understand the two central themes of the book, marriage and deception, and to keep in mind the involuntary nature of Roxana's misdeeds, it is necessary to remember the stylised features of her presentation, notably her nationality and title. Though the name 'Roxana' is conferred well into the narrative, and is not known to all the participants, it is the name by which the reader is invited to consider the narrator. The original Roxana was a Turkish concubine of Alexander the Great, and would have been familiar to Defoe's readers, if at all, through her appearance in Nathaniel Lee's play, *The Rival Queens* (1677). The importance of the name lies in its connotations, rather than its denotations. It is given to the narrator for her Turkish costume, and we may remember Defoe's contemptuous conjunction of Turks and ideas of predestination in *A Journal of the Plague Year* and elsewhere. Roxana's 'Turkishness' is self-created, and shows her culpably seeking to deny responsibility for her own behaviour. Her actual nationality reinforces this notion of irresponsibility. Being French, even if Protestant, the narrator comes under the general condemnation of that nation throughout Defoe's work. In *The True Born Englishman*, the characteristic French vice is seen as ungoverned passion:

> Ungovern'd Passion settled first in *France*,
> Where Mankind lives in haste, and thrives by Chance.
> A *Dancing Nation*, Fickle and Untrue:
> Have oft undone themselves, and others too. . .[11]

Roxana, then, exists at the intersection of irresponsibility and fickleness. Her self-image of Turkishness is an attempt to take on notions of predestination, which lead to her being 'hedg'd up' at the end. Her French background makes her passionate, headstrong and dangerous, and these features together lead to the catastrophe of the ending. By communicating in this stylised way to his readers, Defoe is preparing the ground for the ending, which otherwise looks very abrupt.

From the beginning, *The Fortunate Mistress* appears as a cautionary anecdote about marriage, in keeping with Defoe's other publications around this time. The book invites our attention for the fate of a naturally lively, young girl, trained in manners rather than morals, who is brought to poverty by an ill-judged early marriage. Though it is tempting to read the book in this way as a fictionalised didactic tract, advocating caution, hostile to the French, in praise of responsibility, the narrative reads much more dramatically than that, and it invites more understanding of its heroine than such tracts would seek. Our understanding of Roxana is not wholly to be inferred from some overseeing moral code, but to be arrived at more inductively, through the pattern of withdrawal and involvement which the narrative asks. The admonitory anecdotes in a text such as *Religious Courtship* (1722) have to avoid idiosyncracies of presentation or characterisation, if they are to secure unambivalent moral force. In *Roxana*, however, even more than in *Moll*, the individual personality of the narrator is a most important feature of the reading.

The Fortunate Mistress is also comparable with *Moll* and *Colonel Jack* in its use of the proverb 'Give me not Poverty, lest I steal'. The occasion of Roxana's collapse into poverty is her unwise first marriage. She starts her campaign of reproach, and specifically self-reproach, as soon as her first husband enters the narrative:

> After I have told you he was a Handsome Man, and a good Sportsman. I have, indeed, said all; and unhappy was I, like other young People of our Sex, I chose him for being a handsome, jolly Fellow, as I have said; for he was otherwise a weak, empty-headed, untaught Creature, as any Woman could ever desire to be coupled with: And here I must take the Liberty, whatever I have to reproach myself with in my after-Conduct, to turn to my Fellow-Creatures, the Young Ladies of this Country, and speak to them, by way of Precaution. . . (*Rox*, pp. 7–8)

The first marriage is, then, constructed by Roxana as instrumental to her downfall, and she offers it as a cautionary example. The sense of an audience to be addressed and advised is much stronger here than in the earlier narratives. The overt address to fellow women at the end of the extract is assumed in Roxana's earlier reference to 'other young People of our Sex', where the use of 'our' shows a kind of complicity between narrator and audience. The retrospective view is obviously more prominent, and more coherent than it was in *Moll* or *Crusoe*, and there is a greater sense of purpose than in those tales. Though the narrative opens in this sympathetically admonitory way, presenting Roxana's errors as typical, it soon becomes much more idiosyncratic, and Roxana's misdeeds are seen to be unusual rather than representative. So though the book looks as though it is to be categorised with conduct books, like Defoe's own *Good Advice to the Ladies* (1702) and *Reformation of Manners* (1702), the scandalous tale takes over, and the concentration on the narrator is increasingly prominent.

Roxana's first husband transpires to be a feeble and incompetent businessman, incapable of earning a living through trade, however gallant he might be. As soon as his father dies, the husband manages to dissipate the long-established business. Eventually, after seven years of marriage, omitted from the narrative as unworthy of concentration, he abandons Roxana. She is left with five children and a total wealth of around £70. Though she does not tell us of the seven years marriage (just as Moll omits her time with Robin), she rants against this man's foolishness. It is significant that he was involved in the brewing trade, which at the time was volatile. By diligence and good fortune, it could be very remunerative, by neglect, it could only be disastrous.[12] What emerges from Roxana's description of her early married life is the emphasis on her own innocence and helplessness. She presents the marriage as something over which she had very little effective control from the beginning — 'my Father gave me . . . 25000 Livres . . . and married me to an Eminent Brewer' (*Rox*, p. 7). The sense of herself as a bequest, or as a commodity to be bestowed without resistance, is maintained by her extraordinary passivity during the marriage itself, and forms a startling contrast to her later adventurousness.

Roxana's recollection of her lost innocence, and of her sense of having been cheated, becomes most passionate in her denunciations of her first husband. However, as happened in *Moll*, the early misadventure does not harden the heroine's heart, or turn her towards a cynical view of the world. Later, Roxana becomes much more hardhearted and cynical than any of Defoe's other narrators, but to begin with she tries to hold on for so long as possible to her illusions. The retrospective narrator makes us aware of the naivety of her younger self, and dwells on it to make clearer the abrupt change towards worldliness. Having been left by her brewer husband, in poverty, and with the hindrance of five young children to look after, Roxana's position is very unhappy, and seems far away from the scandalous tale. The narrative importance of these early events is to remove Roxana from a position of security, to set her adrift on the world, with only her genteel training to support her. The scandalous tale then emerges from the confrontation between Roxana and the world she moves into. However, before this can be discussed, she has to free herself of her children. As charitably as possible, she tries to do her best for them by bestowing them on a relative. The decision to part with the children is not reached lightly, but the alternative seems to be either starvation, or putting them upon the mercy of the parish. Roxana arrives at her decision by trying to evaluate what will be best for the children, and responds persistently on an emotional level to their plight. When the suggestion of putting them on the parish is made, Roxana is deeply distressed:

> I was at first, sadly afflicted at the Thoughts of parting with my Children . . . and then a hundred terrible things came into my Thoughts; *viz.* of Parish-Children being Starv'd at Nurse; of

their being ruin'd, let grow crooked, lam'd, and the like, for want of being taken care of; and this sunk my very Heart within me. (*Rox*, p. 19)

It is only the feeling that they will all starve if she does not do something which eventually changes her mind, and she is then established as an emotional character, initially devoid of cynicism. When this episode is compared with Moll's brisk treatment of her offspring, shunted away as irrelevant to her tale, it is possible to see the care being taken to establish the innocence and feeling nature of Roxana.

When she finds a relative to take them in, a very interesting discussion of charity takes place. The wife of the household is against taking the children, seeing them as a burden, and as a needless drain on their resources. Her husband defends charity, but on remarkably self-interested grounds:

Charity is a Duty to the Poor, and *he that gives to the Poor, lends to the Lord*; let us lend our Heavenly Father a little of our Children's Bread, as you call it, it will be a Store well laid up for them ... I only talk of putting a little money out to Interest, our Maker is a good Borrower, never fear making a bad Debt there... (*Rox*, pp. 22-3)

This sense of the pervasiveness of a balance sheet mentality enters the novel through subsidiary characters, rather than through Roxana herself. The conception of a fastidious deity, who is careful with the accounts, is very much more powerful than the rather slapdash deities of *Crusoe* and *Moll*. In the earlier books, the generic forms presupposed that evil was not necessarily punished, though good was probably rewarded. In *Roxana*, the relative suggests a much neater balancing of the books than that, but his views are not upheld by the main narrative, which invites the reader's hesitation over large moral questions.

It is made clear that Roxana, like Moll, falls into her first crimes more through need than through inclination. All Roxana has been trained for is polite matrimony, and without that she has no recourse other than prostituting her graces and social skills. The training she has received is revealed in the narrative to have provided her with all the desirable attributes of a whore, and that becomes the only profession in which she can operate a trade. Initially, though, she is firmly against even the idea of prostitution. Her maid Amy suggests that, when faced with the likely alternative of starvation, it is quite permissible to become a whore. Roxana, however, denounces such a calculating and self-seeking approach to her situation:

> Hitherto I had not only preserv'd the Virtue itself, but the virtuous Inclination and Resolution; and had I kept myself there, I had been happy, tho' I had perish'd of meer Hunger; for, without question, a Woman ought rather to die, than to prostitute her Virtue and Honour, let the Temptation be what it will. (*Rox*, p. 29)

With the wisdom of hindsight, Roxana returns to her earlier moral convictions, and attributes the blame for her unspecified misery to her breach of morality. Whether or not her assessment of herself is trustworthy, or too severe, remains to be seen, but it is clear that both the earliest and latest pronouncements of Roxana are very moral. It is only the intervening behaviour that seems immoral.

A lengthy debate follows that last passage, concerning whether or not Roxana should give in to the landlord. Her hesitations seem overscrupulous, to say the least, just as Crusoe's scruples about taking the gold from the ship seem excessive. Roxana seems to have failed to understand the gravity of her circumstances, and wishes the luxury of moral equivocation. The maid Amy takes the view that if the act is absolutely necessary, then it must be justifiable. We have already seen the exculpatory role of necessity referred to in *Moll*, and Novak's work shows how widespread the claim of necessity is in Defoe's work. However, the issue is contested even within Defoe. In *An Appeal to Honour and Justice* (1715), the plea that necessity can function as extenuation is roundly dismissed:

> Necessity is pleaded by both Parties for doing things which neither Side can Justify. I wish both Sides would ever avoid the Necessity of doing Evil; for certainly it is the worst Plea in the world, and generally made use of for the worst Things.[13]

In retrospect, Roxana seems to agree with this earlier view of her condition, but the point remains that she *cannot* avoid doing evil. It has been argued that Amy's view is the one which would have had Defoe's support.[14] This may be true, and it certainly seems to the reader of contemporary popular fiction that Roxana is extraordinarily severe upon herself. No character in the work of Mrs Manley or Mrs Haywood makes more than token self-recrimination, and Roxana's fervour in the repeated self-castigations is very unusual. It raises the interesting narrative possibility that, just as Moll may be too generous in her estimate of herself, Roxana may be too strict.

The retrospective Roxana's powerfully expressed anguish affects the process of the entire narrative. Her great severity about her possible act of adultery (though, since she does not know if her husband is alive or dead, it might not even be that) leads her to see Amy as 'a Viper, and Engine of the Devil' (*Rox*, p. 38). Such savage outbursts reveal the essential difference between Roxana and the earlier narrators. Unlike them, she originally acts in the confirmed belief that her behaviour is unjustifiable and wicked.[15] Moll and Crusoe were never seen to suffer from any analogous dilemma. Crusoe was helpless in the face of his 'wandering Inclination'; Moll acted from what she saw as pardonable necessity, and was required as narrator to spend little time assessing herself morally. Roxana's much more stringent sensibility, which is established by her religious background, leads her to think of herself as sinning, and so leads to the guilt and misery from which she suffers. It is worth stressing just how unusual this guilt is, within popular fiction.[16] As Roxana herself puts it, 'I was a Double Offender . . . for I was resolv'd to commit the Crime, knowing and owning it to be a Crime' (*Rox*, p. 14). Her cloistered and polite background has given her a moral understanding of events, which seems inappropriate to the circumstances of her narrative, and which leads inevitably to a kind of grim absolutism. After she has committed this first, relatively inoffensive act, she sees herself as wholly corrupted, having forsaken 'all Sense of Religion, and Duty of God, all Regard to Virtue and Honour' (*Rox*, p. 43). It is the inflexibility of her moral position, which cannot distinguish between small offences and great ones, which leads to the catastrophe.

The treatment of this single episode has been extended because of its great importance to the overall shape of the narrative. Roxana's personality, and her partial misconception of the moral status of her own life, are the twin features of the narrating process. Her continuously sustained self-recriminations invite a very different kind of reading from the relatively blithe *Crusoe* and *Moll*, and present the book as tragedy rather than comedy. However, because of the ambivalence of the episode in which Roxana's self-hatred becomes a force, the tragedy may be one of misconception rather than of misdeed. The consequences of Roxana's moral sense are very grave indeed. Having, as she sees it, forsaken all morality and conscience, she feels wholly abandoned. This leads her to act most recklessly, and brings out the paradox that Defoe's most sombrely moral narrator is the one who acts most wickedly. Once she has committed her original sin, she feels no compunction in involving others in her downfall. This is most clearly seen when she puts Amy to bed with her own lover:

> At Night, when we came to go to-Bed, *Amy* came into the Chamber to undress me, and her Master slipt into Bed first; then I began, and told him all that *Amy* had said about my not being with-Child, and of her being with-Child twice in that time: Ay, Mrs *Amy, says he,* I believe so too, Come hither, and we'll try; but *Amy* did not go: Go, you Fool, *says I,* can't you, I freely give you both Leave; but *Amy* would not go: Nay, you Whore, *says I,* you said, if I wou'd put you to-Bed, you wou'd with all your Heart: and with that, I sat her down, pull'd off her Stockings and Shooes, and all her Cloathes, Piece by Piece, and led her to the Bed to him: *Here,* says I, *try what you can do with your Maid* Amy: She pull'd back a little, would not let me pull off her Cloaths at first, but it was hot Weather, and she had not many Cloathes on, and particularly, no Stays on; and at last, when she see I was in earnest, she let me do what I wou'd; so I fairly stript her, and than I threw open the Bed, and thrust her in. (*Rox,* p. 46)

This wonderfully brisk paragraph, with its haphazard punctuation and accumulative style, offers clear insight into Roxana's self-presentation. The single sentence can encompass details about the weather, but includes little of prurient interest. Clearly she is not presenting a salacious, or pornographic tale. The episode is briskly presented then followed by an omission, like Moll's — 'I need say no more . . .' (*Rox,* p. 46). The roles of Amy as corrupter and Roxana as reluctant sinner have thus been effectively reversed, and Roxana has transformed herself from a timid, passive character, into a coercive, aggressive one.

The contrast between this new Roxana, and the earlier submissive wife is very startling, and needs to be examined. Many critics have found it to be psychologically implausible, though emblematically effective. G.A. Starr presents the problem in terms of the author's sympathy with his character — 'Defoe regards his heroine as a damned soul. On the other hand, his imaginative oneness with her often seems virtually complete, and at such times we too may be drawn into a kind of imaginative complicity with her'.[17] David Blewett takes a very different view, and assumes that we remain more distanced from the narrator. In his view, her crime is to disrupt the kind of social order which Defoe persistently advocates, by raising Amy to the status of an equal.[18] Neither of these analyses seems to be completely satisfactory. The problem is not that Roxana is definitely evil, yet the subject of some 'imaginative oneness', or that readers must recognise the exact way in which she is evil. Rather, the problem lies in *her* sense that she is evil, and in our recognition that such a sense may be initially imperceptive. In this narrative, Defoe presents the consequences of a sense of sin, which seems to lead towards sin.

If this argument is acceptable, than readers are not imaginatively in sympathy with Roxana, but remote from her. In the other narratives, the reader is not given pause to assess events, and simply has to be absorbed in the narrator's presentation of them. These earlier narratives also offer a kind of comic structure, so the moment when the narrator becomes redeemable is fairly openly announced. For example, the criminal career of Colonel Jack is brought abruptly to a halt by his sense of the limits of what is tolerable. After robbing an old woman whose condition is as bad as his own, he feels he is betraying his own standards:

> BUT my Heart was full of the poor Woman's Case at *Kentish Town*, and I resolv'd, if possible to find her out, and give her her Money: With the abhorrence that fill'd my Mind at the Cruelty of the Act, there necessarily follow'd a little Distaste of the thing in it self, and now it came into my Head with a double force, that this was the High Road to the Devil, and that certainly this was not the Life of a Gentleman! (*CJ*, p. 67)

Jack's sense of standards, and propriety, thus allows him to redeem himself. This is directly in contrast to the way Roxana's sense of standards becomes the effective agent of damnation. In the other books, the narrators are brought round to resolution by some overt kind of act — there are the thunderclaps in *Captain Singleton* and the *Serious Reflections*, the arrival in Virginia in *Moll*, and the deliverance from the island in *Crusoe*. In *Roxana*, no such return to stability takes place, and the course of the narrative is never impeded.

Rightly or wrongly, each earlier narrator feels warned at some point, and responds to that warning. Before that point, they are barely aware of their own status, and the reader is concerned with following the adventures only sequentially. In those books, readers want to know what is going to happen next; in *Roxana* they want to know what will happen eventually. Roxana sees her enforced decision to sleep with her landlord as the outrageous act which puts her beyond all possibility of redemption. It seems likely that by selecting an act whose moral status is so contested and ambivalent, Defoe is allowing readers to remain remote from Roxana's plight, and he may be offering the possibility of irony much more extensively than anywhere else. If the narrator is under a delusion throughout the narrative, and if it is that delusion which leads to her disasters, then the appropriate mode of reading is irony. After all, Roxana's behaviour is no worse than Moll's and she came to no harm, without agonising. But Roxana feels herself to be depraved, and her casually gratuitous corruption of Amy only confirms her sense of desolation. It may seem paradoxical, but while it is true that Roxana is the most public of Defoe's characters, and the only one with a long-lasting confidante, she is simultaneously the most private and the most isolated.

Roxana makes constant references to the unhappiness and misery which kept breaking in on her, which she sees as both unprovoked and inevitable:

> We liv'd as merrily, and as happily after this, as cou'd be expected, considering our Circumstances; I mean as to the pretended Marriage, &c. and as to that, my Gentleman had not the least Concern about him for it; but as much as I was harden'd, and that was as much, as I believe, ever any wicked Creature was, yet I could not help it; there was, and would be, Hours of Intervals, and of Dark Reflections which came involuntarily in, and thrust in Sighs into the middle of all my Songs; and there would be, sometimes, a heaviness of Heart, which intermingl'd itself with all my Joy, and which would often fetch a Tear from my Eye; and let others pretend that they will, I believe it impossible to be otherwise with any body; there can be no substantial Satisfaction in a Life of known Wickedness; Conscience will, and does,

often break in upon them at particular times, let them do what they can to prevent it. (*Rox*, pp. 48-9)

This remark would not be confirmed by reading Defoe's other narratives. Moll lived a life of comparable wickedness with few pangs. Singleton lived much more wickedly, but there was no mention of sighing. Jack, it is true, did suffer from something like remorse for his crimes, but only once, and that briefly. So Roxana's claim that a wicked life inevitably leads to misery is obviously not consistent with the narrative movements of popular fiction. However, the emphasis on the personal element is significant. Roxana keeps using phrases of personal reference, like 'as I believe'. When she talks of her life as 'a Life of known Wickedness', she is not referring to public knowledge, as Moll would, but to private scruples. Though others can be blithely wicked, Roxana cannot, and it is her sense of guilt which organises the narrative. The pervasiveness of her guilt is even apparent in the phrase about how the 'dark Reflections' are 'thrust in' upon her. The phrase 'thrust in' is a direct echo of the scene where Roxana puts Amy to bed with the landlord, and may show Roxana's obsessive self-examination operating at an unconscious level. Again, both by making this parallel and by keeping Roxana mute about it, Defoe is offering his readers a superior reading of events.

Roxana's guilt entails a sense of continuous jeopardy, which is confirmed by her next adventure. Her sense of the imminence of disaster is borne out when her lover is required to go to Versailles with a foreign bill. He discusses their mutual financial state before leaving, and, despite his reassurances, Roxana is overcome by forebodings. She even thinks of her sense as a kind of prescience, foreseeing the murder of her lover and protector. Second sight, along with various other kinds of prophecy and prediction, appears throughout Defoe's work, and seems to have been seriously entertained by most readers. From the early attention to the supernatural in *A True Relation of the Apparition of one Mrs Veal* (1705) Defoe wrote many pieces solely on paranormal phenomena, all of which seem to have gained a public. As well as *The Political History of the Devil* (1726) and *An Essay on the History and Reality of Apparitions* (1727), Defoe is thought to have written the life of a famous seer, in which he made ironic comments about how the prophet was unable to foresee his own life.[19] The whole issue seems to have engaged both credulity and scepticism. Crusoe's prophetic dreams are taken seriously, while H.F. is caustic about the astrologers who sprang up during the Plague. As a narrative component, rather than as a spectacle in its own right, the supernatural serves to enhance the status of the narrator as recorder of his or her own experience, while making them less potent as an agent. By telling us of her private apprehensions, Roxana sounds more authentic and personal. However, since she seems to detect some supervisory power in experience, which she is unable to influence, it renders her impotent. All the narrators in popular fiction have to balance the conflicting narrative demands of personal aggressiveness and helplessness, and Defoe uses the supernatural to effect this balance, and to introduce a kind of supervised helplessness in his narrators.

Roxana's feelings of foreboding are accurate, and she is left bereaved. However, she is also left wealthy, and her lover's settlement on her removes her from economic hardship. The thought of herself as an eligible, wealthy widow soons dries her tears, and it is not long before she is being courted by a prince. At this point, she recognises that the forces which impelled her into evil were her own characteristics rather than economics or poverty. She offers an analysis of her downfall in terms of vanity and covetousness:

> I have given you the whole Detail of this Story, to lay it down as a Scheme of the Way how Unhappy Women are ruin'd by Great Men; for tho' Poverty and Want is an irresistible Temptation to the Poor, Vanity and Great Things are as irresistible to others. . .
> (*Rox*, p. 64)

The covert plea of necessity is never followed up, and Roxana is lamenting her own behaviour, without trying to excuse it. The sense that she is brought into wickedness by vanity is developed throughout her interlude with the prince. She does still mention the Devil occasionally, and there is some talk of the supernatural, but these are seen as a way of talking about her own impulses, not as a description of some external forces. In a much more self-conscious way than Moll is ever required to speak, Roxana offers a clear analysis of her own emotions, within a moral framework.

She is occasionally surprised in retrospect that she managed to remain sane and calm, throughout her wicked career. As the prince's mistress, she convinces herself (briefly) of the acceptability of her affairs, and describes how odd that acceptance was:

I have, I confess, wonder'd at the Stupidity that my Intellectual Part was under all that while; what Lethargick Fumes doz'd in the Soul; and how it was possible that I, who in the Case before, where Temptation was in many Ways more forcible, and the arguments stronger, and more irresistible, was yet under a continued Inquietude on account of the Wicked Life I Led, could now live in the most profound Tranquillity, and with an uninterrupted Peace, nay, even rising up to Satisfaction, and Joy, and yet in a more palpable State of Adultery than before. . . (*Rox*, pp. 69–70)

This passage of puzzlement makes clear the difficulties in Roxana's view of her own life. The pattern she is striving to find there does not appear. She has claimed that it is impossible to find satisfaction in vice, yet is faced with her own calm acceptance of a state of adultery. In *Moll*, on occasions like the theft of the child's necklace, a disparity between the narrator's professed moral views and her behaviour was obvious. The narrator tried to close that gap, by claiming that the behaviour was *really* moral, after all. It was clearly not, but the narrator's attempts at self-justification became part of the book's comedy. In *Roxana*, the narrator is also aware that there is a gap between her feelings and her principles, but cannot bring herself to re-write the past. Where Moll is in control only of her past, and can plainly distort it to her own advantage, Roxana is the victim of her past, which she sees as damning her inexorably. The only stability she may have is her moral severity, but episodes such as the happy affair with the prince put even that in doubt.

The inconsistency between Roxana's retrospective view of events and her contemporay view of them is not to be seen as simply a failure of technique on Defoe's part. There are a number of slips and clumsinesses in *Roxana*, just as there were in *Crusoe* and *Moll*. For a start, the inaccuracy of the title page is obvious, since Roxana would only have been 12 years old when Charles II died in 1685, and there are a number of similar discrepancies to be found in the narrative itself.[20] However, Roxana's failure to find a coherent shape in her past is a different type of inconsistency entirely, and is clearly to be seen as the narrator's error rather than Defoe's. *Roxana* is a much more thoroughly ironic work than any of Defoe's other extended narratives. It is ironic in that throughout the narrative, readers seem to be aware of much more than the narrator is, and are placed in a position where the limitations of her viewpoint are made obvious.

We see her anguish and despair immediately, but since it is unexplained, we remain remote from it, and seek to evaluate its appropriateness. We see the oddity in the way she castigates herself for things which seem reasonable, much less evil than she presents them to be. We see her world as being competitive, mercenary and corrupt, but also see her intrude into that world a series of moral principles which seem inappropriate. She even draws attention to their inappropriateness by incorporating episodes which seem inconsistent with them.

The remoteness of this kind of reading is only a sporadic feature of the earlier narratives, and rarely appears in such a consistent form in popular fiction, which more often requires involvement of its readers. The kind of irony involved has been widely discussed by critics. John J. Richetti claims that Roxana is 'an ironist who is aware of those two levels of reality: the public image and the private fact, or the social mask and the natural reality'. He goes on to argue that Roxana remains constant throughout her narrative, as he claims all of Defoe's narrators do, and that her 'pretence is that the "natural" self is discovered rather than acquired, an innate rather than a historical entity'.[21] There is much of value in what Richetti has to say. He is pertinent and perceptive on the conflict between public image and private fact, which is central to all the popular fiction of scandal and intrigue. However, his discussion of Roxana and the 'natural' self is hard to follow. It is certainly true that, as an individual, Roxana arrives more fully formed and individuated than any of the others. For that reason, she can be presented as a separate entity, to whom things happen, rather than as a developing consciousness, modified and influenced as events unfold. She presents herself as a reader of her own experience, and sees herself as Macbeth may be seen, as someone who discovers her own evil, and is helpless to do anything about it. But it is still vital to notice that it is Roxana's discovered self, or at least her disclosed fate, which dominates the tone of the book. The retrospection in *Roxana* is of a strategically more important kind than that in the earlier narratives. In those, the narrator was conventionally attempting to provide order for his or her experiences, but the retrospection itself was not an act of importance. Were *Crusoe* to have been written in the present tense rather than in the past, all that would be lost would be the promise that he had survived his exploits. Similarly in *Moll*, events are relived and recreated rather than simply reviewed, and the past tense is only a conventional form of the present. The momentum of events consistently wins out over deliberation or analysis. Roxana, on the other hand, seems to have some wisdom in her hindsight, and is much stricter in her search for pattern and meaning. Of all the narrators, she is the only one who is disquieted by her past, and the only one who is gravely aware of any inconsistency in its interpretation.

Roxana's conscience is a much more strident and powerful voice than was Crusoe's or Moll's. She worries much more about the likely fate of her bastard children than does Moll, but that does not prevent her from continuing to live as the prince's mistress, and to live pleasurably. We are left in no doubt that the prince is an established man of pleasure. We are told, for instance, that he has several mistresses, and that he can cope efficiently with their inconvenient pregnancies (*Rox*, p. 76). All our knowledge of his activities comes from Roxana's speculations about him, and she does seem strikingly unwordly in all her relations with him. Despite the obviousness of his libertine ways, it is Roxana who denounces herself as the wicked one, and even sees herself as the cause of his sins, in a passage of disquietingly neurotic self-reproach:

> such is the Power of a vicious Inclination; Whoring was, in a Word, his Darling Crime; the worst Excursion he made; for he was otherwise, one of the most excellent Persons in the World; no Passions; no furious Excursions; no ostentatious Pride; the most humble, courteous, affable Person in the World; not an Oath; not an indecent Word, or the least Blemish in his Behaviour, was to be seen in all his Conversation, except as before excepted; and it has given me Occasion for many dark Reflections since; to look back and think, that I should be the Snare of such a Person's Life; that I should influence him to so much Wickedness; and that I should be the Instrument in the Hand of the Devil, to do him so much Prejudice. (*Rox*, p. 102)

The extraordinary transition in this single sentence, from seeing the prince as an accomplished rake, to seeing him as a helpless victim of the predatory Roxana, is extremely compressed and self-reflecting. It reveals Roxana's conception of herself as a most powerful agent of evil, able to corrupt otherwise unblemished souls. Given what we have already been told about her lover, this conception must be seen as excessive and grossly inaccurate. After all, who can Roxana fairly be said to have influenced towards evil? She herself thinks she corrupted Amy, but Amy seemed an eager enough accomplice. The prince, too, is a highly unlikely victim. If he is indeed given to whoring, as Roxana admits, then she is the expression of his vice, not the cause of it. Her blatant misunderstanding of his character, and of her role in his life, must raise grave doubts about her reliability as a commentator elsewhere.

In the next few episodes, readers are invited to recognise the power of money, and the mercenary nature of the social world through which Roxana moves. The prince dramatically repents, conscious of having betrayed his late wife. Roxana approves of the chivalry of his conduct, but remains unmoved by his religious penitence. She does take the opportunity to review her position, but thinks of it in only financial terms. In a splendid accumulative phrase, she describes her comfortable situation — 'not only well supply'd, but Rich, and not only Rich, but was very Rich; in a word, richer than I knew how to think of' (*Rox*, p. 110). No longer, then, could she claim financial necessity as a motive for her wickedness, but in fact her wealth leads her on to greater crimes. Being wealthy, and a woman, she has to take steps to protect herself, and these lead to greater and greater deceptions. We see, as she herself does, that her position as a wealthy 'widow' must be a dangerous one. The world she inhabits is too full of sharpers and rakes for her to be able to be honest. In that world, appearance is of paramount importance, and, just like Moll, Roxana is forced to conceal the true nature of her financial position from her suitors and lovers. Money is thus seen to be a necessary condition for decent behaviour — the prince may be able to behave nobly towards Roxana because he has the resources to conduct his departure in proper and formal terms. However, as we can see from Roxana herself, wealth is not a sufficient condition for such fair and decent behaviour. It was obvious in the earlier discussions of charity (*Rox*, pp. 22-3), that the possession of cash was no guarantee of good behaviour. The charitable people behaved well once they convinced themselves that it was a good investment. Roxana's world seems to be dominated by prices, purchases and the pursuit of bargains. Roxana's view of things is so odd because she thinks in terms of values.

Once Roxana's new concern with her own wealth has been established, though her retrospective condemnation is also made clear, there is the curious episode of another storm repentance. Like Crusoe's first repentance at sea, or Moll's temporary penitence in Newgate, this rejection of the past life arises more from fear than from abhorrence. Its role in the narrative is to enhance the understanding of Roxana's constant jeopardy. In a world such as the one she moves through, her position is bound to be persistently precarious. She sees her life as a constant battle to hold on to her wealth, but is now made aware that death is even more of a danger than poverty. We, thus, see the beginnings of the book's dual concentration upon mercantile dealings in the competitive world, and the spiritual concerns which arise from the threat of imminent death. The spiritual concerns are always seen as a potential threat, not as a possible source of solace or comfort. In *Crusoe* and *Moll*, they were only a conventional generic requirement, and not pertinent to the main workings of the narratives. However, they were present in, if not fully coherent with, the rest of the texts. So too, the combination of prostration and practicality can be found in *Captain Singleton*, *Colonel Jack* and *A Journal of the Plague Year*. The narrator of *Roxana* comes much closer to cynicism than any of these earlier ones. She is scathing about life in high places, and is to be read in a genre which invites cynicism rather than credulity. Roxana herself is severe about ideas of honour, chivalry and gentility, but, like Moll, she always retains a kind of innocence and unworldliness. And always behind her overt cynicism there is a sense of foreboding about the spiritual side of life, even if that foreboding blinds the narrator to some of the observable features of her own life.[22]

Throughout her life as narrated, Roxana was seeking a kind of tolerable independence, free from the constraints both of matrimony and poverty. The nearest to this that she managed was the life of the wealthy courtesan.[23] Typical of this life is the stress on appearance, and the power of appearances to take over from reality. When she does her famous Turkish dance, Roxana is adorned in sumptuous-looking jewels, which we know to be fakes. Thus, her pursuit of liberty has become part of a deepening spiral of deception, disguise and fraud. She has by now become so enmeshed in frauds, that she has to resort to increasingly risky feats of subterfuge to maintain her own position. One of her concerns as narrator, as we have seen, is to show how rare true honour is. In the later parts of the book, we see this confirmed in Roxana's ignoble attempts at both personal grandeur and personal safety. She becomes concerned with the meaning of honour for someone in her situation, and says:

> It had for a-while been a little kind of Excuse to me, that I was engag'd with this wicked old Lord, and that I cou'd not, in Honour, forsake him; but how foolish and absurd did it look, to

repeat the Word Honour on so vile an Occasion? As if a Woman shou'd prostitute her Honour in Point of Honour; horrid Inconsistency; Honour call'd upon me to detest the Crime and the Man too, and to have resisted all the Attacks which from the beginning had been made upon my Virtue; and Honour, had it been consulted, would have preserv'd me honest from the Beginning.

For HONESTY and HONOUR, are the same. This however, shews us with what faint Excuses, and with what Trifles, we pretend to satisfie ourselves, and suppress the Attempts of Conscience in the pursuit of agreeable Crime, and in the possessing those Pleasures we are loth to part with. (*Rox*, pp. 201–2)[24]

Notice here Roxana's acknowledgement that her conscience actually troubled her little at the time, and her obsessive worrying over the first loss of innocence. Her interpretation of her current position is also remarkable, in that she feels she has surrendered all moral values, and has no feasible expression of honour. Staying with the 'wicked old Lord' is clearly dishonourable, but leaving him would be a breach of faith, and so would be equally dishonourable. Thus, as Roxana presents things, her life is one in which no positive moral action can be undertaken, and she is deeply disturbed by that prospect.

From that point onwards in the narrative, Roxana declines steadily. Once she has turned down the Dutch merchant's offer of marriage (which, of course, is quite acceptable, since she knows herself to be a widow), the narrative has set itself on a tragic course, and the narrator is doomed. In her decline, she is accompanied only by Amy, and a further secondary character, the 'Quaker'. This very untypical Quaker encourages Roxana in her wickedness, like Moll's governess, or the figure of William Walters in *Captain Singleton*. However, interesting though she may be, the Quaker has only slight force when compared with the renewed strength of Amy. In the earliest parts of the tale, Roxana saw Amy as an agent of the Devil (*Rox*, p. 38). Later, she changes her views abruptly, and sees Amy as a victim of her own evil ways, and blames herself for corrupting her (*Rox*, p. 46). As the tale continues, Amy comes more and more to represent the evil forces at work. It is always Amy who makes the most cynical statements. When Roxana sends her out to inquire about a possible suitor, she returns to say that 'he was poor, and not worth looking after' (*Rox*, p. 231). Amy, indeed, becomes a more loyal example of the picaro as servant, aware of the cruelties of the world, and being prepared to perform whatever is necessary to survive. In her life as servant, she is greatly aware of economic necessity. She also co-operates with her mistress to help her secure her own safety and security, and to maintain their mutually false positions. Whether or not Roxana's view of Amy as the Devil's temptress is accurate is left largely undecided, and is part of the reader's hesitation about Roxana's reliability and sanity. What is certain, and very important for any overall reading of the book, is Amy's major role in the brisk ending.

The truncated ending of *Roxana* has been the subject of a prolonged critical debate. What actually happens is that a forgotten daughter of Roxana's, Susan by name, makes a surprising reappearance. Since Roxana is now permanently in disguise, Susan poses a threat to her security, by being able to reveal her true identity. Though the events are left hesitant and unclear, it is most likely that Amy has Susan murdered, and that this event is thought to bring about Roxana's ultimate downfall. During Susan's fleeting appearance in the narrative, Roxana stresses Amy's power more and more. There is even some striking confusion of identity, with Susan believing Amy to be her mother (*Rox*, p. 269). Roxana's position is frightening, and the narrative moves out of the scandal genre, into the admonitory and confessional types. The emblematic presentation of the heroine is precisely done. The two characters who surround her can be seen to represent two aspects of her developed character. Susan represents the way she once was — young, innocent, friendless and at the mercy of the world. Amy represents what she has now become — cynical, worldly and evil.

In terms of policy and procedure, Amy now takes over, and Roxana cannot control the outcome of events. Amy's casual decision to do away with Susan horrifies the narrator:

> *Amy* was so provok'd, that she told me, *in short*, she began to think it wou'd be absolutely necessary to murther her: That Expression fill'd me with Horror; all my Blood ran chill in my Veins, and a Fit of trembling seiz'd me, that I cou'd not speak a goodwhile; at last, What is the Devil in you, *Amy, said I*? (*Rox*, p. 270)

Despite her initial outrage and horror, Roxana comes to recognise a kind of virtue in Amy's proposal — '. . . it was all of it the Effect of her Excess of Affection and Fidelity to me' (*Rox*, p. 271). Readers are being reminded again here of how responsible Roxana feels for everything that happens, though at the same time thinking how much out of her direct control things have got. Her feeling seems to be that she managed to set in train a whole process of evil, which she cannot direct or divert. It is this sense of ultimate responsibility, coupled with minute lack of control, that frightens her most. Here, for the first time, Roxana's retrospective sense of shame is matched by her contemporary sense of horror. The whole narrative seems to be coming together with the gap between Roxana's past and present sense of herself diminishing.

The reappearance of Susan is a most unusual device, and has few parallels in contemporary popular fiction. As M.E. Novak has pointed out, 'that Roxana's misery arises from one of her few good actions is not without irony'.[25] Indeed, it is true that, unlike Moll, and the adventuring heroines of popular fiction, Roxana has shown some care towards her legitimate and illegitimate children, and that one of them should reappear as a threat is dramatically ironic. It serves to reveal more of the moral complexity of Roxana's life, and to sever the connection between actions and consequences that the book explores. Like the problems of honour, or of Amy's fidelity, this incident shows how, in a wayward world, good thinking and high intentions can lead to danger and depravity. The end of things is never certain, and that applies to the narrative process of the book, as well as to individual events within it. The reappearance of Susan shows that a pattern of reunion is possible, as it is in *Colonel Jack* and *Moll*, but by a combination of wilfulness and mischance, this particular reunion is tragic rather than comic. Mention was made earlier of the lines from *The True Born Englishman* describing the French, which may have prepared a reading of Roxana's character. Even more apposite are the two lines following the ones quoted:

'Prompt the Infernal Dictates to obey,
And in Hell's Favour none more great than they.'[26]

The tragic nature of the ending, brief and enigmatic though it be, serves to confirm Roxana's sense of damnation, and to close the gap entirely between her earlier self and her later one.

Roxana's continual self-reproaches have seemed throughout the narrative to be excessive, particularly those concerned with her enforced decision to sleep with her landlord. The obvious inaccuracy of her statements about misery as a consequence of sin made her seem a more deliberately fallible narrator than either Crusoe or Moll. However, all that irony and remoteness is dissolved by the ending, which dramatically confirms Roxana's self-presentation, and changes the narrative's mode from irony to tragedy. The book's final paragraph is an extraordinarily abbreviated summary of Roxana's later days:

> Here, after some Years of Flourishing, and outwardly happy Circumstances, I fell into a dreadful Course of Calamities, and *Amy* also; the very Reverse of our former Good Days; the Blast of Heaven seem'd to follow the Injury done the poor Girl, by us both; and I was brought so low again, that my Repentance seem'd to be only the Consequence of my Misery, as my Misery was of my Crime. (*Rox*, pp. 329-330)

The narrative ends with these strange words. We are given no indication of what actually took place, or of what is meant by the 'Blast of Heaven'. The sobriety and brevity of these remarks do not allow them to be read as a kind of advertisement for a further volume, as the brief remarks at the end of *Crusoe* can be read. Rather, they seem to come as close as first person narrative can come to the tragic ending, with the heroine destroyed and abased.

As has already been said, this truncated ending has divided and perplexed critical opinion. It is certainly very different from the endings of Defoe's other fictions, where the narrator reverted to a position of some stability, usually being reincorporated into society. Those endings are certainly swift, and do not offer much in the way of moral summary, but since the books are generically adventure tales, such rapidity is appropriate. *Crusoe* ends with the briefest mention of marriage, and the promise of farther adventures. *Moll* ends with the narrator back in the comfort of England, avowing sincere penitence. The avowal may not be psychologically convincing, but it is a generically acceptable way of bringing things to finality. Of the others, *Singleton* simply stops, because of a complete reversal of character; *Jack* ends in comfort and contented matrimony; *A Journal of the Plague Year* ends with the dispersal of the Plague, and some renewed hope for reformation. So even if the endings of the previous narratives can be thought of as conventional and perfunctory, they all conform to a pattern from which the ending of *Roxana* deviates radically. As one critic points out, there are the opportunities for a comic ending here, but the narrative ignores them — 'If *Roxana* were like Defoe's earlier novels, Roxana's marriage to the Dutch merchant would serve as a suitable conclusion'.[27] *Roxana* shares its abruptness with the other books, but its ending has a narrative function other than simply closure; it is meant to change the way the book has been read.

One way of accounting for the oddity of the conclusion is to attribute it to Defoe's technical naiveté. A.D. McKillop claims in this way that Defoe 'shies away from a situation that would naturally force him to follow a tightly-constructed story through to the end'.[28] In essential agreement with this position, though making its teleological assumptions more explicit, is Bonamy Dobrée — '. . . had he been able to carry it through, it might have constituted another step forward in the art; but he abandonned it, feeling perhaps that he was faced with a technical problem, as well as a moral one, that he could not solve'.[29] Speculation about Defoe's reasons for ending are not helpful. It is true, however, that the narrative could have been continued, just as *Crusoe* and *Moll* could have been, and as, indeed, *Roxana* spuriously was by a later hand. Yet it is possible to see the extant ending as being at least as satisfactory as, if not even better than, the endings of the earlier texts. Throughout the main body of the narrative, we have remained distant from Roxana's castigations, and have read the book as a scandalous tale. By dramatically confirming her severity, the book undermines our whole category of reading, and retrospectively transforms the book from its sporadic mimetic, ironic and even comic modes to tragedy. In terms of genre, it demands re-allocation from being a scandalous tale to being a grim confessional, and such transformation of genres may remove it from the world of popular literature, partly, and place it more in the more self-consciously literary world.

Overall, the book is very pessimistic indeed. It shows us a world which is mercenary, corrupt and unpredictable, wherein actions do not lead to the expected consequences, but where disaster alone is inevitable. There is an interesting passage in the *Serious Reflections*, which seems to describe Roxana's career accurately:

> There is an inconsiderate temper which reigns in our minds, that hurries us down the stream of our affections by a kind of involuntary agency, and makes us do a thousand things, in the doing of which we propose nothing to ourselves but an immediate subjection to our will, that is to say, our passion, even without the

concurrence of our understandings, and of which we can give very little account after it is done.[30]

Throughout *Roxana*, this fascinating concurrence of wilfulness and involuntariness is revealed. Roxana never seems to be in full control of her emotions, which for Defoe's readers may have been the expected behaviour of someone both female and French, yet even so she is held responsible for her own behaviour. The world she moves through is, thus, a very bleak one where virtue cannot prosper, and where even the inevitable acts of vice lead to misery.

Any interpretation of the book's conclusion is made more difficult by the ambiguities of the syntax. When Roxana says, 'my Repentance seem'd to be only the Consequence of my Misery, as my Misery was of my Crime', it is hard to understand the precise meaning of the word 'only'. She seems to be suggesting that she was brought so low that repentance was the only feasible possibility. Yet the word only does seem rather dismissive as well. The most likely reading is that her repentance was as inevitable as her downfall, but that it was little source of comfort. The sense that penitence is the final option, and that it only leads to self-castigation and further misery, is the book's final bleakness. Roxana is forced to denounce her former pleasures, while seeing them as the inevitable causes of her destruction. The wisdom that she is presented as having gained is a grim and bleak view of human possibility, and transcends the generic expectations the book has been read within.

The sudden ending is, thus, justified by the dramatic reversal it indicates, and the way it forces readers to reassess their readings. For the reader arriving at *Roxana* either as part of Defoe's work, or as another scandalous romance, such a sudden reversal is both startling and unifying. For the first time in either context, the narrator has much more than a conventional function, and the whole tale becomes much more of a psychological exploration of misery than any other contemporary tale. We get the sense that Roxana is simply *unable* to tell any more, that her obsessiveness has led to the point of being unable to support a narrative. So even the act of closure is to be explained in terms of the narrator's specific personality, rather than in terms of generic necessity. So just as Roxana's ending is the result of both caprice and inevitability, the ending of *Roxana* is arrived at by an analogous process of surprise and hidden predictability.

Given this increased individuality, *Roxana* is the narrative of

Defoe which resides least in any recognised genre. However, for its ending to be potent, and for its narrative to be coherent, it must be read as though it were a scandalous romance. In this case, differently from *Crusoe* and *Moll*, the text derives its significance from the way it is eventually different from its supervisory genres, not from the ways it may be similar to them. Defoe seized upon various possibilities of the scandalous tale, as seen in Manley and Haywood. He exploited the possibility of social criticism, the avenue to reveal the mercenary and corrupt nature of the court, and the concentration upon female vulnerability in the predatory sexual world. However, he also adapted the compendiousness of the supervisory tales, and replaced it with an increased concentration on the interpretative personality of the narrator. Unlike the diffuse, engaging temper of the earlier adventure narratives, the mood of *Roxana* is cumulatively dark, and her telling of her tale is as much a hermeneutic exercise as a recapitulary one. The vividness with which Roxana's mental and moral disintegration is handled is full of detail and haphazardness. However, there is a much greater sense of control in the overall presentation of the narrator. Roxana herself may become incoherent and even mad, but her tale retains coherence throughout. The combination of stylisation and individuation in the narrative is always intriguing, and allows communication between author and reader, ironically bracketing the narrator. The most extraordinary feature of the book is the way it carries on a dialogue between the author and the reader, by means of the manipulation of the reader's expectations. By partly fitting into recognised genres, and partly emerging from them, *Roxana* allows the possibility of extended irony in Defoe's fiction at its most accomplished.

All of Defoe's fiction has, thus, been concerned with the examination of jeopardy, and extreme conditions of one kind or another. From Crusoe in slavery and on his island, H.F. in plague-stricken London, Moll in Newgate and Jack on his plantation, to the deranged Roxana, seeking incriminating patterns in her reckless life, Defoe has offered the reader the satisfactions of vicarious peril. The common reader could participate in the tales by watching the central figures endangered, and then by watching them escape. But in *Roxana*, the eventual escape fails to happen, and the reader is thrown back on the tale to ask why. That story is then organised on a different narrative principle from the others, with the events being causally connected, rather than more simply connected by chronology and contiguity. The increased sophistication of *Roxana* in terms of characterisation and technique makes it less of a popular text, and more of a literary one, and the book deserves to read alongside Richardson, rather than alongside Manley and Haywood. Replacing it in its early popular context, and seeing the ways it adapts popular forms, is essential, to show the emergence of a more subtle kind of psychological characterisation. Once done, it allows us to concentrate on the book's delineation of guilt and calamity, and shows Defoe's greatest achievement in its clearest light.

Notes

1. Though it has been overlooked in comparison with *Crusoe* and *Moll*, this narrative has not been totally ignored. Much of the earlier writing has been summarised in Robert D. Hume, 'The Conclusion of Defoe's *Roxana*: Fiasco or Tour de Force?', *Eighteenth-Century Studies*, III (1969), pp. 475-90. See also the brief bibliography in David Blewett's recent edition, *Roxana* (Harmondsworth, 1982), pp. 30-1.
2. Many nineteenth-century critics seem to have taken the continuation as genuine. For an example of one important reading of the book which depends on accepting the sequel as genuine, see F.W. Chandler, *The Literature of Roguery* (1907).
3. See, for instance, the horrified dismissive remarks in William P. Trent, *Daniel Defoe: How to Know Him* (Indianapolis, 1916), p. 217.
4. It is worth remembering that the title pages of Defoe's narratives are not always accurate descriptions of the books, and may not have been written by Defoe. The point is made in Rodney M. Baine, 'The Evidence From Defoe's Title Pages', *Studies in Bibliography*, XXV (1972), pp. 185-91. Even if Defoe was not responsible for them, the title pages still guided the reader's generic categorisation of the books, and so are as instrumental in the supervision of reading as they would be if they were accurate, or if they were really Defoe's.
5. See the excellent extensive discussion of Mrs Manley, Mrs Haywood, and similar writers in John J. Richetti, *Popular Fiction Before Richardson: Narrative Patterns 1700-1739* (Oxford, 1969), pp. 119-68.
6. The point about the near-contemporary location of the narrative is first made by Rodney M. Baine, '*Roxana's* Georgian Setting', *SEL*, XV (1974), pp. 459-73. It is expanded and very interestingly developed in Paul Alkon, *Defoe and Fictional Time* (Athens, Georgia, 1979), pp. 53-8.
7. The translation used is that available in Defoe's lifetime. See *The Comical Works of Don Francisco de Quevedo*, translated by John Stevens (London, 1707), pp. 346-7.
8. There is a strange recurrence of the year 1683 throughout Defoe's fiction, marking a point of change. It is both the year in which Roxana is said to have arrived in England from France, and that given as the date of composition of Moll's memorandums. It is also the year in which Bob Singleton was born. There is probably no significance in the detail, but 1683 was probably the year Defoe set up in the hosiery business, and it is certainly the year he courted his eventual wife, Mary Tuffley.
9. Defoe, *A General History of the Pyrates* (1724), Manuel Schonhorn (ed.) (London, 1972), p. 95.
10. Defoe, *The Complete English Tradesman* (1725), quoted in Laura Ann Curtis (ed.), *The Versatile Defoe* (London, 1979), pp. 378-9.

11. Defoe, *The True Born Englishman* (1701), in Boulton, p. 57.
12. Though the various government measures to promote local breweries, and so combat the pernicious effects of gin drinking, did not take place until later, the brewing industry of the late-seventeenth and early-eighteenth centuries seems to have been extremely volatile. See. M. Dorothy George, *London Life in the Eighteenth Century* (new edn, Harmondsworth, 1965), Chapter Six, and Peter Earle, *The World of Defoe* (London, 1976), p. 248, for an analysis of Roxana's economic condition.
13. Defoe, *An Appeal to Honour and Justice* (1715), in Boulton, pp. 186-7.
14. See M.E. Novak, *Defoe and the Nature of Man* (Oxford, 1963), p. 82.
15. Though there are very few, if any, instances of such a moral view in early-eighteenth-century popular fiction, a similar attitude can be found in some Puritan writing on marriage. The debate is summarised in Stone, *The Family, Sex and Marriage*, p. 34.
16. This point is illustrated in M.E. Novak, 'Crime and Punishment in *Roxana*', *JEGP*, LXV (1966), pp. 445-65.
17. *Defoe and Casuistry*, p. 165.
18. David Blewett, *Defoe's Art of Fiction* (Toronto, 1979), pp. 116-20.
19. See *The Life of Duncan Campbell* (1720), Aitken (ed.), IV, p. 144. The whole question of the supernatural is discussed thoroughly by Rodney M. Baine, *Defoe and the Supernatural* (Athens, Georgia, 1968). Baine casts severe doubts on the attribution of *Duncan Campbell* to Defoe, but my point is not seriously weakened thereby.
20. Such errors are extensively discussed in E. Anthony James, *Daniel Defoe's Many Voices: A Rhetorical Study of Prose Style and Literary Method* (Amsterdam, 1972), pp. 231-2.
21. Richetti, *Defoe's Narratives*, pp. 198-9.
22. Roxana's cynical and satirical views on matrimony are discussed by E.A. James, *Daniel Defoe's Many Voices*, pp. 240-3. As he rightly points out, Roxana's first marriage is no more or less disastrous than Moll's incestuous union, yet it causes Roxana to reject the notion of marriage utterly. This is a case of Roxana's absolutism, her ungoverned passion, coming into contrast with Moll's opportunism and resilience.
23. For discussions of Roxana as a courtesan, see Blewett, *Defoe's Art of Fiction*, pp. 122-4; Spiro Peterson, 'The Matrimonial Theme of Defoe's *Roxana*', *PMLA*, LXX (1955), pp. 166-91; and Everett Zimmerman, 'Language and Character in Defoe's *Roxana*', *EC*, XXI (1971), pp. 227-35.
24. The line 'For HONESTY and HONOUR are the same' comes from Defoe's *The Character of the Late Dr Samuel Annesley* (1697), which makes it anachronistic in the narrative.
25. Novak, 'Crime and Punishment in Defoe's *Roxana*', p. 454.
26. Defoe, *The True Born Englisman* (1701), in Boulton, p. 57.
27. R.D. Hume, 'The Conclusion of Defoe's *Roxana*', p. 483.
28. A.D. McKillop, *The Early Masters of English Fiction*, p. 37.
29. Bonamy Dobree, *English Literature in the Early Eighteenth Century* (Oxford, 1959), p. 425.
30. Quoted by Martin Price, *To the Palace of Wisdom: Studies in Order and Energy from Dryden to Blake* (Carbondale and Edwardsville, 1964), p. 268.

CONCLUSION: NOVELS AND ROMANCES

Having looked closely at three of Defoe's narratives, and having drawn attention to others in passing, my analysis of his writing has become increasingly progressivist. The qualities of difference I have selected from *Crusoe*, *Moll* and *Roxana* can be seen as part of a general improvement or sophistication on Defoe's part, as a producer of sustained narratives. Starting from the conventional traveller's tale in *Crusoe*, we see Defoe gradually lessening his dependence on generic supervision, until we arrive at the integrated, sophisticated narrative of *Roxana*, self-conscious, ironic and capable of standing on its own. With the benefits of hindsight, we can express this change in Defoe's writing by saying that he started producing chronicles, and ended up writing a novel. In the hectic production of at least eight long narratives between 1719 and 1724, Defoe refined his procedures, it seems, and moved from the para-literary world of traveller's tales, criminal biographies and scandalous chronicles, into the literary world of Richardson and even Fielding.

This progression can be expressed in many different ways. It can be seen in the rejection of compendiousness in favour of greater single-mindedness. Whereas *Crusoe* and *Singleton*, for instance, are digressive, accumulative tales, offering little development of interest, *Roxana* is a more sustained examination of its central figure. The later book sticks to its point much more, and makes less effort to incorporate digressive essays on travel or home economics. Another way of trying to get at this change is to look at how the narrating personality is handled throughout. As I have shown earlier, the change from *Crusoe* to *Moll* is seen in the increased individuation of the later narrator, whose individual personality is given greater prominence. Whereas Crusoe is a blandly representative figure, given only the most stylised motivation, Moll exists more as a character, with idiosyncracies and eccentricities of her own. To some extent, Moll's adventures arise from her specific personality, rather than from the general requirements of the genre, and though this is handled awkwardly at times, leading to the hesitation over ironies, it is still more sophisticated in retrospect than anything attempted in *Crusoe*. In *Roxana*, even more so, the narrator's role is paramount, and the tale becomes an investigation of how Roxana presents her experience, as well as a narrative presentation of that experience.

A different way of putting the same point is to claim that the principle of connection in Defoe's narratives changed from 1719 to 1724. The principle of connection in the earlier tales can be called the 'and then' principle, where events are presented sequentially. Crusoe's life is just one damn thing after another, with only the most perfunctory and unsustained attempts to connect them. The same applies to the narratives of Singleton, H.F. and, for the most part, the Colonel, where chronology is more important than consequence, and where no overview of experience is offered. In *Moll*, however, and especially in *Roxana*, the principle of connection becomes the 'and so' principle, where episode follows episode by implication and causal connection rather than simply by contiguity. The 'and so' principle is used to construct plots, whereas the 'and then' principle constructs stories. To use E.M. Forster's examples, 'The King died, then the Queen died' is a story; 'The King died, then the Queen died of grief' is a plot.[1] In this way of speaking, Defoe's development can be expressed as a move from storytelling to the construction of plots. The advantage of plotting is that it is cumulative, and allows for deferred revelations of the kind which is seen at the end of *Roxana*. It also allows greater concentration on motive and psychology, rather than simply on action and behaviour.

So, from the literary point of view, Defoe improved as he went along. This should not surprise us, as his projecting nature was always concerned with improvement and sophistication of any manufacturing process, storytelling included. From *An Essay Upon Projects* (1967) to *Augusta Triumphans* (1728), Defoe was for ever putting forward schemes to improve the way things were conducted. Very few people paid any attention to these schemes, and many of them look like the kind of over-ambitious, ill-considered schemes which preoccupied the professors of the Academy of Lagado. However, they reveal Defoe's concern to learn from experience, and to put things to rights by the exercise of his projecting imagination. *Augusta Triumphans*, written in what are generally held to have been his embittered final years, is in fact a remarkably buoyant six-point plan showing 'the Way to make London the most flourishing City in the Universe.'[2] Not just Britain, or even Europe, but the Universe! The six points are worth listing:

First, By establishing an University where Gentlemen may have

Academical Education under the Eye of their Friends.
II. To prevent much Murder, &c. by an Hospital for Foundlings.
III By suppressing pretended Mad-Houses, where many of the fair Sex are unjustly confin'd, while their Husbands keep Mistresses, &c. and many Widows are lock'd up for the Sake of their Jointure.
IV To save our Youth from Destruction, by clearing the Streets of impudent Strumpets, Suppressing Gaming-Tables, and Sunday Debauches.
V To avoid the expensive Importation of Foreign Musicians, by forming an Academy of our own.
VI To save our lower Class of People from utter Ruin, and render them useful, by preventing the immoderate Use of Geneva: With a frank Explosion of many other common Abuses, and incontestible Rules for Amendment.

These rather eccentric plans are put forward with 'incontestible Rules for Amendment', and 'Amendment', like 'Reformation' is one of the key terms in Defoe's thinking.

As a writer he was concerned not just with improving the skills whereby he communicated with his audience, or with the internal amendment of literature, but with the broader issues of conduct and manners raised by the events in his narratives. In the catalogue of potential improvements to London given above, it is remarkable how non-partisan Defoe remains. As I argued in the earlier chapters, Defoe was happiest as a polemicist and pamphleteer when he could claim to be rising above party or factional interest, and addressing himself to the common concerns of his readers. In his conduct books, he sought to offer moral guidance, avoiding the political strife which had brought him into trouble so often earlier on. What I see happening in the fiction is the gradual drift from the simple chronicle of adventure to the appropriation of extended fiction as a vehicle for Defoe's moral, improving concerns. To some extent, *Colonel Jack*, *Moll* and *Roxana* use the extended narrative form as a way of exploring Defoe's persistent concern with crime, education and manners. The first-person narratives allow him to avoid direct personal commitment, a more successful strategy of evasion than the construction of an alternative moralising personality such as 'Andrew Moreton, Esq.'. Also, the popular form made it possible for Defoe to take his views directly to the reading public, without the dangers of interventionism.

For readers, Defoe's narratives not only offer versions of their own lives, outside the operative constraints, they also provide accessible ways of debating issues of general moral concern, outside political faction. Even *Crusoe* offers some discussion of patriarchy and sovereignty, and where Defoe's narratives emerge from the popular genres in which they awkwardly reside is in their insistent address to general issues of the day. However obliquely, Defoe manages to introduce his usual subjects into his fictions. *Colonel Jack* deals with the treatment of Jacobites and servants; *Moll* deals the treatment of the children of criminals; *Singleton* deals with foundlings; *Roxana* with moral absolutism and licentiousness in high places. In the early works, various subjects are just touched on in passing, and are not made prominent, but later, Defoe discovered the possibilities of using the extended narrative as a way of looking in depth and detail at one issue. What we remember from *Crusoe* are the various adventures, with occasional superb moments of evocation — such as the discovery of the flotsam, or the footprint. From *Moll*, we remember more of Moll's character and resilience, with all its evasions and ebullience — episodes like the theft of the child's necklace, or the careful presentation of the various bills of laying-in, stay in the mind to show Moll's combination of impulsiveness and shrewdness. From *Roxana*, we remember the overall dark, sombre tone, with its bizarrely anticlimatic ending. The interest of the tales moves from the broadly logistical to the psychological.

The point I want to emphasise, however, is that no matter how psychological Defoe's narratives become, and no matter how well they may stand up on their own, they are still intimately connected to his public and political concerns, and to the popular discourses available to readers. The move from romances to novels may look like a process of detachment from contemporary concern, but it is in fact a process of displacement. Defoe was every bit as concerned with popular issues in *Crusoe*, through its subdued references to a body of travel writing, as he was in *Roxana*, through its analysis of a specific psychology. Each text is allusive, though the manner of its allusion, and the objects of its allusions, are very different. For Defoe, the whole enterprise of fiction was a way of dealing with public concerns safely and remuneratively, and the progress from *Crusoe* to *Roxana* was a refinement of his ability to treat public issues in a displaced way. Different kinds of displacement, of course, are visible in different books. The earlier narratives did not deal with the issues of mobility, or crime, or the individual's control over his or her fate, as individual texts, but rather as members of a class of narratives, all addressed to these questions. The individual narratives make indirect contributions to an area of thinking, made more direct by the recognition of similarity to and difference from other contributions to that class of narratives. Where Defoe's narratives most importantly emerge from their supervisory genres is initially in the choice handling of detail and the rhythm of recovery and frustration that is so important to *Crusoe*. Later, the combination of the amatory and the criminal in *Moll* allows greater development of the effects of behaviour and circumstance. Finally, in *Roxana*, the single-mindedness of the narrator allows full exploration of the defects of one set of ideas.

I talked earlier of the surprising omission of historical detail in most of Defoe's narratives — his characters seem to inhabit a geography much more obviously than a history. The reason for this is now, I hope, clearer. There is no need for the direct intrusion of historical or political detail, since Defoe was striving after a universalist analysis of human character. The shaping influence of place was more important to him than the shaping influence of time. Sudden disaster could strike at any time, in Defoe's view, whether on board ship in the Tropics, or in quiet London before the plague. The fiction explores this state of constant endangerment, and examines its protagonists as they respond to their setbacks. The notions of imminent disaster, and the slow recovery are made important to Defoe by the intersection of his religious sensibility and his political views. An eminently practical man in sensibility, however harebrained some of his proposals look to us, Defoe was always concerned with recovery rather than acceptance, with encouragement of others rather than with the exploitation of their weaknesses. When failure was presented, in *Roxana*, it was offered as a warning, as a kind of admonitory case history. In the other narratives, we see the eagerness and energy of both narrator and narrative being directed to the enumeration of reconstruction and survival.

What I have been trying to do throughout this study is to reinsert Defoe in his time, and to see if the form of his tales can be explained by the known features of his religious or political views, and the literary world of the time. I am conscious that in doing so, I have made the reading of Defoe sound extremely difficult. His books now look clearer to this reader, but I seem to have put a great many weighty and cumbersome obstacles in the way of the 'general reader', whose enjoyment may wane at the appearance of critical terminology, or, indeed, at the mention of any word ending in '-ology'. Further, my recent remarks that Defoe improved after *Crusoe*, rising to his greatest achievement with *Roxana*, look immediately suspect. If that is the case, why did everyone read *Crusoe*, a book of enduring popularity, and hardly anyone read *Roxana*? And why is all this discussion necessary, when *Crusoe* is so eminently readable?

Two different kinds of reading are involved here, and two different estimates of Defoe. I have been trying to offer a synchronic estimate of the books, comparing them to other features of their contemporary world. But it is also possible to look for a diachronic estimate of Defoe, and to try to put him into a literary tradition somehow or other. Most people who read Defoe at all are unworried either about synchrony or diachrony as they read, and are probably more interested in whether Crusoe's boat will sink. In a very telling remark, Robert Louis Stevenson said that 'fiction is to the grown man what play is to the child'.[3] To most early readers of Defoe, and I think to most later ones as well, the element of play in reading must be very prominent. Defoe's popular narratives are probably best thought of romances than as novels, for they transport uncritical readers back to a childlike state of anticipation and receptivity. In 'A Gossip on Romance', Stevenson has a lovely tale about the kind of devotion that Defoe could inspire late in the nineteenth century:

> But perhaps nothing can more strongly illustrate the necessity for marking incident than to compare the living fame of *Robinson Crusoe* with the discredit of *Clarissa Harlowe*. *Clarissa* is a book of far more startling import, worked out on a great canvas, with inimitable courage and unflagging art. It contains wit, character, passion, plot, conversations full of spirit and insight, letters sparkling with unstrained humanity. . . And yet a little story of a shipwrecked sailor, with not a tenth part of the style nor a thousandth part of the wisdom, exploring none of the arcana of humanity and deprived of the perennial interest of love, goes on from edition to edition, ever young, while *Clarissa* lies on the shelves unread. A friend of mine, a Welsh blacksmith, was twenty-five years old and could neither read nor write, when he heard a chapter of *Robinson* read aloud in a farm kitchen. Up to that moment he had sat content, huddled in his ignorance, but he left that farm another man. There were day-dreams, it appeared,

divine day-dreams, written and printed and bound, and to be bought for money and enjoyed at pleasure. Down he sat that day, painfully learned to read Welsh, and returned to borrow the book. It had been lost, nor could he find another copy but one that was in English. Down he sat once more, learned English, and at length, and with entire delight, read *Robinson*. It is like the story of a love-chase. If he had heard a letter from *Clarissa*, would he have been fired with the same chivalrous ardour? I wonder. Yet *Clarissa* has every quality that can be shown in prose, one alone excepted — pictorial or picture-making romance. While *Robinson* depends, for the most part and with the overwhelming majority of its readers, on the charm of circumstance.[4]

The comparison of Defoe and Richardson is delightful, in the light of the recent radical reappraisal of *Clarissa*. For whatever has been discovered or rediscovered in Richardson, the element of enthralling play has not been very prominent.

Stevenson's anecdote brings out the problem for academic readers of Defoe. If we wish to go beyond naive involvement, how are we to talk? After all, fiction may be to the adult what play is to the child, but it was more work than play for its author, as it is for me, and as I suspect it must be for you, gentle reader, if you have read this far. A recurrent strategy has been to place Defoe in front of a long string of novelists, and to proclaim him as a founder, or antecedent of the English novel. I discussed some problems in this method earlier, but it deserves another look. The feature of Defoe's work which most often qualifies him to stand at the head of the queue is what Ian Watt called his 'formal realism'.[5] This refers to Defoe's plainness of style, his pseudo-factuality, and his delight in detail. By being so concerned with the appearances of fact in works of fiction, Defoe is said to initiate the tradition of realism in English prose, albeit clumsily.

By now, a great deal of print has been taken up in seeking to define Defoe's realism, and I agree that there is some point to it. However, if pressed to give a diachronic rendering of Defoe's fiction, I would prefer to emphasise the function of this technique, and to see Defoe as a fantasist rather than a realist. What Stevenson's Welsh blacksmith friend recognised in Defoe was not realism, but compelling fantasy, fantasy sufficiently grounded in the details of day-to-day life that it otherwise contradicts. Defoe's early works of fiction deal with the absorbing issues of danger and escape, in a manner which is at once plausible and strange, simultaneously down to earth and dreamlike. Stevenson himself learned a great deal from Defoe, in the treatment of jeopardy, and in the intermixing of detail and fantasy in *Treasure Island* and *Kidnapped*. What Defoe was excellent at in *Crusoe* was maintaining the balance between corroborative detail and extraordinary adventures. Were there too much detail, the tale would become boring, as anyone brave enough to try to read *Swiss Family Robinson* will discover. Were there too little detail, the tale would become risibly implausible, as perhaps the *Farther Adventures* seem. This view of Defoe does not put him at the beginning of the English novel, but somewhere near the start of the sporadic romantic adventure tradition. His successors are not Richardson and Fielding, but Stevenson and Scott, and a host of forgotten popular authors. It becomes more important to emphasise the quest pattern in his fiction than its presentation of psychology, and we can try to find common feeling with 'honest Dick and Doll' in our delight in Defoe's escapist yarns.

So there are two ways of coming to terms with Defoe's career as an author of extended fictional narratives. We see the development from the apparently simple chronicle to the more complex psychological novel. We note the persistence of Defoe's characteristic features — the delight in detail, the geographical exactitude, the love of dialects and terminologies, or whatever — and then, if pressed, we have to decide whether he gained or lost by this change. But we only have to decide if pressed, and there is no need to seek after a more rigorous definition of Defoe's work than it will support. The point must remain that Defoe's fiction is varied, uneven and difficult to assess. This leads to the paradoxes involved in trying to pin him down once and for all. Either we then decide to define his career somehow or other, exalting tidyness over indecision, or we do what I have sought to do in this study — to try to cope with Defoe's variety without evaluating his achievement in the light of our own concerns. Hindsight has its benefits, but also its drawbacks. If we interpret the past only by what it has passed down to us we are likely to receive a very distorted version. And if we interpret eighteenth-century fiction only by what has 'survived the test of time' we remove Defoe far too much from the culture which nourished him. I hope that my attempt to reinsert him in his culture has helped to articulate the fictions, and to give a clearer picture of Defoe himself, without doing too much violence to his readability or energy.

Notes

1. See E.M. Forster, *The Rise of the Novel* (1926), Chapter One.
2. See Michael F. Shugrue (ed.), *Selected Poetry and Prose of Daniel Defoe* (New York, 1968), p. 310.
3. Robert Louis Stevenson, 'A Gossip on Romance', in *Selected Short Stories of R.L. Stevenson*, Ian Campbell (ed.) (Edinburgh, 1980), p. 30.
4. Ibid., pp. 27-8.
5. See Ian Watt, *The Rise of the Novel*, Chapter One.

INDEX

Act of Union (1707) 26
Addison, Joseph 38, 55
Adolphus, Gustavus 5-9, 31
Aesop 38
allegory 3-4, 62, 120
'Ancients' 16-18, 38
Anglesey, Earl of 35
Anne, Queen 3, 21, 23, 34, 154
Annesley, Samuel 15
anonymity 18, 35-6, 57
Applebee's Weekly Journal 27
Aristotle 38, 60, 62
Arnold, Matthew 45, 56; *Culture and Anarchy* 45
Augustine, St. 38

Barthes, Roland 57-8
Behn, Aphra 155
Benjamin, Walter 51-2
Bigsby, C. W. E. 45
Blewett, David 171
Boileau 38
Bonnet, Major Stede 161
Boswell, James 54
Bunuel, Luis 75
Bunyan, John 38, 44; *Pilgrim's Progress* 7, 27; *The Life and Death of Mr Badman* 116-17
Butler, Samuel 38

Candide 73, 86
Charles II 5, 15, 154, 157, 175
Chateaubriand 73
Chaucer, Geoffrey 38
'Chevy Chase' 55
Cicero 38
Civil War 15, 31, 149
Clare, John 74
Congreve, William 38
Cowley, Abraham 38
Culler, Jonathan 68

Dante 1
Davis, Lennard J. 53
Defoe, Daniel, works by: *And What if the Pretender Should Come?* 26; *Appeal to Honour and Justice, An* 20, 25, 168; *Argument Shewing, that a Standing Army, with Consent of Parliament, is not Inconsistent with a Free Government* 20; *Atlas Maritimus and Commercialis* 30; *Augusta Triumphans* 16, 28, 190-1; *British Visions, The* 37; *Captain Singleton* 3, 32, 52, 63, 65-6, 73, 77, 79-80, 82, 89, 90, 92-3, 95, 98, 106, 110, 114n40, 126-7, 129, 136, 146, 158, 171, 173, 179, 180, 183, 189, 192; *Colonel Jack* 3, 5, 7, 16, 32-3, 65, 77, 80-2, 105, 113n20, 118-19, 124-6, 129, 133, 136, 138, 146, 153, 158, 165, 171, 173, 179, 182, 186, 192; *Complete English Gentleman, The* 129; *Complete English Tradesman, The* 11, 162; *Consolidator, The* 37, 73; *Due Preparations for the Plague* 85; *Elegy on the Author of the True Born Englishman* 34; *Essay on the History and Reality of Apparitions, An* 173; *Essay on the Regulation of the Press, An* 36; *Essay Upon Projects, An* 16, 101-2, 190; *Every-Body's Business is No-Body's Business* 28; *Family Instructor, The* 27-8, 32, 50, 54; *Farther Adventures of Robinson Crusoe* 91, 107, 109-10, 158, 196; *General History of the Pyrates, A* 77, 161; *Giving Alms No Charity* 36; *Highland Rogue, The* 33; *Good Advice to the Ladies* 165; *History of the Union, The* 31, 36; *Hymn to the Pillory, A* 23-5, 36, 42; *Journal of the Plague Year, A* 3, 6, 31, 39, 85-8, 95, 110, 146, 153, 158, 164, 179, 183, 186; *Legion's Memorial* 10-11, 23; *Letter from a Gentleman at the Court of St. Germains, A* 37; *Life of Duncan Campbell, The* 173; *Memoirs of a Cavalier* 5, 31-2, 39, 119; *Military Memoirs of Capt. George Carleton, The* 31, 57; *Moll Flanders* 1, 3, 5, 7, 16, 32-3, 37, 43, 48, 52, 54, 61, 65, 70, 80, 82, 89, 101, 112, 115, 115-53, 155-7, 158, 164-7, 169-73, 176-9, 180, 182-4, 192; *New Voyage Round the World, A*

73; *Parochial Tyranny* 28; *Political History of the Devil, The* 173; *Protestant Monastery, The* 28; *Reasons Against the Succession of the House of Hanover* 26; *Reformation of Manners* 165; *Religious Courtship* 129, 164; *Review* 9, 14, 16, 17, 25-7, 33-7, 86; *Robert Drury's Journal* 73; *Robinson Crusoe* 1, 3-8, 14, 17, 27, 32-3, 37, 42, 47-53, 61, 65-6, 69-70, 73-115, 117, 118, 120, 122-3, 124, 126, 130-1, 133, 135-6, 139-140, 142, 145-6, 148, 149, 153, 155-7, 160, 165, 167, 169-73, 176-9, 184-6, 189-90, 192-6; *Roxana* 3, 5, 6, 16, 32, 42, 54, 65-6, 70, 80, 101, 133, 138, 141, 149-50, 153-89, 192, 193; *Second Thoughts are Best* 28; *Serious Reflections . . .* 3-4, 114n27, 120, 171, 184-5; *Shortest Way with Dissenters, The* 3, 22-4, 36; *Some Thoughts upon the Subject of Commerce with France* 10; *Storm, The* 31-2; *System of Magick, A* 28; *Tour thro' the Whole Island of Great Britain, A* 8, 29-30, 42; *True Born Englishman, The* 18, 21, 24, 36, 83, 119-20, 164, 182; *True Collection* 13n11, 19, 36; *True Relation of the Apparition of One Mrs Veal, A* 94, 173; *Vindication of the Press, A* 19, 37-8
Deloney, Thomas 55
Demosthenes 38
Derrida, Jacques 72n8
Dickens, Charles 56, 58
Dobrée, Bonamy 184
Donoghue, Denis 147-8
Don Quixote 53
Dryden, John 38
Dublin Journal 48
Dunton, John 14

'English' 42-6
English Rogue, The 59, 146

Farquhar, George 38
Fielding, Henry 48, 55, 189, 196; *Amelia* 153; *Jonathan Wild* 62; *Joseph Andrews* 55, 62; *Tom Jones* 63, 73, 153
Flying Post, The 35
Foe, James 15
Ford, G. H. 56
Forster, E. M. 190

Frye, Northrop 60-2, 68

Gay, John 15
Gildon, Charles: *The Life and Strange Surprizing Adventures of Mr D- De F-, of London*, 4, 7
Godolphin, Earl of 25-6
God's Revenge Against Murther 7
Greene, Robert: *A Notable Discovery of Cozenage* 115-16

Hall, John 56
Hardy, Thomas 62
Harley, Robert 4, 11, 25-6
Haywood, Eliza 154-6, 169, 187
Hazlitt, William 43, 48
Hervey, Lord 49
Hill, Christopher 77-8, 115
History of John Bull, The 62
Hobbes, Thomas 78
Homer 38, 66
Hopkins, Gerard Manley 19
Horace 38
Hunter, J. Paul 76

irony 2, 22-4, 61-2, 91, 101, 107, 117-18, 124-7, 140, 145-6, 176, 183

Jack and the Giants 54-5
Jacobitism 35, 103, 192
James, Henry: *Portrait of a Lady* 147-8
Johnson, Samuel 14, 49-50, 54-5, 74; *Rasselas* 54, 62, 73
Jonson, Ben 38: *Volpone* 116
Juvenal 38

Kentish Petition 10-11
Koonce, H. L. 146

Lawrence, D. H. 58
Lazarillo de Tormes 61
Leavis, F. R. 39, 58
Lee, Nathaniel: *The Rival Queens* 163
Lee, William 7
Libel Act (1792) 35
Lindamira 137
Livy 38
Locke, John 38
London Gazette 25, 32
Long Meg of Westminster 146
Lucretius 38

McBurney, W. H. 64

MacDonald, J. R. 56
Macherey, Pierre 76, 100-1
McKillop, A. D. 184
Malcolmson, Robert W. 115
Mallarmé, Stéphane 58
Manley, Mary de la Rivière 154-7, 169, 187
Martin, Terence 145-6
Marvell, Andrew 38
Maynwaring, Arthur 14
Mercurius Politicus 27
Michie J. A., 146
Milton, John 38, 66, 76
Mist, Nathaniel: *Weekly-Journal* 27
'Moderns' 16-18, 28-30, 38, 63
Monmouth, Duke of 2, 23
Montagu, Lady Mary Wortley 48-9, 54
Moonstone, The 7
'Moreton, Andrew, Esq.' 28-9, 32-3, 50, 191
Morris, Sir Lewis 19
Morton, Charles 16

Natural Law 43, 76, 135, 137, 139, 146
Neuburg, Victor E. 50
'New Criticism' 66
Newgate 3, 23, 48, 122, 123, 133, 142, 144, 178, 186
Novak, M. E. 76, 81, 135, 142, 146, 168, 183

Oldsworth, William 38
Orwell, George 14
Otway, Thomas 38
Ovid 38
Oxford Book of Eighteenth-Century Verse, The 19

Phillips, Ambrose 38
picaresque novel 78, 96, 130-1, 160, 181
Plato 38
Plutarch 38
Pope, Alexander 15, 19, 38, 47-8, 163; *Dunciad, The* 15, 16, 48, 55, 163; *Rape of the Lock, The* 19, 66
popular fiction 42-73
Practice of Piety, The 7
Prior, Matthew 38
Propp, Vladimir 64
Proust, Marcel 58
Providence 77-104, 122-3, 137, 141, 142
Pufendorf 135

Puritanism 1, 3, 15-17, 28-30, 42, 53, 76

Queen, Ellery 59
Quevedo, Francisco de: *El Buscon* 160

regulation of the press 33-6
Religious Tract Society of London, The 27
Restoration 15
Richards, Frank 14
Richardson, Samuel 69, 187, 189, 196; *Clarissa* 62, 69, 194-5; *Sir Charles Grandison* 153
Richelieu, Duc de 36
Richetti, John J. 64-7, 76, 176
'robinsonaden' 47
Rogers, Pat 76
Rousseau, J.J. 56
Rowe, Nicholas 38

Sachervell, Henry 11, 22
Salisbury, Sally 48
Scott, Sir Walter 48, 196
Seven Wise Man of Gotham, The 54
Shakespeare, William 18, 38, 62; *Macbeth*, 176
Sheppard, John 48, 162
Smollett, Tobias: *Humphry Clinker* 73
Somerville, Lord 54
Spence, Jonathan 49
Spenser, Edmund 38
Stamp Tax (1713) 26
Starr, G. A. 76, 81-2, 95, 127, 171
Steele, Richard 38
Sterne, Laurence: *Tristram Shandy* 62
Stevenson, Robert Louis 194-6; *Kidnapped* 196; *Treasure Island* 196
Stone, Lawrence 132, 135
Suckling, Sir John 38
Swift, Jonathan 6, 15-17, 22, 47-8; *Battle of the Books, The* 16; *Gulliver's Travels* 17, 61, 62, 66, 73, 107, 190; *Modest Proposal, A* 22; *Tale of a Tub, A* 16, 19, 55, 63
Swiss Family Robinson 196

Tacitus 38
Thomas, Keith 115
Thompson, E. P. 56, 115
Todorov, Tzvetan 72n43, 96
Tompkins, J. M. S. 45-6
Tory Party 3, 12-18, 21-7, 35, 154, 163
Treaty of Ryswick 20
True Born Hugonot, The 21

Tutchin, John 14, 20; *Foreigners, The* 20
Two Apprentices, The 27

Valery, Paul 58
Van Ghent, Dorothy 117, 140, 146
Virgil 38, 66

Walpole, Lady 49

Watt, Ian 47, 69, 76, 79, 82-3, 97, 117, 153, 195
Whig Party 9-12, 15-18, 21-7, 30, 162
Wild, Jonathan 162
William III 3, 9, 20, 21, 24, 37
Williams, Raymond 65
Wilmot, John, Earl of Rochester 38
Wilson, Edmund 58
Wordsworth, William 55